Sports Law

PRENTICE HALL STUDIES IN BUSINESS PAPERBACK SERIES

Levy/Paludi, *Workplace Sexual Harassment*
Kubasek/Silverman, *Environmental Law*
Jones, *Sports Law*

Sports Law

Michael E. Jones
University of Massachusetts Lowell

PRENTICE HALL, Upper Saddle River, New Jersey 07458

For Professor Robert H. Waters
School of Law
University of Miami

A great teacher, leader, and friend

Assistant Editor: John Larkin
Editorial Assistant: Paula D'Introno
Editor-in-Chief: Natalie Anderson
Marketing Manager: Debbie Clare
Production Coordinator: Maureen Wilson
Managing Editor: Dee Josephson
Manufacturing Buyer: Ken Clinton
Manufacturing Supervisor: Arnold Vila
Manufacturing Manager: Vincent Scelta
Design Manager: Patricia Smythe
Cover Design: Kevin Kall
Front cover photos: AP Worldwide Photos—Top: L. M. Otero; Middle: Paul Carter;
    Bottom: Greg Gibson
Back cover photo: Katarina Jones
Composition: D&G Limited, LLC

Library of Congress Cataloging-in-Publication Data

Jones, Michael E.
    Sports law / Michael E. Jones
        p.   cm.
    Includes index.
    ISBN 0-13-676545-9
        1. Sports—law and legislation—United States.   I. Title.
    KF3989.J66   1999
    344.73'099—dc21   98-33823
                                                        CIP

Prentice-Hall International (UK) Limited, London
Prentice-Hall of Australia Pty. Limited, Sydney
Prentice-Hall Canada, Inc., Toronto
Prentice-Hall Hispanoamericana, S.A., Mexico
Prentice-Hall of India Private Limited, New Delhi
Prentice-Hall of Japan, Inc., Tokyo
Prentice-Hall Asia Pte. Ltd., Singapore
Editora Prentice-Hall do Brasil, Ltda., Rio de Janeiro

Printed in the United States of America
10 9 8 7 6 5 4 3 2

Contents

Preface

In the early months of 1998, the nation watched an appeals board overrule the disqualification of a Canadian snowboarder at the Nagano Olympics after he tested positive for marijuana, listened to Latrell Sprewell explain to a *60 Minutes* audience why he was pleased over an arbitrator's ruling that his professional basketball team could not terminate his contract even after he attacked his coach, and read about spy novelist Tom Clancy's ill-fated attempt to acquire the Minnesota Vikings football team for slightly more than $200 million. Each of these incidents involved sports, legal disputes, and resolutions of these disputes by adherence to rules of law.

Nearly seventy years ago, the esteemed legal educator Karl Llewellyn wrote that what the "officials" of the law do about disputes is the law itself. In the context of this book, it is the league commissioners, sports arbitrators, judges, athletic directors, coaches, and NCAA administrators who serve as the "officials" of the law of sports. The rules of sport laid down by Congress or the NCAA or the International Olympic Committee are the heart of law. For today's fans and students of sport, following what these "officials" do about legal disputes that arise on the playing field, outside the arena, and in the boardrooms of team owners is, in the words of Llewellyn, the "main thing."

The environment of sports at the professional, intercollegiate, and amateur levels has changed. The actions of sports "officials" are the "main thing" in terms of their interpreting the language of collective bargaining agreements, recruiting student-athletes, complying with Title IX, avoiding antitrust charges, licensing team logos, compensating injured players, saving franchises, and stopping domestic violence by athletes. Readers will learn about the body of laws, rules, and regulations governing intercollegiate sports, Olympic sports, professional athletes, and management.

This book, intended to reach two audiences, undergraduate and graduate students enrolled in a standard Sports Law course and lay persons who are interested in learning more about the subject of sports and the law in contemporary society, begins by providing a basic introduction to sports law issues involving intercollegiate sports as "regulated" by the NCAA. It is followed by an analysis of key disputes focusing on eligibility, opportunity to participate, and drug testing at the Olympic and amateur levels. Title IX, which commenced a tidal wave of changes in the landscape of sports competition for women, is explored in a separate chapter.

The next few chapters provide an insider's look at the legal aspects of the professional sports industry. This section starts with a detailed look at the relationship between antitrust and labor laws. The latest collective bargaining agreements in the major team sports are highlighted. Salary caps, college drafts, and free agency are an integral part of this study. The role of player agents who negotiate everything from player contracts to "tell-all" books is covered. The "underbelly" of dishonest agents is exposed.

The extra hard hits on the playing field and boorish behavior by players that have led to an explosion in tort litigation are covered. Al Davis' years of litigation against the NFL are chronicled in the next to last chapter on the business side of professional sports teams. The difficult societal issues of race, violence, and athletes as role models are thoughtfully examined.

In the appendices, several relevant documents related to chapter materials are included. Excerpts from the Amateur Sports Act and The Olympic Charter, a sports waiver document, an NFL player contract, the NFLPA's agent certification requirements, a state statute governing agent conduct, and a list of the major college sports management and sports administration programs are offered as resources.

ACKNOWLEDGMENTS

I would like to thank the following family members, friends, and colleagues for their support, assistance, and counsel throughout the process of researching and writing this book:

Family members: Carolyn Jones, Elka Jones, Katrina Jones, Larry Jones, Ken Jones, Cynthia Lange, Brenda Jones, and Craig Jones.

Friends: William Carvalho, Jean Daigle, Brad Hill of Goodales, Julie Carr Scully of PowerBar, Christopher Georgia of Riteway Products East, John Nadeau of Grip Shift, Chris Polster of Breathe Right, Mary DeLuca of GT Bicycles, John Runckel, Jr. of Barracuda, Tom Cox of Intra-Nutria Sports, Dan Nall of Blackburn, Beth Simpson of Polar, Matt Zimmer of TYR, Dena Link of Continental, Mark Vandermolen of Profile, Andrea Sandy of Croakies, Coach George Davis, Guy Esposito, Mary Ann Esposito, and Dan Malone.

Researchers: David Cote, Peter Stocks, Esq., Mireille Vartanian, George Dokos, Gerry Vass, Sarah Heffernon, Allison Cunha, James Richards, Esq., Dennis Feeble, and Jennifer D'Amour, plus many students from my Sports & Entertainment Law classes at the University of Massachusetts Lowell.

Reviewers: Professor Gregory Cermignano (Widener University), Mr. Richard Kenney (Compliance Officer-University of Massachusetts Lowell), Mr. Mark Garneau (Mississippi State University), Professor Robert Waters

(University of Miami School of Law), Professor Glen Wong (University of Massachusetts Amherst), Professor William Weston (Florida Coastal School of Law), and Professor Ken Shropshire (The Wharton School, University of Pennsylvania).

Attorney James Richards substantially contributed to the chapter on torts and sports. Mireille Vartanian and David Cote offered superb research and writing assistance. A special acknowledgment is extended to my academic colleagues at the university including William Burke, Russell Karl, Ernesto Sands, Dean Nancy Kleniewski, and Provost Robert Wagner, all of whom were supportive of this publishing effort. Finally, recently retired Prentice Hall sales rep Dave Cole was instrumental in bringing me together with senior editor Don Hull and the fine editorial staff at Prentice Hall including Maureen Wilson.

MICHAEL E. JONES

ABOUT THE AUTHOR

Michael E. Jones, or Judge Jones as he is known to many, is an associate professor at the University of Massachusetts Lowell and a Special Justice at the Salem (NH) District Court. He teaches courses in sports law and international law.

Before joining the faculty at University of Massachusetts Lowell, he taught at the Whittemore School of Business, University of New Hampshire. Judge Jones worked in the sports and entertainment field for many years. He was elected to four terms in the New Hampshire legislature.

Judge Jones has published more than 25 business and law review articles. These publications have appeared in journals such as *Business Law Review*, *New England Law Review*, *Bar Journal*, and *Midwest Law Review*. He edited a well-known book, *Current Issues in Professional Sports*, that was used by many of the leading sports management and sports law programs in the country.

He is a former chair of the International Sports Division of the Forum Committee on Sports and Entertainment Law (ABA). He was a founding member of the first national organization to accredit sports agents, the Association of Representatives of Pro Athletes (ARPA). He has lectured throughout the country on a variety of sports law issues at universities and on television and radio.

Judge Jones is a sponsored athlete who is considered one of the leading masters athletes in the world. He is a former world ocean swimming champion and one of the top 8km masters runners in the world. He has achieved a ranking as high as fourth in the world at the ITU age-group triathlon championships. He loves to surf.

CHAPTER I

The National Collegiate Athletic Association

A basic purpose of this Association is to maintain intercollegiate athletics as an integral part of the education program and the athlete as an integral part of the student body and, by so doing, retain a clear line of demarcation between intercollegiate athletics and professional sports.

— Article I, Constitution, NCAA

Case Study

During the spring, members of the football coaching staff began contacting student-athletes at another university about transferring. The coaches asked the student-athletes not to mention anything to their current coaches or the NCAA, if asked. If the students elected to transfer, their parents would each receive two free round-trip airline tickets to one away game per season plus accommodations. The coaches promised the student-athletes that they would receive a full financial aid package for every year they played so long as they didn't miss more than three practices a season. Do any of these actions constitute violations of NCAA rules? Would the violations be deemed major or secondary? What different penalties might the NCAA impose?

INTRODUCTION

This book begins by exploring the relationship between law and intercollegiate sports. On college campuses sports have developed into an industry generating millions of dollars in income each year. Sources of revenue include ticket sales, booster gifts, television and licensed merchandise sales. Conflicts have arisen over regulating not merely the rules of intercollegiate play and participation, but the shape, form, and amount of benefits flowing into athletic departments.

I

This chapter discusses the regulatory bodies that have stepped forward to balance the need for maintaining a level playing field for amateur intercollegiate athletic programs for men and women against the demands of winning and balancing athletic department budgets. The chapter's primary focus is on the National Collegiate Athletic Association (NCAA) as the premier intercollegiate regulatory body.

THE HISTORY OF REGULATING INTERCOLLEGIATE ATHLETICS

In the early days of football played on the campuses of Yale, Princeton, Cornell, and Michigan, it was not unusual for schools to recruit larger, stronger, nonstudent "ringers" or "tramp athletes" to play for the real student-players. Before the dawn of the forward pass, the only "thing" that was thrown were the ball-carrying players who were frequently picked up and hurtled over the opposing defensive line. The well-known "flying wedge" and gang tackling contributed to a horrible number of on-the-field casualties. Finally, in 1906, after 18 deaths and 149 serious injuries the year before, President Teddy Roosevelt called upon leading college presidents to police the sport of football. Heeding the call of the White House, the National Collegiate Athletic Association (NCAA) was formed.[1]

Today the NCAA is the primary rule-making body for intercollegiate sports. Its role has expanded into offering championship events, negotiating television contracts, formulating policies, and enforcing rule compliance.

Nearly 1,200 institutions comprise the NCAA. Membership is available to any accredited intercollegiate four-year school that meets its standards. Non-upper division junior and community colleges are not eligible to join the NCAA, but many have formed their own regulatory body called the National Junior College Athletic Association (NJCAA). Numerous Christian schools have united to form the National Christian Collegiate Athletic Association (NCCAA). Nearly 500 four-year schools have elected not to join the NCAA and instead are members of the National Association of Intercollegiate Athletics (NAIA).

The NAIA is similar in many ways to the NCAA. It creates rules for member institutions to follow for recruiting, eligibility, and championship play for men and women. NAIA schools historically have opted to avoid participating in "big-time" college football. Top NAIA athletic schools include the University of Sioux Falls, Montana Tech, Findlay, Westminster, Simon Fraser (British Columbia), Flagler, Willamette, and Rockhurst. Unlike the NCAA, Canadian colleges may join the NAIA.

Beyond the college walls, other regulatory bodies impact amateur sports. Certainly, at the high school level, nearly every state has created rule-making athletic associations that occasionally are the sources of controversy. In some states, for instance, the sport of competitive swimming is a coeducational athletic activity. However, in other states, schools offer swimming as a single-sex sport. Even the time of the year when swimming is offered—fall, winter, or spring—varies considerably from state to state. In the state of Texas, the policy of "no-pass, no-play" for high school athletes paved the way for other states to impose tougher academic standards to the dismay of many coaches and students.

Some high school conferences operate within the context of statewide association rules that require student-athletes to pass a drug test prior to participation. Despite right to privacy concerns, the U.S. Supreme Court recently endorsed one high school's decision to impose drug testing as a prerequisite to playing in the interest of sending a message to all students. [2]

At the national and international levels almost every organized sports group from mountain biking to beach volleyball has an association that creates rules for the sport, defines amateurism and professional status, lists eligibility requirements, and hosts championship events. Many of these associations are closely connected to Olympic participation and eligibility standards. Jurisdictional overlap, not to mention constitutional due process and equal protections concerns, between the NCAA and what is known as the national governing body (NGB) for each Olympic sport frequently places the student-athlete in an untenable regulatory conflict.

Frequently, colleges that are geographically linked or share common academic standards combine to form a league or conference. The Pacific Athletic Conference (PAC) combines 12 top-flight large public and private universities from the far western states; the Big 10, which after the recent addition of Penn State to the major flagship universities of the midwestern states, actually consists of 11 schools. Well known small college conferences include the Ohio Conference, consisting of outstanding academic schools like Denison and Kenyon, and the Great Lakes Conference combining competitive programs at Kalamazoo and Ripon and other exceptional liberal arts schools.

All of these conferences have in common the establishment of standards of eligibility, championship play, and sportsmanship conduct that at a minimum must meet, and frequently exceed, the requirements of the NCAA. The constitution of the NCAA at Article 3.3.4.1 requires conferences to "agree to administer their athletic programs in accordance with the constitution, bylaws and other legislation of the Association (NCAA)."

The member institutions of the NCAA are grouped into divisions: Division I, which is further divided into I-A and I-AA; Division II; and Division III. Athletic scholarships serve as inducements for students to attend a particular college. A separate agreement known as a *letter of intent* initially binds a student to a particular school during the recruitment period. Thereafter, the financial aspects of the student's relationship with the school on a year-to-year basis are found in the actual athletic scholarship. Not all schools grant athletic scholarships. Division III schools are not permitted to issue scholarships based on athletic prowess, although students certainly are eligible for academic financial awards and loans. Division II schools may offer a limited number of athletic scholarships but only 36 in football. Division I-AA schools consist of college programs that agree to a lower limit on football scholarships while retaining the higher limits for other sports. The largest football programs compete at the Division I level in all sports regardless of gender and offer the highest number of football scholarships at 85.

The NCAA is one of the most powerful athletic regulatory bodies in the world. Much of its authority over intercollegiate sports is historical, but its control over the television contracts of its member institutions, especially in basketball and through conference affiliation in football (except in the case of Notre Dame where it has contracted separately with NBC), makes the NCAA godlike but not infallible in the eyes of seasoned observers.

CONSTITUTION OF THE NCAA

The constitution of the NCAA contains six main articles.[3] Collectively these articles refer to the general organizational makeup of the NCAA, the legislative and amendment process, and the principles guiding the conduct of intercollegiate athletics.

The cornerstone of the constitution is the *principles* section. A basic NCAA principle is that each member institution *promises to maintain institutional control over the activities that occur within its athletic-academic community.*[4]

Not long ago, Texas A&M University, College Station was penalized by the NCAA Committee on Infractions for failing to prevent a prominent member of the school's booster club for the second time from paying student-athletes for work never performed. Because both students and an active alumnus under the direction and control of the school failed to abide by NCAA rules, the NCAA determined Texas A&M had breached the *principle of institutional control.*[5]

Contrast the Texas A&M case with that of UMASS, Amherst when men's college basketball player of the year Marcus Camby was found to have violated the *principle of amateurism* (discussed later) by accepting money illegally from an agent while still a college player.[6] In this instance, university and NCAA investigators failed to show that UMASS knew or had reason to know of Camby's infractions. So unlike Texas A&M, which was placed on probation for five years and excluded from bowl and television appearances for one year, UMASS received a less severe penalty of voiding its 1996 Final Four basketball appearance and returning $151,000 in revenue because there was no finding of loss of institutional control. Violating the principle of institutional control is deemed a more serious NCAA violation than breaching its rules of amateur status and agent dealings.

Controversy

One of the most controversial contemporary principles surrounds the notion of the application of *institutional gender equity*. The NCAA Manual, which serves as the bible for college presidents and athletic administrators, states that "it is the responsibility of each member institution to comply with Federal and state laws regarding gender equity." [7] Furthermore, the NCAA is supposed to enact legislation to enhance schools' compliance with gender-equity laws. This issue is explored more fully in the chapter on women's sports.

Another contested principle that springs from the early days of inter-collegiate sports is the notion of *amateurism*. In an era of seven-year, billion-dollar NCAA men's basketball television contracts and football bowl winners walking away with more than $11 million, the obvious question of the student-athletes somehow sharing in this largess is raised. The NCAA plainly took a page from Teddy Roosevelt's 1905 White House speech to college presidents when he declared that " . . . play is not a business, and it is a very poor business indeed for a college man to learn nothing but sport." [8] The NCAA Manual declares that "intercollegiate athletics is an avocation, and student-athletes should be protected from exploitation by professional and commercial enterprise." [9]

Concerns arose regarding the unfairness of not allowing student-athletes to work part-time for pay after the season while in school. Revelations of incredible payments to coaches for activities like winning tournaments, meeting modest graduation goals, signing Nike or adidas shoe contracts, appearing on television and radio shows, running sports camps, and fulfilling speaking engagements forced the NCAA to act.

The NCAA's response was not to limit payments to coaches like Florida's football coach Steve Spurrior receiving a base salary of $950,000 plus two free cars, 24 home game tickets, and money from television shows and speeches totaling $2 million a year; Duke's Coach K (Kryzewski) accepting a $1 million bonus from Nike for switching from endorsing adidas apparel and shoes; and Arizona's NCAA winning basketball coach Lute Olson receiving a month's salary if three-fourths of his players graduate. Instead the NCAA response was to permit student-athletes on full athletic scholarships to work for pay, but compensation may not exceed $2,000 during the school year.

In 1991, the NCAA in a cost-cutting move capped the earnings of certain athletic coaches to $16,000 a year. Seven years later the 1,900 coaches affected were awarded nearly $67 million in treble damages for unlawfully restricting their earnings in violation of federal antitrust laws. This decision may signal future limitations on the regulatory power of the NCAA.

Voluntary Membership

When viewing the rules and regulations of the NCAA, it is imperative to remember that the member schools *voluntarily* choose to join this organization.

The NCAA does not enact laws but legislates *bylaws*. These bylaws try to guarantee equal opportunity of participation in the spirit of amateurism without necessarily assuring athletes the same rights normally associated with the U.S. Constitution whenever government entities or state actors are found. Adherence to bylaws by colleges protects a level playing field of competition. Forms, signatures, contractual agreements with or without hearings, and banishments for violators instead of public trials and imprisonment are the norm.

Consider an individual accused of illegal drug use under the public, criminal legal system versus the NCAA. The individual suspected of violating a state- or federal-controlled drug statute (use or possession of steroids, illegal stimulants, etc.) is subject to arrest based on probable cause, arraignment, bail hearing, appointment of counsel, presumption of innocence, trial by jury or judge, fines, incarceration, and the right to appeal an adverse verdict.

This same individual in an NCAA setting prior to any practice or competition must sign a drug-testing consent form (see appendix for sample drug-testing waiver). Automatically, as a condition to sport participation, the student-athlete waives any right to a presumption of innocence and agrees to testing on demand in the absence of any probable cause or evidence the athlete has committed any wrong! Under the criminal code, giving blood or providing a urine sample upon demand might be viewed as a constitutional violation of the right to be free from unreasonable searches or seizures. No such constitutional protection exists before the NCAA.

The NCAA drug-testing form also requires the student-athlete to abide by the NCAA bylaws. A positive banned drug test immediately makes the student-athlete ineligible to participate for the remainder of the school year and one year thereafter under the bylaws.[10]

Schools are obligated to inform immediately conference affiliate members and the NCAA of any drug testing violations. Failure to do so could lead to the imposition of further penalties by the conference and the NCAA against both the individual and the school.

Notice the differences in rights and privileges and even presumptions between the two systems. The public legal system guarantees minimum constitutional protections for everyone regardless of the person's athletic status or membership in an organization. Public laws are enacted to guarantee advance notice prior to arrest and punishment. Fair and open hearings, assignment of counsel at government expense, speedy trials and equality of rights and privileges for all are constitutionally guaranteed. In contrast, participation in intercollegiate sports is viewed as a privilege, not a constitutional right. Membership in the NCAA means voluntary membership in a private, selective association without the same protections for athletes and coaches found in the public legal system. The following case involving longtime NCAA nemesis Jerry "The Tark" Tarkanian and the NCAA explores these differences more fully.

NCAA v. Tarkanian, 488 U.S. 179 (1988)

- Coach Tarkanian sued the NCAA alleging that it deprived him of both property and liberty interests protected by the the U.S. Constitution and that he was not afforded due process before he was suspended by his employer—the University of Nevada, Las Vegas (UNLV). These constitutional rights apply whenever a government or state actor or body is found. Tarkanian's punishment arose because of 10 NCAA basketball recruiting violations.
- The Nevada Supreme Court held that the NCAA had engaged in state action when it basically gave UNLV an ultimatum to remove Tarkanian as coach of the highly successful basketball program to avoid even harsher penalties from the NCAA.
- The NCAA was joined in an appeal to the U.S. Supreme Court. The Court denied Tarkanian's request to find that UNLV, a public school where state action is always found, delegated its powers to the private, voluntary, nonstate body known as the NCAA. The Court noted, impractical as it might seem, that UNLV could always withdraw from the NCAA if the school didn't like conducting its athletic program under the policies adopted by the NCAA. The Court reversed the Nevada judgment in Tarkanian's behalf on a 5–4 vote. Tarkanian lost his case.
- Justice White, a former All-America and outstanding professional football player, wrote a dissenting opinion. White believed that the NCAA and UNLV acted jointly to suspend and demote Tarkanian. This joint enterprise meant that the NCAA was indeed acting as a state entity.
- If White's dissenting view were ever to become the majority opinion of the U.S. Supreme Court, then whenever the NCAA seeks to impose sanctions or penalties that affect a coach or administrator working for a state or public school, the NCAA must follow the ground rules of procedural and substantive due process before instituting disciplinary procedures.
- In 1998, the NCAA reached an out-of-court settlement with Tarkanian ending all litigation between the two parties. Tarkanian received $2.5 million.

Key Considerations

- The NCAA is the leading intercollegiate amateur athletic regulatory body.
- The NCAA offers championship events for men and women, negotiates television contracts on behalf of its members, formulates athletic and academic policy, and enforces compliance with its rules.
- Membership in the NCAA is voluntary.
- The NCAA is grouped into divisions.
- The Principles section dealing the amateurism and institutional control, gender equity, and others is the cornerstone of the NCAA Constitution.

BYLAWS

The legislation adopted by the membership of the NCAA meeting annually is known as the *operating bylaws*. The bylaws are meant to promote the constitutional principles and purposes of the NCAA. [11] The NCAA Council and Board of Directors (previously the Executive Committee) are responsible for enacting *administrative bylaws* or policies and procedures required to implement the operating bylaws. Administrative bylaws are subject to review by the full membership of all participating colleges.

There are 14 operating bylaws. The major bylaws are broken down into the following categories, each of which will be discussed at length:

1. Ethical conduct
2. Amateur eligibility
3. Financial aid
4. Recruiting
5. Academic standards

Ethical Conduct

Athletes, coaches, and administrators are expected to compete honestly and display sportsmanship at all times. An assortment of evils is spelled out, which athletes must avoid to retain eligibility or the opportunity to participate. Knowingly falsifying college transcripts, cheating on an SAT or ACT exam, misleading administrators investigating a possible NCAA violation, and accepting an improper inducement or benefit to attend a college are all deemed *ethical violations*.

Perhaps no unethical conduct negatively affects the integrity of college sports more than students who gamble on intercollegiate events. A few years ago, Tulane University's basketball program was shut down after it was learned that certain players shaved points off games to assist known organized gamblers. Arizona State's basketball coach, Bill Frieder, was forced to resign in 1997 when a handful of players pleaded guilty to point shaving charges. Law enforcement officials were alerted when several of the Arizona State basketball games had unusual betting patterns in Las Vegas. A conspiracy to commit sports bribery charge looms over Northwestern University's men's basketball program. The team's top 3-point shooter has been implicated in fixing the outcome of three games during the 1994–95 season.

Boston College's Division I football program was rocked by the revelation that thirteen players had placed bets on college games through Boston and New York bookmakers. Even more alarming was that two of the thirteen players placed bets against their own team in a game against Syracuse University. These two players were permanently barred from competing for Boston College. The other eleven were temporarily suspended.

Shortly before the Boston College gambling incident became public, a research project conducted by the University of Cincinnati discovered that over 25 percent of the male Division I basketball and football players randomly surveyed admitted to gambling on sporting events.[12] Another four percent placed bets on events in which they participated.[13] These findings are troubling both because of the high incidence of athletes gambling on college campuses and the opportunity for organized gamblers to influence the outcomes of games. Bookmakers frequently have connections to organized crime figures, which creates its own set of safety issues for student-athletes who gamble.

It is illegal in all states, except Nevada, to place a bet on college games. Generally, in the criminal justice system, it is a misdemeanor offense for the gambler and a felony for the bookmaker. Student-athlete violators lose their eligibility under NCAA rules.[14] The NCAA has advised athletic departments to add materials on the hazards of college and professional sports betting to preseason athletic seminars. Unsuccessfully, the NCAA sought to deny press passes for championship events to any reporter for newspapers that carried gambling lines on college games.

Amateur Eligibility

Article 12 of the NCAA bylaws clearly states that only *amateur* student-athletes are eligible to compete. Administratively, the NCAA has sought to create a clear line of demarcation between college sports and professional sports. Keeping these lines clear in the midst of a commercial, sponsor-filled, for-profit world has not been an easy task for athletic departments.

Amateur status in a particular sport is lost whenever a college athlete signs a contract with a professional sports team. Lonnie Shelton, a college basketball player attending Oregon State University, signed a professional basketball contract. Oregon State, an NCAA member school, declared him ineligible even though Shelton argued that his pro contract might be unenforceable because he was induced to sign it under duress and fraudulent circumstances.

Shelton challenged the NCAA rule on amateurism in federal court. The court held that this particular college bylaw was rationally related to a legitimate purpose of promoting and protecting amateurism and did not, therefore, violate the equal protection clause of the U.S. Constitution.[15] After the Shelton decision, the NCAA modified its bylaws to read that merely signing a professional contract "regardless of the legal enforceability or any consideration received" from an agent or pro club will cause a student-athlete to lose eligibility.[16]

Additional acts under the NCAA bylaw on amateurism (Article 12) that can lead to loss of amateur college status include:

1. Using athletic skill directly or indirectly for pay in that sport or where overall athletic skills are on display (e.g., participating in "SuperStars" or "Toughman" or "Toughwoman" contests).

2. Accepting a promise of pay where the payment is to commence after college eligibility expires.
3. Receiving any kind of payment or reimbursement of expenses from a professional sports organization except as permitted by the NCAA. (An example of a permissible exception is, prior to enrolling in college, accepting reimbursement of actual out-of-pocket expenses for one tryout with a pro team.)
4. Competing on a professional sports team.
5. Signing with an agent or entering into a professional sports draft. (Note NBA exception discussed later.)

According to the NCAA bylaws, track or cross-country college runners who compete during the summer in off-season road racing and accept payment for winning or placing lose their eligibility. A college soccer player who plays on a semipro summer soccer team loses his or her eligibility by playing on a team with paid professionals. For the college soccer player it doesn't matter that he or she receives no actual compensation. Why, under these same rules and logic, doesn't the college runner who competes in the Boston or Los Angeles marathon where the winners receive paychecks lose eligibility?

The NCAA bylaws do not address the dichotomous treatment between soccer players and runners. It has carved out specific exceptions for college tennis and golf players. A student-athlete in these two particular sports may play against professionals provided no payment is received.

Former Stanford University standout Tiger Woods could compete against pro golfers Greg Norman and Jack Nicholas at the U.S. Open without the threat of losing college eligibility so long as he didn't accept any payment for playing. However, when Tiger accepted a dinner invitation from Arnold Palmer after playing in a pro-amateur golf tournament, he found himself in violation of an NCAA bylaw that prohibits receiving an "extra benefit" by virtue of his athletic status. Tiger's penalty was to repay Arnold Palmer for the value of the meal and sit out a handful of intercollegiate golf matches.

There exist a number of written exceptions to the NCAA's rules on amateur eligibility. Recently, the NCAA revised its rules so as to permit a student-athlete to participate as a professional athlete in one sport while retaining amateur college status in a different sport.[17] Today it is not uncommon for an outstanding two-sport athlete to sign a minor league baseball contract while competing in college basketball or football. For example, two-sport high school standout Kenny Kelly of Tampa signed a grant-in-aid (athletic scholarship) to play college football at the University of Miami. A few months later he was drafted in the second round by baseball's newest franchise, the Tampa Bay Devil Rays. Subsequently, he signed a minor league baseball contract. A different NCAA bylaw requires Kelly to forgo his athletic grant-in-aid, but he may still play college football as an amateur. His professional baseball team will pay for his college tuition and other expenses.

Nearly every spring some potential Heisman candidate speculates openly about skipping his final season of college eligibility and declaring himself available for the National Football League (NFL) draft. NCAA Bylaw Article 12.1.2.1 was enacted to encourage athletes to stay in school and minimize the financial risk of a career-threatening, college-related injury. This particular bylaw permits a student-athlete to purchase insurance against a disabling injury or sickness. An athlete may even borrow against future earnings potential from an accredited commercial lending institution to pay for his or her insurance premiums. Former college players like Florida State's exceptional running back Warrick Dunn, Wake Forest's basketball star Tim Duncan, and Tennessee's quarterback sensation Peyton Manning are three well-known professional athletes who took advantage of this provision while in college.

In the mid-1990s the NCAA amended its amateur rules solely for basketball players.[18] Once, while they still retain eligibility, college basketball players may make themselves available for a professional basketball draft. If a player isn't subsequently drafted or doesn't like his or her draft position, then that player has 30 days after the draft to return to college play without loss of amateur college eligibility. Ironically, if this same player retains an agent or receives some benefit from an agent to assist in assessing the likelihood of professional success, then eligibility is lost under Bylaw Article 12.3, prohibiting the use of agents by amateur athletes.

A longtime contemptuous issue in hockey is whether or not participation on a junior A team constitutes play on a professional team. The NCAA's position is that teams classified as major junior A clubs by the Canadian Amateur Hockey Association are deemed professional clubs.[19] For a major junior A player who wishes to play college hockey the NCAA allows a player to petition for restoration of amateur status.[20] Restoration includes loss of one year of intercollegiate hockey eligibility.[21]

Compounding the problem of amateurism on the college level is the relaxation of the concept of amateurism by other sports organizations. The U.S. men's and women's Olympic basketball teams are now fielded largely by professional athletes. Track star Donovan Bailey won $1.5 million for defeating two-time Olympic gold medal winner Michael Johnson in a 150-meter showdown at the Sky Dome in Toronto. However, both athletes remain eligible for Olympic and other international competitions. The U.S. Olympic swimming team now rewards swimmers financially on the basis of their Olympic performance with winnings placed in a trust fund for those athletes who desire to continue their swimming careers in college.

In a sign that both the NCAA and United States Olympic Committee (USOC) need one another to help train competitive athletes for international events, the USOC announced that it would give nearly $8 million to the NCAA and affiliated conferences and associations. This money is earmarked to help support NCAA championship events for Olympic sports lagging in intercollegiate participation. Water polo, cycling, rowing, archery, and gymnastics are among the 12 sports named to receive modest funding over a four-year period.

Key Considerations

- Student-athletes who engage in ethical violations, including sports-related gambling, may lose their eligibility to compete.
- Receiving pay for sports participation may lead to loss of NCAA eligibility.
- Student-athletes may become professional athletes in one sport yet retain their amateur athletic status in a different sport.

FINANCIAL AID

A gifted student-athlete may be awarded financial aid based on athletic ability. To qualify, a student must meet not only a coach's standards of performance but also satisfy school, conference, and NCAA academic eligibility requirements for intercollegiate participation.

Typical athletic grant or athletic scholarship awards include aid covering the cost of tuition, room and board, textbooks, and student fees. Certain outside government grants are excluded when calculating the value of a student's financial aid package. Social security benefits, G.I. bill of rights payments for veterans, and military reserve paychecks are not counted against a student-athlete's total awards package, which normally cannot exceed the cost of attending that college institution. Until the mid-1990s, Pell Grant awards not exceeding the value of a full grant-in-aid plus $2,400 at a Division I school or $1,500 at a Division II school were permissible. Recent changes in the law now state that Pell Grant awards may not exceed the grant-in-aid limit. Monetary assistance from parents and legal guardians is always allowed under the NCAA bylaws.

Nonathletic awards based on academic achievement (National Merit Scholarship Award or United Negro College Award) or service (Rotary Club Community Service Award or Junior Achievement Award) are permitted under Bylaw Article 15.2.5.2.

The concern the NCAA has regarding a nonathletic award is that a university booster club doesn't "back door" financial aid under false pretenses to a talented athlete. Additionally, a 1995 amendment to the bylaws recognized the symbiotic relationship between the USOC and the NCAA. The rules revisions enable a student-athlete to receive educational expenses awarded by the USOC so long as the expenses don't exceed the value of a full grant-in-aid.[22]

Athletic-based financial awards must also conform to the rules and regulations of the college awarding the aid and the college's conference affiliation. All awards must state in writing the amount, duration, conditions, and terms. Athletic awards are renewable annually. A student-athlete must be given notice and an opportunity for a hearing in the event an athletic award is reduced or canceled. Ground for not renewing financial aid might include a student-athlete fraudulently misrepresenting pertinent information an application for admission (e.g., age or years of college eligibility remaining), voluntarily quitting the team, engaging in criminal misconduct, and becoming ineligible for intercollegiate competition. Interestingly, during the course of an academic award year, the NCAA prevents a coach or school from taking away an athletic scholarship for poor play, lazy practice habits, or even injury.

Only Division I and II institutions may award financial aid to a student-athlete based on athletic ability, as discussed earlier in the chapter. Division III institutions may grant financial aid to a student who participates in intercollegiate sports upon a showing of financial need. The methodologies used by Division III schools to determine financial need must conform to established federal, state, and institutional guidelines.

A financial aid award is different from a national letter of intent. the NCAA establishes national signing dates for different sports. This signing date is the first day that a prospective college student may sign an institutional or conference letter of intent to attend a particular school. The Collegiate Commissioners Association administers the national letter of intent program. A separate award agreement may be made by a college to a student-athlete after the letter of intent signing.

NCAA Bylaw Article 16 seeks to ensure that a student-athlete does not receive an extra benefit or award not authorized by the NCAA by virtue of athletic status. The test the NCAA has established is quite simple. If the benefit received is not generally available to other student members of the institution or a particular segment of the student body (e.g., foreign students or Hispanic-American students) and it is not authorized by NCAA legislation, then it is deemed improper. Improper awards or benefits predictably subject a student-athlete to loss of eligibility and an institution to penalties including loss of scholarships, bowl sanctions, and no television appearances.

In the early 1990s a University of Miami athletic department representative was charged with providing extra benefits to football players by waiving admission charges to a local nightclub. Miami was placed on probation and lost numerous scholarships over a two-year period. The University of California, Berkeley was placed on three years' probation and lost two scholarships when head basketball coach Todd Bozeman admitted to the Committee on Infractions that he agreed to pay a basketball recruit's family $15,000 a year for each year that the recruit played. Whereas the Berkeley penalties were imposed in 1997, a few months later the NCAA accepted the internal investigations conducted by the University of Michigan when it was discovered that an athletic booster offered a basketball player's family free airline tickets—an illegal extra benefit.

Certain extra benefits are specifically provided for under NCAA legislation. Complimentary game tickets, postseason awards not exceeding defined dollar limits, medical and training expenses related to sports' participation, tutoring, drug rehabilitation programs, counseling costs tied to treatment of eating disorders, student development and career counseling, per diem meal and housing expenses on away trips, entertainment (e.g., complimentary tickets to professional sporting contests) on away games, and transportation costs while representing the institution all fall within permissible limits.[23]

Extra benefits deemed improper are reimbursement for travel to practice, non-sports-related travel apparel, an automobile, and athletic dormitories or athletic blocks where at least 50 percent of the residents are student-athletes unless the school can demonstrate that its housing assignment policies are nondiscriminatory.[24]

One particular extra benefit that has received serious debate over the years relates to an institution paying for the transportation, housing, and meal expenses of a student-athlete to visit or care for a parent or immediate family relative who is in a life-threatening situation. So long as the person who is ill or has just died is with a 100-mile radius of the college campus, then the institution may safely pay for these expenditures.

Many observers felt this rule is particularly harsh on financially strapped student-athletes who generally have limited sources of outside assets or income to pay for an unexpected life-challenging event. An assistant coach at the University of Kansas was reprimanded for taking money out of his own pocket to pay for a bus ticket for a student-athlete who had no money to attend a family funeral more than 100 miles from campus.

Besides limiting the dollar package award for an individual student-athlete, the NCAA (grants-in-aid limitations Bylaw Article 15.5) restricts the total number of athletic awards an institution may issue. Individual schools and conferences may limit these total awards even further. A partial list of maximum awards for selected Division I and II sports follows:

Sport	Division I		Division II	
	Male	Female	Male	Female
Basketball	13	15	10	10
Football	85		36	
Football (I-AA)	63			
Swimming	9.9	14	8.1	8.1
Volleyball	4.5	12	4.5	8
Baseball	11.7		9	
Softball		11		7.2

The fractional financial awards enable coaches to split scholarships. Not every student-athlete receives a full scholarship. In some cases, a student-athlete may receive a tuition waiver or free housing and books. This flexibility enables a coach to spread out financial awards over a larger student base.

Recruiting

The recruiting of athletically talented student-athletes is one of the starting points for any successful college program. NCAA Bylaw Article 13.1.2 permits the recruitment of a prospect or the prospect's relatives or legal guardian only by authorized school members. Generally, authorized school or staff members include designated faculty, administrators, and coaches. Colleges may not employ talent scouts or evaluators to help recruit. Members of a school booster club are barred from recruiting prospects.

A college athletic prospect normally falls within one of two categories: (1) a high school student who has completed his or her junior year of classes or (2) a junior college student who seeks to enroll in a four-year school. Occasionally, an enrolled intercollegiate student-athlete in a four-year school seeks to transfer to another four-year school. In this instance, a student's original college must grant permission for another college to recruit the athlete or release the athlete from his or her scholarship unless the original school has been placed on probation or dropped the sport.

One-time standout Marshall University wide receiver Randy Moss initially planned to begin his college career at Notre Dame University. Some off-the-field high school altercations led Notre Dame not to admit him. Moss enrolled at Florida State where a drug possession charge convinced Coach Bobby Bowden to release him from any commitment to the school. Moss then joined the Division I-AA Marshall team where he could begin play immediately. Normally, a student-athlete transferring from one Division I school to another Division I school must sit out a year. However, in Moss's case, because he transferred from a higher-division (I-A) football school to a lower-division (I-AA) football school, he did not have to wait a year to play ball. Ironically, Marshall had already arranged to move into the Division I-A Mid-American football conference before he elected to transfer.

The reasons for the NCAA imposing detailed requirements for student-athlete recruitment is to eliminate a litany of common practices used to lure prospects to major colleges. For instance, a few years ago a Federal Express driver inadvertently delivered an overnight letter from a Kentucky assistant basketball coach to a person other than the intended basketball recruit. The letter contained thousands of dollars of cash. The coach was suspended and the prospect was deemed ineligible to attend Kentucky.

Besides outright offers of cash, other improper recruiting inducements include co-signing a car loan, finding a job for the prospect's mom or dad,

merchandise discounts, gifts of equipment or clothing apparel, and free or reduced housing. Even providing publicity or media announcement of a
prospective student-athlete's campus visit may constitute an illegal recruitment activity.

The NCAA bylaws clearly make the prospect responsible for knowing
the rules surrounding the recruitment process.[25] A student-athlete violator is
subject to penalties ranging from loss of eligibility to loss of amateur status.
An institutional violation by faculty, administration, or staff depending on
the severity of the offense may lead to eliminating or curtailing recruiting
privileges, loss of scholarship, and placing the sports program on probation.

The NCAA has very specific recruiting periods limiting the times when
coaches can contact, evaluate, phone, and recruit players on campus. A freshman is not available to play a varsity sport until the NCAA Initial-Eligibility
Clearinghouse certifies the student's high school core course work as meeting the NCAA's eligibility standards.[26] This procedure is often slow moving
and controversial because the NCAA has, in essence, become "the super
school board in the sky." The NCAA's Student-Athlete Advisory Committee
recommendation that individual high school principals certify the high school
core courses incoming college students must successfully complete to compete in order to speed up the process has recently been accepted.

Key Considerations

- Financial awards may be given based on athletic ability but only at
  Division I and Division II schools.
- A National Letter of Intent is not the same agreement as an athletic
  scholarship.
- Improper awards or benefits may mean loss of eligibility and institu-
  tional penalties.
- Schools must authorize staff members who are eligible to help recruit.
- Students are expected to know the rules surrounding recruiting.

ACADEMIC STANDARDS

In 1986 the NCAA fielded about 400 questions a week regarding its rules for
eligibility. Today it receives more than 1,000 calls, letters, and faxes a day
from parents of prospective college student-athletes. That's because the
NCAA does not permit a student-athlete to participate in intercollegiate
competition unless all applicable academic eligibility standards are met.

To compete as a college freshman at the Division I and II levels a student-
athlete must have completed a minimum of 13 core high school courses in
designated academic disciplines.[27] Core subjects include four years of English, two years of mathematics, two years of natural science, two years of social science, one additional year of English, math, or natural science, and two

years of either a foreign language, computer science, or philosophy course. Currently, an Iowa City-based clearinghouse organization reviews the curricula of more than 24,000 U.S. high schools and identifies core courses as meeting or not meeting the eligibility standards established by the NCAA Academic Requirements Committee.

High school students register with the clearinghouse as a first step in meeting initial intercollegiate eligibility. The clearinghouse then certifies the core course work and standardized test results to the NCAA. Before deemed eligible to compete, students must earn a "C" or better average in these 13 academic courses. In response to the concerns of many African-American educators, the NCAA bylaw on eligibility imposes a sliding composite scale of high school core grades and SAT or ACT scores.[28] For a student-athlete to qualify for freshman sports participation with a minimum 2.00 core grade point average (GPA), a 1010 recentered SAT or 86 ACT is required. A prospective freshman with a 2.50 GPA needs a minimum 820 recentered SAT or 68 ACT to qualify.

These academic standards were fully debated at numerous NCAA conventions prior to ratification. Some academic scholars were concerned that these scholastic standards created an unfair hardship on high school members of the minority community who historically have not tested as well as other ethnic groups on standardized tests. Not achieving these academic standards might mean loss of athletic scholarship opportunity.

The full NCAA membership voted to impose these new standards for a freshman to compete at practice and games, and to become eligible for financial aid. A freshman in this category is called a *qualifier*.[29]

Heeding the concerns of many minority educators, a *partial qualifier* category was created.[30] This status permits an incoming freshman who did earn a "C" or better in core courses but did not achieve a high enough SAT or ACT score to receive financial aid. A partial qualifier may practice with the team but may not play in competition.

A third category known as a *nonqualifier* is for an incoming freshman who failed to meet the core course work and standardized test requirements.[31] Nonqualifiers are ineligible to practice and play and may not receive an athletic-based financial aid award.

Students in all three categories are expected to have earned a high school diploma. A Division I student-athlete partial qualifier or nonqualifier loses one year of intercollegiate eligibility under these same bylaws.

Over the past few years, since the imposition of these new freshman academic standards, the NCAA has become known for some as the "National Collegiate 'Arrassment Association." As reported by a leading newspaper, Jason Taylor, an outstanding high school linebacker with a 3.85 GPA and a more than satisfactory SAT score, was declared academically ineligible by the NCAA four days before his first college football game at the University of Akron when it was learned he was homeschooled by his mother.[32] The

NCAA bylaws refused to recognize grades earned in core subjects when taken at home. Taylor appealed the NCAA's initial decision to the Eligibility Committee, the last line in decision making for student eligibility problems. The NCAA agreed to reverse itself when it learned the core courses were monitored by an outside homeschooling accrediting association and the courses were approved by his local high school.

The New York Times highlighted the controversy regarding the NCAA's zeal to stand strictly behind its academic bylaws when it printed the following copy of a fax sent to an honors high school student whose college scholarship was placed on hold when the clearinghouse failed to approve a critical reading honors-level English course: "Thank you for you (sic) fax regarding 'Essential Communications.' Do (sic) to the vocational aspect of the course, we are unable to approve this course as a core course. Therefore, the decision remains unchange (sic) for student named above."[33]

Although the NCAA admits it was publicly embarrassed by these incidents, it points to two reasons for continuing to place a priority on academic preparedness. First is the need to assure the public that college sports is about amateur students competing in sports. Second, the graduation rates for student-athletes have appreciably improved since these new standards went into place.

For instance, in 1984, 52 percent of all student-athletes graduated in five years.[34] By the early 1990s the rate had improved to 58 percent with female student-athletes graduating at a substantially higher rate than their male counterparts.[35] However, the stricter academic standards have increased the percentage of ineligible black student-athletes from 11 percent to 27 percent according to the most recent figures.[36] But more African-American student-athletes are graduating each year than did before the latest standards were enacted.

Nevertheless, the NCAA continues to remain under siege regarding its academic eligibility standards. A class-action lawsuit brought by Trial Lawyers for Public Justice on behalf of minority student-athletes against the NCAA has asked the court to strike down these rules as discriminatory on the basis of race. A separate class of students sought relief from the U.S. Justice Department. Learning disabled student-athletes claimed victory when the NCAA's application of academic standards was deemed in violation of the Americans with Disabilities Act as too inflexible especially as it relates to core courses. Yet, the NCAA won a victory in a 1998 decision when a federal judge held that the NCAA need not accept the ACT scores from a high school student who took an untimed exam.[37] The student unsuccessfully argued that he had an anxiety disorder that caused nervousness while taking timed tests. The court did rule that the NCAA, even though it is a private entity, is subject to the Americans with Disabilities Act.

Once enrolled, a student-athlete must meet institutional and conference eligibility standards. A student-athlete at all institutions is expected to "be enrolled in at least a minimum full-time program of studies, be in good academic standing and maintain satisfactory progress toward a baccalaureate or equivalent degree" (NCAA Bylaw Article 14.01.2). The general course requirements for meeting these ongoing academic standards are left to the individual academic authorities (faculty, deans, and administrators) of each member institution. As the following case scenario reveals, this can lead to serious problems of underachievement and misguided missions.

University of Georgia Scandal

- Jan Kemp was the coordinator of the English section of Georgia's developmental studies program. She was fired after refusing to change the grades of six failing student-athletes. Her supervisor irately asked her, "Who do you think is more important to this university, you or a very prominent basketball player?"
- Kemp fought back. Despite suffering from severe depression over the school's attempt to blackmail student-athletes into making false accusations against her, she sought her job and dignity back in court. After listening to hours of sworn testimony describing Kemp as a caring, professional educator and hearing horror stories of student-athletes attending Georgia for years with no realistic chance of graduating, the jury awarded Kemp over $2 million in punitive damages along with nearly $300,000 in lost wages and compensation for mental distress. Ultimately those individuals responsible for education "malpractice" were dismissed themselves.

At a minimum, "good academic standing and satisfactory progress" means completing an average of 12 semester or quarter hours of credit per semester or its equivalent, or earning 24 semester or its equivalent credit hours since the beginning of the prior season of competition.[38] Summer school credit may count toward this requirement; however, the course(s) and credit hours must be acceptable at the student-athlete's college.

A last-semester senior who has fewer than 12 semester credits remaining to graduate falls within a special NCAA bylaw exception–permitted play. A 1995 amendment to the bylaws carved out a special exception to the 12 credit hours per semester rule for a learning disabled or handicapped student-athlete who can objectively demonstrate a course load of less than 12 credits or its quarterly equivalent is considered full-time status by the student-athlete's school for reasons of accommodation.

By the start of a student-athlete's third year of school work a major must be declared leading to a specific undergraduate degree. A student-athlete must have successfully completed at least 50 percent of the program of study or major requirements by the start of the fourth year of college. GPA requirements vary from institution to institution, but generally a student must maintain an overall "C" or better average by the end of his or her sophomore year and thereafter to retain eligibility to compete in sports.

Many of the requirements were imposed after the University of Georgia academic scandal.

NCAA Bylaw Article 14.2 grants a Division I student-athlete five years in which to complete four seasons of intercollegiate competition. Time off for missionary service, which is common among Mormon student-athletes, military duty, or the Peace Corps does not count against the five-year rule. A one-year extension of the five-year rule may be granted to a female student-athlete for pregnancy. A top-flight student athlete trying out or competing for a national or Olympic team may seek a time waiver through a two-thirds majority vote of NCAA Council members present and voting. A Division I or II student-athlete has 10 semesters or 15 quarters to complete athletic eligibility. A pregnancy waiver is available for non-Division I student-athletes too. It is permissible for a student-athlete to enroll in a graduate course of study during the fifth year and retain eligibility to participate when all four years of competition have not expired. All of these exceptions are found within the bylaw article on eligibility and satisfactory progress.

In a 1984 federal court case entitled *Butts* v. *NCAA & LaSalle University* a college student challenged NCAA Bylaw 14.2.4.4 that states that "any participation . . . in organized sports competition . . . after the student's 20th birthday and prior to full-time enrollment in a college institution shall count as one year of varsity competition in that sport."[39] (Note: In 1995 this rule was changed to read a student's twenty-first birthday, but at the time of the Butts case the bylaw read twentieth birthday). Butts had enrolled in prep school after high school to improve his grades and found himself turning twenty after the completion of his extra prep school year, causing him to lose one year of basketball eligibility at LaSalle. The court sided with the NCAA in holding that the bylaw served a legitimate, nondiscriminatory purpose of promoting equality of competition by preventing older players from dominating intercollegiate sports.

Another NCAA bylaw that has been unsuccessfully challenged in court deals with a rule that states that a Division I transfer student is ineligible to compete for another Division I college until after a full academic year in residence at the new academic institution. The historic genesis of this rule is quite amusing. Fielding Yost was enrolled as a law student at West Virginia University. On the Wednesday before Lafayette College was scheduled to play football on Saturday against the University of Pennsylvania Quakers, Yost enrolled as a transfer student. He helped Lafayette defeat Penn and then withdrew from classes. By the Monday after the game he was reenrolled once again at West Virginia!

The leading court decision upholding the voluntary NCAA rules hampering student-athletes from freely transferring and immediately playing for another school is *English* v. *NCAA*.[40] In this instance, the federal court determined that there are sound nondiscriminatory policy reasons for restricting the recruiting of a student-athlete by another competing institution.

The financial pressures on NCAA member institutions to turn a profit in their athletic programs are enormous. In 1997 the athletic director and president of New Mexico State University were released because of a $700,000 shortfall in athletic revenue over expenses. Only about 50 NCAA schools turned a financial profit according to the most recent accounting. Perhaps it is these pressures that lead schools to search not only for the best high school talent around but also for the best disgruntled college-athlete talent around that have led to the restrictive transfer rules. It is difficult to imagine not allowing a nonathlete transfer student from participating in student government activities or from joining the computer club at his or her new school, yet the NCAA and even the NAIA have in place such judicially supported transfer rules regarding intercollegiate athletics.

Exceptions do exist to the stringent NCAA transfer rules. The time rule is waived when a student-athlete's school drops his or her intercollegiate sport or reclassifies the sport from Division I to Division III status.

The NCAA Eligibility Committee yearly reviews a number of "hardship" cases where special circumstances warrant granting an extra year of intercollegiate eligibility. By far the most common request occurs when a student-athlete suffers a season-ending injury or comes down with an incapacitating illness. Historically, this committee has been reasonable in granting deserved waivers.

ENFORCEMENT

The major administrative bylaw regarding enforcement policies and procedures is found in Article 32 of the NCAA Manual. Unlike some of the operational bylaws that may apply only to some schools based on their division classification, the enforcement bylaws apply across the board to all member institutions and conferences. Procedurally, the Committee on Infractions proposes enforcement legislation subject to approval by the general policy board of the NCAA: the 46-member council. The full membership of the NCAA has an opportunity to consider for passage the recommendations of the council.

The Committee on Infractions headed by longtime NCAA staffer David Berst is arguably the most powerful NCAA body. The committee not only recommends new enforcement legislation but investigates allegations of rules violations. Remember that each member school and conference promises to fully comply in the administration of its athletic programs with the NCAA's constitution, bylaws, rules, and regulations. When an individual college learns of a possible violation, it is duty bound to inform the Committee on Infractions immediately.

A common scenario especially among intercollegiate football and basketball programs is for a competing school to bring to the attention of Berst's committee possible irregularities in recruiting or offering aid at another institution. Occasionally the Committee on Infractions will initiate its own investigation of a potential rules violation usually on the basis of a parent of a recruit calling the NCAA or something a member of a committee reads in a newspaper or views on a television broadcast of a college sporting event. The committee has at its disposal a paid staff of investigators to look into allegations of rules abuse.

Once the enforcement staff makes a determination that there is reason to believe a violation has occurred, a letter is forwarded from the NCAA to the president or chancellor of the school, the athletic director, the school's faculty representative to the NCAA, and the head of the school's conference. The letter serves two purposes: to inform the school of the nature of the charges and to request full cooperation in its investigation.

Violations are classified as either major or secondary. A *secondary violation* is usually unintentional, inadvertent, and harmless in the sense that no competitive athletic or recruiting advantage is gained.[41] For instance, a college coach attending a high school baseball game to watch a recruit lent his jacket to the mother of the recruit when she complained that she was "freezing." The lending of the coat to the recruit's mother was deemed an "illegal contact" but was classified as a secondary violation under NCAA Bylaw Article 19. No hearing before the Committee on Infractions was required. No institutional penalty was imposed.

Not all secondary violations go unpunished. Penalties may include suspending a coach or an athletic staff member for one or more games, imposing a fine from $500 to $5,000, forfeiting a contest, restricting future recruiting activities, losing a recruit who may be at the center of the violation, reducing financial aid award packages, requiring the school to recertify compliance with NCAA rules and procedures, and a public reprimand. A school's voluntary disclosure and reporting of a secondary violation increases the likelihood of a less severe penalty, which is what occurred when Colorado reported that one of its reserve football players had already used his five years of eligibility when he played in all 11 games during the 1997–98 season. The violation was deemed secondary. Colorado's sole penalty was to forfeit all of its 1997 football wins.

If a violation is not of a secondary nature, then it must be a *major incident* calling for serious presumptive penalties, which allows for a hearing before the Committee on Infractions and an appeal of the committee's finding and penalties.[42] The NCAA's newsletter known as *The NCAA News* is a good source for finding examples of major violations and penalties imposed. A few examples follow. A perennial top-10 football school failed to follow its own institutional drug policies and procedures when it permitted three players who had tested positive for marijuana use prior to an end-of-the-season bowl game to play. School policy called for their immediate suspension. Additionally, the head coach at the time failed to inform his superiors of the drug test finding until well after the national championship bowl game was played. School procedures required immediate disclosure to the athletic director. The principles of amateurism were at stake when football student-athletes contributed to a pool of money for the purpose of providing a cash payout to the player who made the best game tackle. Collectively, these major incidents all occurring at the same school suggested a lack of institutional control.

Once an investigation turns out a finding of a major violation, and after any hearing before the final appeals board, the council, upholding the finding, must comply with Bylaw Article 19.6.2, which demands the imposition of *all* of the following penalties for the sport involved, subject to some discretionary powers to ameliorate the penalty by the committee:

1. A two-year probationary period;
2. A one-year reduction in the number of expense-paid recruiting visits;
3. A one-year prohibition in off-campus recruiting by coaches;
4. For a coach or staff member who knowingly engaged in or condoned the illegal activity subject to termination, a one-year suspension without pay, reassignment of duties, or other disciplinary action;
5. A reduction in the number of financial aid awards;
6. Sanctions precluding postseason (bowl) competition;
7. Institutional recertification of compliance with all NCAA regulations.

Furthermore, the penalties imposed for a secondary violation may also be applied to an institution that engages in a major violation.

In the preceding example of the three players who tested positive for drug use, the school received the following penalties from the NCAA: a one-year ban from postseason play, a two-year probation, and a reduction in 24 financial aid awards, putting the team at a recruiting and player personnel disadvantage. The players in question who tested positive had either opted to leave school early, including first-round NFL draft choice Warren Sapp, or their eligibility had expired. The head coach in question, Dennis Erickson, chose to leave the college football fraternity and join the professional Seattle Seahawks as head coach. The school that was penalized, the University of Miami, suffered further public indignation when *Sports Illustrated* in a cover story recommended that the entire football program should be disbanded.

The NCAA bylaws do contain a provision to shut down a college's football program for repeat major violations found within five years following the starting date of any major penalty. Bylaw Article 19.6.2.3 is better known as the "death penalty" clause. Not all repeat violations lead to the cancellation of a school's sport for a maximum of two years' application of the "death penalty." Lesser repeat violation penalties may include a two-year loss of financial aid awards, no recruiting for two years, and a four-year loss of voting privileges in the NCAA including university officials' resignation from NCAA committees and offices. In 1987 Southern Methodist University (SMU) became the first and only NCAA school to date to receive the "death penalty" for flagrant, ongoing alumni booster violations. The NCAA imposed a one-year ban on any football competition. SMU voluntarily tacked on a second year. The football program has never fully recovered from the ban.

Key Considerations

- High school students register with the clearinghouse as a first step in meeting academic intercollegiate eligibility.
- The initial-eligibility clearinghouse certifies "core" courses that meet the minimum 13 core high school requirements for freshmen eligibility with the assistance of high school principals.
- Students are labeled Qualifiers, Partial Qualifiers, and Nonqualifiers.
- Enrolled students must meet minimum academic standards and make satisfactory progress toward a college degree.
- Generally, students have five years to complete four years of athletic eligibility.
- The Committee on Infractions investigates rules violations, which are either major or secondary.
- Repeat violators may face the "death penalty."

SUMMARY

The NCAA is a powerful regulatory body charged by its member institutions with the responsibility of maintaining the amateur status of student-athletes and ensuring a level playing field for intercollegiate athletic programs for men and women. The constitution of the NCAA contains six main articles that provide for the body's organizational structure, rule-making process, and principles guiding the conduct of fair play. Annually the members of the NCAA adopt and modify operating bylaws that are meant to promote the organization's guiding principles.

The major bylaws concern ethical conduct, amateur eligibility, financial aid, recruiting, and academic standards. The practical application of these operating bylaws presents challenging issues to the NCAA ranging from due process rights, drug testing, gambling, racial bias, rights of the learning disabled, and fundamental fairness to general administrative misconduct. Special-interest groups have frequently contested in court the bylaws promulgated by the NCAA.

For Reflection

1. Under what circumstances can a student-athlete participate as a professional athlete without losing amateur intercollegiate status?
2. What is the difference between a qualifier and a partial qualifier?

3. List examples of situations when the NCAA bylaws will allow a student-athlete five years to complete four seasons of intercollegiate competition.
4. What is the basic purpose of the NCAA?
5. What is the purpose of the NCAA bylaws?
6. Describe four acts by a college athlete that can lead to loss of amateur intercollegiate status.
7. Which is the most powerful NCAA committee, and why?
8. What is the difference between a major violation and a secondary violation?
9. What steps does the enforcement staff of the NCAA take after notice of an infraction?
10. Why is the NCAA so concerned about student-athletes gambling?
11. Does a student-athlete enjoy the same constitutional protections as a nonstudent in the public sector?
12. Why did the U.S. Supreme Court rule against Jerry Tarkanian?
13. Has the "death penalty" ever been imposed?
14. What is the role of the clearinghouse?
15. May an NCAA student-athlete compete in the Olympics and not lose intercollegiate amateur status?

Useful Web Sites

1. http://www.xcscx.com/colsport/
2. http://uscollegehockey.com/
3. http://football.yahoo.com/ncaaf/
4. http://www.ncaa.org/
5. http://www.soconline.org/WATCH/

Notes

1. See Walter Byers and Charles Hammer, *Unsportsmanlike Conduct (Exploring College Athletes)* (Ann Arbor, MI: The University of Michigan Press, 1995) for a historical overview of events leading to the formation of the NCAA.
2. *Veronia School District v. Acton*, 115 S. Ct. 2386 (1995).
3. NCAA Manual, Constitution, Art. 1–6 (1997–98).
4. Ibid., Art. 2.1 (Principle of Institutional Control and Responsibility).
5. The NCAA News, February 12, 1994, p. 21.
6. *The Boston Globe*, May 9, 1997 at 1.
7. NCAA Manual, Art. 2.3 (Gender Equity).
8. From Byers and Hammer, *Unsportsmanlike Conduct*, p. 39, quoting

an extract from Theodore Roosevelt's speech, February 23, 1907, as reported by the *New York Sun*.

9. NCAA Manual, Art. 2.8.
10. Ibid., Art. 10.1 (Unethical Conduct) and Art. 10.2 (Knowledge of Use of Banned Drugs).
11. Ibid., Art. 5 (Legislative Authority and Process).
12. From NCAA funded research conducted by professors Frank Cullen and Edward Latessa, University of Cincinnati, reported in a number of sources including *Union Leader*, November 9, 1996, at D3.
13. Ibid.
14. NCAA Manual, Art. 10.1 (Unethical Conduct) and Art. 19.6 (Penalties).
15. *Shelton* v. *NCAA*, 539 F 2d 1197 (9th Cir. 1976).
16. NCAA Manual, Art. 12.1.3 (Professionalism).
17. Ibid., Art. 12.1.4 (Amateur Status if Professional in Another Sport).
18. Ibid., Art. 12.2.4.2.1 (Exception—Professional Basketball Draft).
19. Ibid., Art. 12.2.3.2.4 (Major Junior A Ice Hockey).
20. Ibid., Art. 12.2.3.2.4.1 (Limitation on Restoration of Eligibility).
21. Ibid.
22. Ibid., Art. 15.2.4.2-(e).
23. Ibid., Art. 16,2–16.8.
24. Ibid., Art. 16.5 (Housing) and 16.8.2 (Nonpermissible).
25. Ibid., Art. 13.1 (Recruiting).
26. Ibid., Art. 14.1.2.1 (Initial-Eligibility Clearinghouse).
27. Ibid., Art. 14.2.9 (Qualification Status).
28. Ibid.
29. Ibid.
30. Ibid., Art. 14.3 (Summary of the Definition and Partial Qualifier). Recently, a class-action suit was filed against the NCAA claiming that its initial-eligibility rules discriminate on the basis of race. See: http://www.ncaa.org/news/97 0120/active/3403 no.4.html.
31. Ibid.
32. As reprinted in *Sports Illustrated*, "Inside the Moat," by Steven Ruskin, March 3, 1997, at 78.
33. Ibid.
34. *USA Today*, June 27, 1997, at 10C.
35. Ibid.
36. Ibid.
37. As reported in *Sports Illustrated*, February 16, 1998, p. 30.
38. NCAA Manual, Art. 14,4 (Satisfactory Progress).
39. 751 F. 2d 609 (3rd. Cir. 1984).
40. 439 So 2d 1218 (La Ct. App. 1983).
41. NCAA Manual, Art. 19.02.2 (Types of Violations).
42. Ibid., and at Art. 19.5.1 (For Major Violations).

CHAPTER 2

Global Amateur Sports

M any of life's disappointments, even major ones (like not having the opportunity to participate in the Olympics), do not enjoy constitutional protection. This is one such instance.
—Judge David Pratt,
DeFrantz v. USOC 492 F. Supp. 1181

Case Study

Susan Powers, a top track star, was suspended by the national governing body for U.S.A. Track & Field for testing positive for a banned substance. Prior to the drug test, Susan had called the U.S. Olympic Committee's "drug hot line" to ask about some medication her personal physician had prescribed. She was told the ingredients in the medication were not illegal. After placing well at a national meet, she was randomly selected for a drug test where she tested positive for a banned amphetamine.

Should Susan be barred from track participation for taking a drug she did not know was banned? What responsibility should the U.S. Olympic Committee accept for dispensing the wrong information?

INTRODUCTION

The summer and winter Olympic games catch the fancy of the viewing public every four years. In between these years, dozens of individual athletic associations hold local, regional, national, and international championships. Subject to certain parameters, a sports association or body is free to establish rules for participant eligibility, hosting of events, and codes of conduct. A national sports body is contractually a part of a larger, comprehensive international federation. At times conflicts arise between these two distinct governing groups. This chapter explores the legal relationship that exists between international governing organizations and national sports bodies. Special focus is directed toward the most current areas of tension including political boycotts, drug testing, gender discrimination, and overcommercialization of Olympic sports.

OLYMPICS: AMATEUR SPORTS ACT OF 1978

The name *Tonya Harding* became synonymous with the 1994 winter Olympics in Norway when the U.S. figure skating community faced the daunting task of deciding whether to keep Harding off the U.S. Olympic team. Harding faced allegations that she had helped mastermind a violent clubbing attack on fellow skater Nancy Kerrigan. The public was captivated by the day-to-day stories surrounding the January 6, 1994 attack on Kerrigan by Harding's bodyguard Shawn Eckardt. The assault took place at the U.S. national championships in Detroit, which served as the qualifying meet for selecting the U.S. Olympic figure skating team.

By following the trail of money, criminal investigators were led to Harding's ex-husband, Jeff Gillooly, and ultimately to Harding herself. Long after the conclusion of the Olympics, Tonya Harding pleaded guilty to hindering the criminal prosecution of the matter. Later the U.S. Figure Skating Association found Harding in violation of its ethical code of conduct, stripped her of the title she won when the injured Kerrigan was unable to compete at the national championships, and banned her for life from competing.

The tangled legal, ethical, and political web of competitive figure skating, the Olympic movement, and the rights of Harding and Kerrigan were exposed for all the world to view. The answer to the question of why Harding was permitted to participate in the winter Olympics during the criminal investigation examining her involvement in assaulting a fellow teammate rests with an understanding of the legislation surrounding international amateur sports.

Under federal law the U.S. Olympic Committee (USOC) is the governing body charged with supervising the participation of U.S. athletes in Olympic games.[1] It is a private corporation. The international governing body for the summer and winter Olympics is the International Olympic Committee (IOC), chartered as a nonprofit, private society under Swiss law. The IOC recognizes the USOC as the sole national Olympic committee for the United States.

The USOC has scores of different amateur sports associations under its jurisdiction. Examples of recognized amateur sports associations include the aforementioned U.S. Figuring Skating Association (USFSA), USA Cycling Federation, US Swimming, USA Baseball, and the recently created USA Triathlon Association. These sports bodies and many others serve as the national governing body (NGB) for each Olympic sport. The Amateur Sports Act of 1978 mandates that the USOC select the sports association that will serve as the NGB for a particular Olympic and Pan American sport based on legislative criteria.[2] An excerpted copy of the Amateur Sports Act is found in the appendix along with the Olympic Charter.

The Amateur Sports Act also guarantees certain substantive and procedural due process rights to amateur and Olympic athletes. It is because of these statutory rights that Tonya Harding was not immediately dismissed from the U.S. Olympic team on the basis of an allegation of criminal activities against a teammate without first granting her the right to a series of hearings.

Tonya Harding's victory in Detroit initially sealed her place on the U.S. Olympic team. However, the USFSA (as the NGB for that sport) first had to officially place her name before the USOC. Almost one month after the assault incident, the USFSA convened a hearing to determine whether disciplinary action, including but not limited to keeping her off the Olympic team list, for violating the sport's ethical conduct rules should be imposed. On February 5 the panel found reasonable grounds for an ethical violation without hearing from Harding. Under the Amateur Sports Act, she was entitled to a hearing no earlier than 30 days from the USFSA's findings or no sooner than March 5. Meanwhile, the women's Olympic figure skating championships were slated to begin on February 23, nearly two weeks before Harding's first hearing date. Additionally, Harding had a right to appeal any adverse finding to the USFSA's executive committee and then to request another hearing before an American Arbitration Association arbitrator.

Fearful of a civil lawsuit seeking lost commercial endorsements and personal appearance fees, the USFSA acting as the NGB decided to put Harding's name forward as an Olympic figure skating team member, along with Kerrigan's, before the USOC. This occurred just before the January 31 deadline. The USOC then elected to convene its own disciplinary hearing, apart from the USFSA hearing and apart from the ongoing criminal investigation by state authorities. This hearing was scheduled about a week before the Olympic skating competition. The legal issue was whether Harding had discredited her teammates, the USFSA, the USOC, and the U.S. by her alleged criminal conduct.

Harding immediately sought injunctive relief in a state court in her home state of Oregon, seeking to prevent the USOC from conducting its hearing just prior to the skating competition. A judicial review, but absent any explicit finding, suggested the USOC's disciplinary rules applied to conduct while a member of the U.S. Olympic team and did not apply to activities prior to joining the Olympic team. The USOC agreed not to go forward with its pending disciplinary hearing. Before a global audience of millions of television viewers Harding skated. She captured eighth place while Kerrigan took home the silver figure skating Olympic medal.

Little judicial precedent exists for a bizarre set of circumstances intertwining brazen behavior, an obsession to win at any costs, federal amateur sports rules, threats of damage suits, and a worldwide audience all watching and wondering where it will all end. In 1924 a stockbroker by the name of

William Silkworth competed in the Paris summer Olympic games notwithstanding an outstanding criminal charge of investor fraud. He won a gold medal in the team trap shooting event for the United States. When he returned home, he was criminally convicted. Harding has not returned to the amateur world of figure skating since her criminal conviction and the finding by the USFSA that she violated its ethical code of conduct.

Key Considerations: Amateur Sports Act of 1978
- The USOC is a private corporation.
- The Amateur Sports Act mandates that the USOC select the national governing body for each Olympic sport.
- Procedural and substantive due process rights are assured U.S. amateur athletes by the Amateur Sports Act, including a right to a hearing and an appeal.
- Tonya Harding tested the limits of sportsmanship and hearing rights.

DRUG TESTING

The subject of testing athletes for drug use is fairly new to Olympic sports. At the 1960 Olympic games in Rome a cyclist died as a result of taking amphetamines. In response, doping controls were established at the 1964 Olympics in Tokyo. Three years later the IOC created a medical commission to identify classes of drugs deemed illegal, eradicate the use of these banned drugs, and propose sanctions for violators. Prior to Olympic participation, an athlete must agree to comply with the IOC Medical Code.

Currently, the IOC lists the following five prohibited classes of drugs or substances as follows:

1. Stimulants
2. Narcotics
3. Anabolic agents
4. Diuretics
5. Peptide and glycoprotein hormones and analogues

Under present standards, the detected presence of certain stimulants (e.g., ephedrine, pseudoephedrine, phenylpropaolamine, and cathine) found in connection with a competition constitutes a prima facie case of doping. The burden then shifts to the athlete to refute this rebutable presumption. The legal standard, as is seen in some of the following cases, requires a showing that the banned substance was present under circumstances that were not intended nor the result of gross negligence, willful negligence, or imprudence. More recently, the IOC Medical Commission has added masking agents like epistosterone and probenecid to the list of banned substances. Epistosterone takes center stage in the Mary Decker Slaney case found later in this chapter.

Before Slaney's controversial drug-testing matter, another U.S. track star was subject to years of lost competition. World record holder Butch Reynolds engaged in a series of arbitration hearings and judicial litigation over the power of the international track establishment to ban him from performing on the basis of a claim of testing positive for an illegal performance-enhancing drug. The IOC in conjunction with the formal Olympic committee for each country and the international federation for each sport posts a list of banned doping drugs and illegal drugs that seek to camouflage drugs on the banned list. However, the lists do not always contain the same drugs nor do they always agree on the amount necesssary to reach an illegal level. Reynolds at a track meet in Monaco was randomly selected for a drug test after competing. His urine tested positive for nandrolone, an androgenic anabolic steroid banned by the International Amateur Athletic Federation (IAAF). The IAAF is an unincorporated association based in England that coordinates global track and field events.

The IAAF immediately suspended Reynolds from competition and later on went so far as to threaten to bar from competition, including Olympic competition, any athlete who competed in an event in which Reynolds might participate. Initially, Reynolds sought relief in a U.S. federal court, but then fearful of not exhausting his administrative remedies first, he sought an arbitration hearing in the United States following the procedures outlined in the Amateur Sports Act. The American arbitrator ruled that strong evidence existed that the urine samples sent to the French lab did not come from Reynolds. The IAAF refused to acknowledge the arbitration decision because the hearing was not conducted under the auspices of the IAAF's rules and procedures.

Reynolds then appealed to the U.S. national governing body, the Athletic Congress of the United States, Inc., or TAC as it was known before changing its name to USA Track & Field. TAC conducted a hearing and found "substantial doubt on the validity of (Reynold's) drug test."

The IAAF failed to act on TAC's findings and convened its own arbitration hearing in England. The drug tests were deemed valid and Reynolds's two-year suspension was upheld.

Reynolds successfully sued TAC and the IAAF in an Ohio federal court, winning the opportunity to compete for the United States in the Olympics and earning monetary damages for loss of business opportunities and defamation of character. These decisions were then appealed all the way to the U.S. Supreme Court.[3] The Court permitted him to compete in the Olympics but refused to hear an earlier appeals court's decision reversing his $23.7 million judgment against the IAAF. The appeals court determined that U.S. courts in this instance had no personal jurisdiction over the IAAF.[4] The IAAF indicated it would be amenable to English courts reviewing its arbitration ruling, but not U.S. courts.

Four years after the disputed drug test Reynolds was out of money and could proceed no further. His case did bring about reforms. The existing

International Council of Arbitration for Sport (ICAS) became the exclusive and final binding arbitrator via the Court of Arbitration for Sport (CAS) for disputes between international governing federations and athletes. Beforehand, individual national governing bodies, such as TAC in the case of Reynold's, conducted a hearing. Yet, as in Reynold's case, the international governing body (IAAF) sometimes refused to acknowledge TAC's findings. The ICAS also was divided into a trial and appeals division, ensuring greater due process rights for amateur athletes.

Organization of the Court of Arbitration for Sport

- The arbitration division resolves sports-related disputes.
- The appeals arbitration division resolves disputes concerning the decisions of disciplinary tribunals or similar bodies of federations, associations, or other sports bodies.
- Nonbinding advisory opinions are given at the request of the IOC, international sport federations and national Olympic committees or governing bodies, and the Olympic games organizing committees.
- There are 150 arbitrators.
- Headquarters is located in Lausanne, Switzerland.

In the appendix readers will find a copy of the Court of Arbitration for Sport Waiver form that all athletes competing in the Olympics and world championship sporting events in an Olympic sport must sign prior to competition.

The newly constituted CAS was called upon to resolve a drug-testing controversy involving a teenage swimmer from New York. Jessica Foschi tested positive for the banned steroid drug mesterolone (a synthetic male hormone that lets your body recover quickly from strenuous workouts) at the 1995 summer national championships. The international governing body for swimming, Federation Internationale de Natation (FINA), imposed a two-year ban. Foschi went before the board of directors of U.S. Swimming (USS), the national governing body for U.S. swimming, seeking relief from the two-year sanctions. This board concluded that she had tested positive for the doping drug, but that she "lacked knowledge of the manner in which the banned substance entered her body." Her family believed that perhaps her water bottle had been tampered with during the swim meet. The board gave Foschi a two-year probation with periodic drug testing.

The USS to the surprise of the swimming community appealed its own board's decision. Under the Amateur Sports Act, the matter was then placed before an arbitration panel. Foschi was deemed innocent of any knowledge as to how the illegal drug entered her body. All sanctions were removed, even though FINA rules called for a full two-year suspension. This conflict led to the CAS hearing the dispute. In the spring of 1997, the CAS as the "court of last resort" imposed a retroactive suspension of six months from competition.

In the aftermath of the perplexing manner in which the fifteen-year-old Foschi tested positive for a banned drug that she adamantly denied ever taking, the swimming community agreed to undertake measures to ensure that swimmers' drinks would not be tampered with. All poolside containers of water and sports drinks are to be secured prior to the start of any major meet. However, at the most recent national swimming championships, meet officials discovered beverage containers unsealed and unattended a full 45 minutes after the first race started.

Also, although U.S. Swimming was criticized in many quarters for appealing the domestic arbitration ruling against one of its own swimmers, this same organization has openly and harshly complained about the lax drug testing of the former Eastern bloc swimmers and, even more recently, of the Chinese women swimmers who set disputed world records. Even Irish swimming sensation, Michelle Smith, who captured a handful of Olympic medals in 1996, but failed to capture public approval for her accomplishments, is still the subject of reports of taking illegal performance-enhancing drugs.

In late 1997 a handful of former East German swimming coaches were criminally charged with giving anabolic steroids to 17 teenaged girls from 1974 to 1989. Besides suspension from coaching Olympic athletes that occurs to any coach or trainer, and not just an athlete, who violates the IOC Medical Code, these former East German coaches were suspended by their current national sport federations. FINA once suspended an Australian coach for two years for failing to know that a prescription headache tablet he gave to his star performer, Samantha Riley, contained a banned substance.

The battle over drugs to improve race performance, testing procedures, confidentiality, and the appeals process reached a new low when USA Track & Field (USATF) suspended longtime middle distance running star Mary Decker Slaney. For many years Slaney has been an outspoken critic of elite athletes who use banned drugs to enhance results. At the 1996 Summer Olympic trials, Slaney registered a testosterone-to-epitestosterone (T/E) ratio higher than the IOC allowable 6–1 ratio.

Testosterone is a naturally occurring male sex hormone unlike the artificial anabolic steroid Ben Johnson illegally used at the 1988 Olympics. Testosterone can be artificially introduced, although it is difficult to segregate the real hormone from the artificial hormone. Dr. David Black, a leading Nashville forensic toxicologist, does not believe the T/E test is a reliable means to indicate testosterone use in a female. Many experts conclude that there doesn't exist sufficient research on what might affect testosterone readings for women. Slaney has publicly argued that at the time of the drug testing she had just begun taking birth control pills and was at a point in her menstrual cycle that adversely influenced her T/E readings.

Slaney was allowed to compete at the 1996 summer Olympics and subsequent national track championships in 1996 and 1997 pending confidential review and appeal of the drug tests and any sanctions. Rumors persisted among fellow competitors that she had tested positive for a banned substance. During the summer of 1997 Slaney's name was leaked to the press by unknown sources as having tested positive for an illegal drug. Shortly thereafter, USA Track & Field suspended her from further competition. For Slaney, a driven athlete who has set 17 world records and 36 U.S. records, she sought complete vindication and an apology for gross violations of the Amateur Sports Act rules on confidentiality.

Finally, in the fall of 1997, the USATF's doping hearing board after two days of expert medical testimony cleared Slaney. Nike chairman Phil Knight financially supported Slaney's legal efforts to exonerate herself. Slaney's international eligibility is now in the hands of the IAAF.

Many of these high-profile drug-doping cases involve charges, countercharges, and controversy. Jurisdictional disputes between national and federal governing bodies are the norm. In Slaney's case the IAAF suspended her even before her national federation, the USATF, had an opportunity to fully investigate her urine sample. The USATF then felt compelled to issue its own suspension after a brief hearing, notwithstanding Slaney's loud protestations of innocence. Fortunately for Slaney, the Amateur Sports Act and the U.S. Olympic Committee constitution grant all U.S. amateur athletes a hearing and an appeal from the initial hearing in accordance with due process.

Due process in matters involving illegal "street" drugs or performance-enhancing drugs means assuring an amateur athlete that the testing procedure is accurate, the results are confidential, a timely and fair hearing and appeals process is in place, and the sanctions are noncapricious, nondiscriminatory, reasonable, and fair. Any tests conducted must also recognize and respect an athlete's right to privacy.

The USOC policy stipulates that all athletes are tested for drugs at the Olympic trials. The IOC policy is to test the winners and randomly test all others. In many ways the drug policy regarding Olympic athletes is similar to the NCAA's random, mandatory testing in postseason competition of college athletes. None of these organizations are deemed state actors for constitutional law purposes, thereby limiting the protections that otherwise might be available. Both policies differ from those found in professional sports. Drug policies and programs in these instances are negotiated as part of the collective bargaining process between management and players associations.

Canadian snowboarder Rass Rebagliati became the center of controversy at the 1998 Nagano Olympics where he became the fifth winter Olympian to test positive for illegal drugs at the games. After winning the first snowboarding Olympic gold medal, Rebagliati tested higher than 15 nanograms per millileter of marijuana. The International Ski Federation, which served as the international federation for snowboarding, allows up to 15 nanograms per milliliter. The IOC doesn't allow any level of marijuana.

Rebagliati claimed the drug traces came from secondhand exposure to marijuana. After the IOC voted to strip him of his gold medal, the CAS reinstated his win. The CAS ruled that because the IOC lacked an agreement with the International Ski Federation governing marijuana use, it could not strip Rebagliati of his medal. The CAS called for the creation of an explicit set of rules governing marijuana use by athletes in international competition, including the Olympic games.

U.S. bobsledder Mike Dionne lost his appeal before the CAS when he was suspended from competition by the International Bobsled Federation (FIBT) for three months just before the start of the Nagano Olympics. Dionne had tested positive for ephedrine, a stimulant frequently found in nonprescription cold medicines.

Key Considerations: Drug Testing

- Drug testing among Olympic athletes first began in 1964.
- The IOC lists five prohibited classes of doping drugs.
- A positive test for an illegal drug generally results in a prima facie case of illegal drug use.
- Butch Reynolds lost his suit against the track establishment, but his case led to the establishment of the International Court of Arbitration for Sport (CAS).
- CAS has become the final and exclusive binding arbitrator for drug disputes.
- Disputes still arise among athletes, national governing bodies, international federations, and the IOC over classifying drugs, due process rights, and penalties.

OLYMPIC BOYCOTTS AND BEYOND

Many Americans remember the tremendous success U.S. athletes had at the summer Olympics of 1984 in Los Angeles, which the Soviet Union elected to boycott. Four years earlier the USOC had decided not to send a team of American athletes to the Moscow Olympics as a response to the Soviet Union's invasion of Afghanistan. A group of American athletes who had qualified for the Olympic team sued the USOC for abridging their constitutional rights.

In *DeFrantz* v. *USOC* 25 athletes, including world record holder Jesse Vassallo, who gave up the opportunity to swim for Puerto Rico to swim for the United States, failed to convince the court that they had a statutory right under the Amateur Sports Act to compete in the Olympics.[5] The court refused to accept their argument that any decision to boycott the Olympics must be based on "sports-related considerations," not politically based motivations.

President Jimmy Carter had put incredible pressure on the USOC to boycott the Moscow games, going so far as to send Vice President Mondale to address the USOC voting delegates, threatening to revoke the USOC's tax-exempt status and bar any athletes from traveling to the Olympic games. The court found that the USOC had the authority to decide not to send an American team for non-sports-related reasons. Finally, the court noted that the USOC was an independent body, not a government or state actor, and nothing in its charter gave the government the right to control its decisions. The USOC was viewed not to have violated any constitutionally protected rights of the athletes, including any rights attributed to the Amateur Sports Act.

The *DeFrantz* decision for amateur U.S. athletes is equivalent to the *Tarkanian* decision for college athletes where the court found the NCAA is not a state actor. These sports governing organizations, the USOC and NCAA, have greater latitude in making decisions that might otherwise run afoul of constitutional due process and equal protection guarantees for private citizens by government officials.

In a non-Olympic event the cyclists of the 85th Tour de France in 1998 staged a boycott to protest what they perceived as harassment by the media and Tour organizers. The 150 cycling competitors reacted to innuendo and rumor that they all might have used an illegal drug known as erythropoietin (EPO), a hormone that stimulates the production of oxygen-bearing red blood cells. The boycott occurred after a handful of Tour riders confessed to using performance-enhancing drugs and following the arrest of some cycling officials for illegally supplying EPO, anabolic steroids and masking agents.

OLYMPIC SEX DISCRIMINATION

The 1984 Olympic games in Los Angeles led to a lawsuit of a different nature than the 1980 *DeFrantz* case. A group of women runners sued the IOC, USOC, and IAAF for failing to include the 5,000-meter and 10,000-meter running events for women in the summer Olympic games.[6] Both track events were included in Los Angeles for men runners. The women contended the lack of equal medal opportunities for women violated their constitutional rights to equal protection.

The court was extremely reluctant to pass judgment involving U.S. constitutional principles on an international event organized and conducted under the auspices of the Olympic Charter. The appeals court supported the lower court's determination that there was little likelihood the women would win their equal protection claims. The move to force the 1984 Olympic organizers to immediately include these two women's track events failed.

Subsequently, they have been added to the Olympic menu. The court pointed out an administrative procedure does exist for adding and deleting Olympic sports.

The passionate closing remarks of federal circuit Judge Alarcon, who concurred in the overall findings but wrote a separate opinion, follows.

> The IOC made concessions to the widespread popularity of women's track and field by adding two distance races this year. (But not the 5,000 and 10,000 meters.) The IOC refused, however, to grant women athletes equal status by including all events in which women compete internationally. In so doing, the IOC postpones indefinitely the equality of athletic opportunity that it could easily achieve this year in Los Angeles. When the Olympics move to other countries, some without America's commitment to human rights, the opportunity to tip the scales of justice in favor of equality may slip away. Meanwhile, the Olympic flame—which should be a symbol of harmony, equality and justice— will burn less brightly over the Los Angeles Olympic Games.[7]

COMMERCIALIZATION OF THE OLYMPICS

For some the 1996 Atlanta summer Olympics was viewed as a mixture of plastic and street hawker. The city of Atlanta licensed unprecedented numbers of merchandise vendors that sold nonlicensed rival Olympic clothing and souvenirs immediately beyond the official Olympic venues. Although the Atlanta Olympic organizers raised $1.6 billion for the games, many IOC observers believe this event marked the first time the Olympics became an advertising and promotional tool for big business sponsors.

Critics of the Atlanta games point to the 1992 Barcelona Olympics where all city contracts with vendors had to receive approval by the regional and national Olympic organizations. It is expected that the IOC will seek to corral at the local level the commercialization of Olympic-related merchandise at the summer Sydney Olympics. However, the IOC and other Olympic organization committees will continue to rely heavily on advertising revenue from the sale of broadcasting rights to the major networks. NBC bid nearly $4 billion for the exclusive Olympics broadcasting rights through the year 2008. CBS paid $375 million for the television rights to the Nagano Olympic games.

Major Olympic advertisers, including Coca-Cola after having paid an average of $500,000 each for 30-second prime-time spots, were appalled at the use of "ambush" advertising by many athletes at the most recent summer Olympic games. Jamaican track sprinter Merlene Ottey was captured on television wearing earrings in the shape of the Puma logo. Gold medal winner Claudia Poll was seen wearing a Pepsi-Cola T-shirt under her track suit top during the medal ceremonies. Coca-Cola, as the largest financial sponsor of the Atlanta games to the tune of $62 million, was incensed that Poll was watched by millions wearing a rival's corporate logo. The IOC bans advertising logos on an athlete's clothing. Stadiums, too, are free from advertising under IOC rules. The IOC expects to issue a new policy with sanctions for those who engage in what has become known as rogue advertising.

As early as 1997, the organizing committee for the Sydney Olympics began broadcasting the list of authorized, official sponsors for the year 2000 games. The committee asked viewers to watch out for "ambush advertisers" or companies that hadn't paid licensing fees yet give the appearance of Olympic sponsorship through corporate slogans and imagery. During the 1998 Nagano Olympics, past ambush advertisers including Nike were prominently inconspicuous.

Key Considerations: Boycotts and Commercialization
- The *DeFrantz* decision mirrored the *Tarkanian* decision in holding that the USOC is a private, independent body and not a state or government actor.
- The IOC is reported to issue new policies to prevent unlicensed advertisers from competing with licensed Olympic sponsors.

IRONMAN BATTLES THE WORLD

In the late 1970s a group of military men decided to invent the most challenging set of physical activities imaginable. They envisioned a swim of 2.4 miles, a bike route of 112 miles, and a marathon distance run all conducted on the island of Kona, Hawaii. The sport of triathlon was born.

In 1978 the World Triathlon Corporation (WTC) was formed to organize, franchise, license and promote "Ironman triathlon races." Two years later the Hawaii Ironman Triathlon World Championship was annually broadcast on ABC and later NBC. To protect the company's goodwill, it secured a federal service and trademark for the names *Ironman World Triathlon Championship* and *Ironman Triathlon World Championships*. The Ironman Triathlon brand name has been since licensed to numerous consumer products including the top-selling Timex Ironman Triathlon watch.

More than 10 years after the WTC was established, the International Triathlon Union (ITU) consisting of nearly 40 national triathlon federations was born. The ITU began operating its own set of triathlon races around the world, albeit at different distances than the Ironman. By 1994 the sport of triathlon had grown sufficiently in public appeal and participation levels by men and women of all ages to gain admission into the Sydney Olympic Games. The ITU was recognized by the IOC as the official international federation for the sport of triathlon.

The USOC recognized USA Triathlon (USAT) as the official national governing body for the sport of triathlon. For years USA Triathlon sanctioned the annual Hawaii Ironman Triathlon World Championship race. According to the WTC, a few weeks before the start of the 1997 Ironman event, the IOC threatened to remove the USAT "good standing" status unless sanction of the 1997 race was withdrawn.

Loss of IOC status could mean no U.S. triathlon team may compete in Sydney and cessation of USOC funding. The WTC's concerns were multiple. It was afraid athletes who competed in a nonsanctioned race may be suspended from participation in ITU events. Additionally, it viewed the ITU's pressure tactics as a means of eliminating event management competition in the sport, ultimately causing the WTC a loss of licensing and franchise revenue.

In a short-term compromise to retain USAT sanctioning, the WTC agreed to change the name of its 1977 race to the *Ironman World Championship* from the former *Ironman Triathlon World Championship*. It then sued the ITU in federal court, and the USAT indirectly, alleging numerous counts of antitrust violations, defamation, and tortious interference with business relations and trademarks. The suit seeks monetary damages and relief from predatory monopoly practices.

SUMMARY

Tanya Harding rocked the international sports world with allegations of criminal harm against a fellow skater to improve her own chances of making the U.S. Olympic team. Harding's case highlighted the administrative and organizational complexity of global amateur sports. The starting point for gaining an understanding of the legal relationships between national and international sports federations is the Amateur Sports Act. Unlike deciding purely domestic legal issues at the intercollegiate level, courts are reluctant to participate in resolving athletic disputes with legal ramifications beyond the boundaries of the United States.

Arbitration as established by the international sports movement has become the latest means for resolving eligibility and drug-doping disputes. The Court of Arbitration for Sport is poised to act as the final arbitrator. Conflicts still abound charging unequal treatment of women whether in the number of Olympic sports offered or failing to understand the aging female body in applying drug-doping standards. Critics continue to demand greater protection of an athlete's privacy while due process standards are balanced against the need to keep sports "clean." The overcommercialization of the 1996 summer Olympic games led many observers to ask whether sports has become a mere tool or gimmick for marketing *Fortune 500* firms to a global televison audience.

For Reflection

1. Are there any good legal or ethical reasons the USFSA could have cited to keep Tonya Harding off the U.S. Olympic team?
2. If a state or federal court actually had convicted Tonya Harding of a crime before the January 31 team announcement date, then do you think the USFSA legally could have kept her off the team? Would your answer be the same if she was convicted of a crime unrelated to her sport?
3. Athletes are sometimes smeared by drug use innuendo, yet society for many years was blind to the cheating by Eastern German athletes. How do we balance the rights of athletes to have some semblance of privacy against the need to ensure a level playing field among all competitors?
4. In *DeFrantz* the U.S. government placed an inordinate amount of political pressure on the so-called nongovernmental USOC entity. What laws could be changed to help prevent athletes from serving as political pawns between governments?
5. Should any athlete who tests positive for a banned substance receive an automatic suspension from participation pending a hearing, or should the athlete receive a hearing before any suspension? What is the practical and legal due process difference between the two?
6. Are there any situations where international sports federations should be subject to a U.S. state or federal court jurisdiction? List plausible factual and legal patterns.
7. Do you think there may exist a gender and age bias against older female athletes when it comes to drug testing? Why?
8. Should Olympic athletes be allowed to compete even when their country is boycotting the games?

Useful Web Sites

1. www.olympic.org/medical/efdop.html
2. www.olympic.org/eftas.html

3. www.gatekeeper.ausport.gov.au/intbods.html
4. www.rohan.sdsu.edu/dept/coachsci/swimming/drugs/death.html
5. www.sportsline.com/u/olympics/events/duraway/j11896.html

Notes

1. 64 Stat 902, 36 U.S.C. sections 371–383.
2. The Amateur Sports Act of 1978, 36 U.S.C. section 371 et seq.
3. *Reynolds* v. *IAAF*, 112 S. Ct. 2512 (1992).
4. *Reynolds* v. *IAAF*, 23 F. 3d 1110 (1994).
5. *DeFrantz* v. *USOC*, 492 F. Supp. 1181 (1980).
6. *Martin* v. *IOC*, 740 F. 2d 670 (9th Cir. 1984).
7. *DeFrantz* v. *USOC*, 492 F. Supp. 1181 (1980).

CHAPTER 3

Women's Sports

W hen I was a little girl, I wanted to be a boy because I thought that was the only way I could play professional basketball.

—Former Connecticut star and current WNBA pro Rebecca Lobo

Case Study

An exceptional female soccer player wants to try out for the men's collegiate soccer team even though a women's program is available. Should she be allowed to try out for the men's team, and if so, does it necessarily follow that a male athlete should be given a similar opportunity if he wishes to try out for the women's team?

INTRODUCTION

The year 1999 marked the twenty-seventh anniversary of the passage of the landmark legislation known as Title IX. This federal legislation bans gender discrimination in sports or any other educational activity at federally funded schools. Title IX is one of many statutory sources seeking to bring equity to women in educational opportunities. The U.S. Constitution through the equal protection clause of the Fourteenth Amendment prevents discrimination on the basis of sex at schools that receive any federal funding. Court decisions interpreting the application of antidiscrimination laws have added to the emerging body of gender equity in sports law. The recent growth in amateur athletic opportunities for women has encouraged corporations like Sears, Reebok, and Lee Jeans to sponsor professional sports leagues for women. This chapter explores the development of amateur and professional opportunities for women.

GENDER EQUITY: TITLE IX

Title IX was signed into law when Richard Nixon was president. Surprisingly, the statute, which is an amendment to the 1964 Civil Right Act, doesn't even mention the word *sports*, yet its primary association over time has been in seeking parity for women in college sports. Quite simply, Title IX [20 U.S.C. section 1681 (a)] provides that:

> No person in the United States shall, on the basis of sex, be excluded from participation in, be denied the benefits of, or be subjected to discrimination under any education program or activity receiving Federal financial assistance . . . .

The Department of Education (previously the Department of Health, Education, and Welfare) is charged with implementing this congressionally mandated legislation. Administrative regulations accompanying Title IX state that the law makes it illegal to deny athletic opportunities and benefits on the basis of sex, subject to some exceptions. The term *athletic opportunities* means varsity sport participation and club and intramural activities.

Once the administrative regulations for Title IX were implemented, schools had three years to comply. Mass confusion over how colleges were to fulfill these mandates led the Office of Civil Rights (OCR), which is the administrative body charged with enforcing the law, to establish a three-part test for schools to follow:

1. Are opportunities for female and male athletes proportionate to their enrollment?
2. Does the school have a history of expanding athletic opportunities for the underrepresented sex?
3. Has the school demonstrated success in meeting the needs of those students?

Although there have been numerous challenges to Title IX since these regulations were promulgated in the late 1970s, they are still good law today. Theoretically, schools need to pass only one of the three prongs to fulfill the compliance mandate.

THE GROVE CITY COLLEGE CASE

Grove City College launched the first major attack on gender equity when it successfully argued before the U.S. Supreme Court that Title IX applied only to specific programs or activities that received federal financial assistance. Therefore, if the OCR could not demonstrate that a specific program, such as the athletic department, received federal funds, then Title IX didn't apply to that department. This 1984 court case, *Grove City College* v. *Bell*, 465 U.S. 444, was overturned by Congress. The Civil Rights Restoration Act of 1987 broadened the definition of Title IX to include all programs or activities in any institution that accepts federal financial assistance (29 U.S.C. 1687).

The first test case after Congress overrode the *Grove City College* decision occurred in *Haffer* v. *Temple University*.[1] The women intercollegiate athletes at

Temple filed a class-action suit alleged that the women's athletic programs were not equal to the men's programs. They charged that there was disparity in almost every conceivable fashion, including the allocation of opportunities to compete, recruiting, coaching, travel, uniforms, equipment, housing and dining, academic tutoring, supplies, and publicity. After eight years of litigation, Temple consented out of court to increase the women's proportion of all its student-athletes to around 45 percent, award athletic scholarships in proportion to women's athletic participation, and maintain budgetary expenditures for women's programs within 10 percent of women's athletic participation.

The Temple story takes an interesting twist. From the beginning of Title IX many leading coaches, athletic administrators, and groups like the American Football Coaches Association have made two major arguments. First is that Title IX should not apply to the revenue-producing intercollegiate sports of men's basketball and football. This issue was addressed in May 1974 when U.S. Senator John Tower, of the proud football state of Texas, proposed an amendment to exempt revenue-producing sports from Title IX coverage. The Tower amendment was defeated by Congress. The second argument is that strict application of the proportionality test (one of the three prongs of the OCR) as the primary barometer of compliance leads to eliminating opportunities for men athletes. In the aftermath of Temple's out-of-court settlement the school's faculty voted to eliminate intercollegiate football to assist in bringing parity to the men's and women's programs. Led by well-placed alumni including television star Bill Cosby, the administration slated the potential of great, new sources of revenue becoming available now that Temple had joined the Big East football conference as a reason for retaining football. Temple did, however, hire Ron Dickerson, the only African-American head football coach at a Division I school at that time, to lead its football program. The matter of reducing intercollegiate athletic opportunities for men remains a concern of many administrators.

OCR FACTORS

Fast tracking to 1996, a clarification of the original 1979 policy interpretations of the OCR was implemented to assist OCR investigators in evaluating whether academic institutions are in compliance.[3] The following program factors are now part of the review process:

1. The selection of sports and levels of competition to effectively accommodate the interests and abilities of members of both sexes.
2. The provision of equipment and supplies.
3. Scheduling of games and practice times.
4. Travel and per diem allowance.
5. Opportunity to receive coaching and academic tutoring.

6. Assignment and compensation of coaches and tutors.
7. Provision of locker rooms, practice, and competitive facilities.
8. Provision of medical and training facilities and services.
9. Provision of housing and dining facilities and services.
10. Publicity.

Recently, the Women's Sports Foundation, a nonprofit educational organization that promotes the lifelong participation of all girls and women in sports and fitness, issued a report entitled "Gender Equity Report Card." Its findings, although demonstrating a substantial improvement in opportunities and expenditures for women, also showed a lack of parity in opportunities and expenditures between men's and women's athletic programs. For 1995 to 1996, based on 767 NCAA schools that responded out of 962,

	Division I		Division II		Division III	
	Male	*Female*	*Male*	*Female*	*Male*	*Female*
Athletic Participation	65%	35%	64%	36%	61%	39%
Scholarship Allocations	65	35	63	37	none	
Recruitment Spending	76	24	68	32	68	32
Operating Expenditures	78	22	66	34	62	38

Women constituted 53 percent of all undergraduate students during the survey period.

The Equity in Athletics Disclosure Act

The daily newspaper, *USA Today*, using public reports required to be submitted since 1995 by the passage of the Equity in Athletics Disclosure Act,[3] found that the number of women athletes has increased 22 percent from 1992, but that women receive only $1 for every $3 spent on men.[4] Colleges without intercollegiate football programs were four times more like to comply with the substantial proportionality test than universities with football teams.[5] Division I football programs with more than 80 scholarships to grant on roster sizes of 100 or more cause compliance difficulties because of vast sums of money spent on coaching, recruiting, building, and maintaining indoor and outdoor football complexes, medical and training expenses because of injuries, and publicity for potential all-star and Heisman candidates. More than 90 percent of the Division I schools with football and basketball programs fail to provide athletic opportunities for women in substantial proportion to a school's full-time undergraduate enrollment.[6] Out-of-court settlements suggest coming within 5 percent meetsthe substantial proportion test, however, for the first time in 1998 the OCR defined this particular compliance test by stating that spending should be within 1% of the school's player rates for each sex. A school that has 65 percent of its athletes as men under the OCR guidelines should spend no more than 66 percent of its athletic scholarship budgets on men.

Vocal critics of recalcitrant athletic administrators and the OCR charge that schools continue to ignore gender equity laws with impunity. The OCR does have the right to terminate a college's federal funding for noncompliance, yet it has never done so. The NCAA responds by citing that in 14 of the 17 NCAA-recognized championship sports offered for men and women, scholarship levels are higher for women than for men. It is expected that the Collegiate Women Athletic Administrators will propose additional changes in the way the NCAA conducts its business to help encourage greater female sports participation and to enhance athletic administration and coaching opportunities for women.

During the 1990s a number of significant court challenges brought gender equity into focus. Indiana University of Pennsylvania lost a Title IX suit when a federal court ruled that it failed all three prongs of the OCR's compliance test.[7] The school's female athletes sued after their gymnastic and field hockey teams were eliminated.

The University of Texas settled a class-action suit after women athletes charged gender-equity violations, citing the fact that females constituted 47 percent of the school's undergraduate enrollment but received only 23 percent of the athletic funding.[8] Women from club programs in softball, crew, gymnastics, and soccer brought the suit when the school refused to elevate the programs to varsity status. Texas promised to bring female athletic participation to within 3 percent of female enrollment and expand athletic scholarships to fall within 2 percent of athletic participation.

The most recent statistics issued indicate that Texas falls short of completely fulfilling its promises. Female students now comprise 49 percent of the undergraduate student body. Forty percent of the school's student-athletes are females who receive 36 percent of the recruiting budget. Texas has not publicly released the percentage of athletic scholarships devoted to women, which appears to violate the Gender in Equity Disclosure Act requiring schools to submit to the Department of Education annually information on male-female participation rates, recruiting costs by gender, and financial support.

Colgate University was forced to move the women's ice hockey program from a club to varsity status.[9] The federal court held that there was no requirement for Colgate to fund the women's team at the same level as the men's ice hockey team, but there was a mandate under Title IX to provide women with equivalent athletic benefits and opportunities. The court's conclusions seem contradictory in light of recent interpretations of gender equity that focus on equivalent expenditures based on the proportionality test. The *Colgate* decision was also somewhat unusual insofar as women's ice hockey, unlike men's ice hockey, is not an NCAA-sponsored sport, so the opportunities for competition are more limiting for women than for men.

Gender equity issues apply to employment and the coaching fraternity, too. The cases have had conflicting results. California State, Fullerton announced it was dropping women's varsity volleyball. Led by coach Jim Huffman, the varsity women players sued the school, alleging breach of Title IX.[10] A few months later the school and the athletes reached an out-of-court resolution. Coach Huffman was then fired. He turned around and sued the college for violating his free speech rights, arguing that his dismissal was in retaliation for his supporting the Title IX suit. The jury awarded him $1.35 million in damages plus an undisclosed punitive judgment.

Another set of facts led to a different result when women's varsity basketball coach Marianne Stanley sued the University of Southern California in federal court alleging that the school violated the Equal Pay Act when it refused to pay her the same amount of base salary and perks as the men's head basketball coach (George Raveling who has since left USC and joined the television commentators' business) received.[11] In denying her claim, the court pointed out that the men's basketball team generated 90 times more revenue than the women's basketball program. Raveling's qualifications, experience, and job responsibilities, including speaking before booster clubs, and his reputation as a national coach and goodwill ambassador for USC were all cited as legal reasons for the pay differentials.

Nearly every school is now sensitive to pay disparity issues between women and men coaches performing the same or similar jobs. At the University of Tennessee the women's varsity basketball coach, Pat Summit, receives more base pay and perks than the men's head basketball coach. This is clearly an exception based on her many years of experience and success at NCAA championship events. The norm is that women receive less pay than men for similar or identical work whether it involves coaching or administrating. The average salary for a male varsity coach is more than 200 percent greater than for a female varsity coach at the college level.[12] The revenue-producing nature of a particular sport carries little or no weight on Title IX matters. Schools are required to submit data on average salaries for head and assistant coaches for men's and women's programs under the Equity in Athletics Disclosure Act. This reporting requirement doesn't demand gender pay parity; however, the day seems near at hand when this will become a reality.

In another late 1990s case, a decision was handed down by a Knoxville Tennesee, federal court on a gender bias case that seems more likely to have occurred in the 1890s.[13] Assistant Tennessee women's volleyball coach Ginger Hineline mentioned to head coach Julie Herman that she wanted to start a family. Reportedly, Coach Herman discouraged Hineline from becoming pregnant. At one point Hineline asked, "Does this mean it might come down to (not) having a baby or losing my job?" Answer back from Herman: "It might." Four months after getting pregnant Hineline was fired purportedly for poor job performance. Hineline's job file did not reveal any reports of bad performance. Hineline was awarded a $150,000 judgment for discriminatory firing.

Key Considerations: Title IX

- The landmark federal legislation known as Title IX bans gender discrimination in sports or any other educational acitivity at federally funded schools.
- Schools must meet at least one part of the three part test established by the OCR to meet Title IX: opportunities proportional to male/female enrollment, history of expanding opportunities for women, meeting the needs of students.
- Congress refused to exempt revenue-producing sports from the reach of Title IX.
- Program factors are a part of the OCR's renew process.
- Women continue to lack the same opportunities for sports participation as men.

THE *BROWN UNIVERSITY* DECISION

Astute readers have noticed by now that in the area of gender equity the real gains have come about through litigation. In this way, the plight of women in sports is similar to the gains experienced by African-Americans in the aftermath of landmark civil rights legislation granting equality of opportunity regardless of one's race. African-Americans can point to the historic *Brown v. Board of Education*, 347 U.S. 483 (1954) desegregation case as the real starting point of government-supported claims of equality based on race. For female athletes the milestone case of the gender equity era began in 1991 when Brown University cut funding for two women's sports teams. Through a series of lower court rulings, the U.S. Supreme Court in *Brown University v. Cohen*, 117 S. Ct. 1469 (1997), elected to let stand a finding of gender bias by Brown in its sports offerings.

In some ways the *Brown* decision is noteworthy simply because this Ivy League academic institution is viewed as having one of the largest and most equitable women's athletic programs. At the initial lower court doorstep, the university was found not to have met any part of the three-prong OCR compliance test. Brown appealed. It argued that, although it did not meet the proportionality test, it did conform to the historical expansion of opportunities for women and accommodation of the interests and abilities of women (second- and third-prong) compliance tests. The appeals court found that in recent years Brown had failed to expand its women's sports programs and that it did not satisfactorily demonstrate an accommodation of women's athletic interests. The lawsuit was filed by women athletes who were affected by Brown's decision to eliminate funding for gymnastics and volleyball for women. The men also lost funding for two sports: water polo and golf. On April 21, 1997 the U. S. Supreme Court let stand the appeals court verdict.

That same day Brown announced a plan, subject to court approval, to increase the number of slots available to women athletes by about 60 so as to adjust the number of women and male athletes to mirror the ratio of women to men in the undergraduate student body (54 to 46).

Donna de Varona, an Olympic swimming gold medalist and past president of the Women's Sports Foundation, hailed the *Brown* decision as "the greatest single legal victory in the history of women's sports."[14] Deborah Brake, an attorney for the National Women's Law Center who argued the appellate court case for the women athletes, remarked that the U.S. Supreme Court "sound(ed) the death knell for a battle over Title IX that should have been over long ago."[15]

Brown seeks full Title IX compliance under the current legal tests by meeting the proportionality test. Yet, despite the euphoria surrounding the *Brown* decision, serious questions remain for the future of intercollegiate sports. For college programs that offer the full complement of 85 football scholarships plus non-scholarship walk-ons, there is no equivalent sport for females that comes anywhere close to offering a 100 or more athletic participation spots. The Supreme Court had the opportunity to help football schools determine how to meet the proportionality test, yet did not offer any advice for administrators.

A review of the latest published literature on athletic budgets and male to female participation rates at NCAA Division I football schools, indicates that only a few schools, specifically the service academies comply with the proportionality test. A few more schools including Akron, Arizona State, Southern Mississippi, Western Michigan, Louisiana Tech, Alabama, and Indiana spend on the average about the same on female and male athletes. The vast majority of major universities do not, and cannot, under the current scholarship/sports configuration comply unless a couple of changes occur.

Schools can dramatically cut men's programs or severely limit the number of male athletes who can participate in sports. By reducing the male sports population, the percentage of women participating automatically increases. Addition by reduction. No additional women's athletic opportunities, just fewer opportunities for men. Good math. Bad policy. From 1982 until 1996 the NCAA counted men's program cuts of 32 in gymnastics, 27 in swimming, and 42 in wrestling. The courts apparently are willing to allow schools to pare the number of male athletes to help narrow the gender equity gap. These program cuts do not run afoul of sex discrimination against men so long as the men's participation in athletics on the whole is substantially proportionate to their presence in the school's student body.

A second possibility is to add more teams for women. For many colleges and universities this is plausible, although it is financially costly to add more scholarships, coaches, travel and recruiting budgets, medical and trainers' staff time, and facilities. Remember, though, the financial aspects of providing equivalent athletic opportunities for women is not an administrative law factor in determining compliance. This is a step well-meaning athletic administrators should embrace.

Skipping the coeducational NCAA sports of rifle shooting and skiing, the NCAA sponsors 15 sports for women. At this time Stanford University and Ohio State are the only schools that offer all 15 female sports. About 44 of the 108 Division I big-time football and men's basketball programs offer at least the equivalent number of sports teams for both sexes. Even so, the vast majority of these schools fail the proportionality test, yet might fulfill one of the other two tests. Adding more team sports opportunities for women is a viable option for heading in the right direction of compliance. Yet, some athletic administrators argue that the revenue generated from football and men's basketball at some institutions (especially those schools that compete in major conferences with NCAA television tie-ins) funds educational opportunities for other male and female student-athletes. Any cuts here adversely affect an athletic department's overall revenue pot available to spend. At many schools football and basketball are not merely vehicles for fund-raising and marketing, but provide community excitement and goodwill not commonly found in other sports for men or women.

Donna Lopiano of the Women's Sports Foundation argues that the major football schools could easily reduce the number of scholarships to 60 or so without any drop-off in on-the-field quality of play. A reduction of 25 or so men's football scholarships along with limiting a football squad size to 80 or 85 players would mean more resources for women and help schools meet the proportionality test. The board of trustees of the American Football Coaches Association has countered by asking Congress to hold public hearings on Title IX with an eye toward convincing the legislative body to exempt the sports of football and men's basketball. Penn State's football coaching icon, Joe Paterno, finds any talk of reducing football athletic grant-in-aids below 85 as an act of self-destruction. The newly formed National Coalition for Athletics Equity seeks "to restore Title IX to its original intent to stop discrimination in sports" especially as the law applies to non-revenue-producing sports, as reported in *NCAA News*.

In perhaps a sign of the times to come for schools that compete in football, Boston University after more than 90 years of gridiron play effective 1998 dropped football. The university's board of trustees cited a lack of campus interest and the requirements of Title IX. Administration officials noted that Boston University spent about $3 million annually on football while generating revenue of less than $100,000 from game receipts and alumni donations.

According to Richard G. Sheehan, author of *Keeping Score: The Economics of Big-Time Sports*, most men's college sports programs follow Boston University's pattern and do not earn a profit. About a third of all Division I and I-AA football programs turn a profit. On the average, football generates 37 percent of an athletic department's revenue, whereas women's sports bring in about 2 percent.

Duke, Vanderbilt, Brigham-Young, Hampton, and Bethune-Cookman were among 25 colleges and universities that the Women's Sports Foundation filed complaints against with the Department of Education. Based on the disparity in scholarships between female and male student-athletes at these schools, as revealed by the latest data from the Equity in Athletics Disclosure Act, they are alleged to have discriminated against women in education in violation of Title IX. It is expected that an administration review and findings will not be reported until the year 2000.

Gender equity concerns are not merely the province of athletic departments but also extend to recreational programs. For instance, the University of Iowa has issued the following guidelines related to pickup basketball games on all campus courts:

BASKETBALL—Women's Priority Courts

1. To ensure gender equity, courts 1, 3, and 5 are designated "Priority for women."
2. Men may play on courts having women's priority, but they must yield should women wish to play. The following demand scale will be used to determine priority.

Number of Women Present	*Court Number (in order of priority)*
8–19	Court #1
20–35	Court #3
36 or more	Court #5

3. All challenges on female courts must be accepted when a) at least four women are challenging and b) no more than one male is on the challenging team.
4. When the number of female participants decreases below the number required to have court priority, courts will return to regular challenge courts in reverse order of priority.
5. The preceding policy would not exclude women from coed rec play.

Iowa's court policy came about after women complained to the university's recreation services department about the lack of basketball playing opportunities.

Key Considerations: The *Brown University* Decision
- The U.S. Supreme Court let stand a finding of gender bias by Brown University in its sports offerings.

- Increasing the athletic opportunities, participation, scholarship allocations, recruitment spending and overall operating expenditures for women in proportion to the ratio of women to men at school meets the Title IX gender equity requirements.
- Many men are fearful that their sports programs are being cut as a means of complying with Title IX and the *Brown* decision.

EQUAL PROTECTION

The U.S. Constitution and the constitutions of some individual states provide another means of protecting women against discrimination on the basis of sex. Specifically, the Fourteenth Amendment provides that "no State shall make or enforce any law which shall . . . deny to any person . . . the equal protection of the laws." This post–Civil War amendment to the Constitution initially applied to male African-Americans who had just gained equal status under the law as citizens. Today it is also used by other groups and individuals who believe a state or governmental entity has denied them equal treatment.

Federal and state courts apply different standards of equal protection review depending on the group or class of individuals claiming a violation and the interest affected by the classification. For discussion purposes assume a classification based on race, such as requiring a school to field a "blacks only" team and a "whites only" team simply because the parents of the players don't want the races to mix. Another series of examples that will be discussed later occurs when a school elects to classify all "contact" sports teams as male only and all "noncontact" teams as coeducational (male and female) or mixed gender. The question raised by these examples is whether or not and under what circumstances these race-based and sex- or gender-based classifications are constitutionally lawful.

The U.S. Supreme Court has ruled that all government classifications for equal protection purposes based on race, alienage, and national origin are "suspect" requiring "strict scrutiny."[16] By this the courts mean that a school must demonstrate a "compelling government purpose" for creating a group classification based on race, alienage, or national origin.[17] The preceding example of separate sports teams for blacks and whites fails to meet a so-called "compelling government purpose" test of keeping the races apart by fielding separate teams based on race. The "strict scrutiny" test also applies whenever a "fundamental right" is at stake. To date the courts have not deemed participating in any sports activity as a "fundamental right."

For sex-based classifications the courts have failed to endorse the "strict scrutiny" standard. Historically, the case law has suggested that if a school wishes to classify all "contact" sports teams as male only, then it has to demonstrate that this classification must serve an important government objective and also must be "substantially related" to meeting this government objective.[18] A Colorado school district that wished to bar high school girls from trying out for the boy's soccer team because the statewide h igh school association deemed it unsafe for girls to play soccer against boys on the basis of differences in strength and speed was struck down. The Colorado court in *Hoover* v. *Meiklejohn*, 430 F. Supp. 164, did state that the equal protection clause would not have been violated had the school created separate teams for males and females where the programs were supported substantially equally.

More recently in 1996, the U.S. Supreme Court in *United States* v. *Virginia*, 116 S. Ct. 2264, visited the issue of gender bias in a case involving whether the establishment of a male-only publicly funded military school denied equal protection of the laws to women. The High Court reiterated the prevailing standard but then added that gender equity cases invoke "heightened scrutiny" in determining the validity of the sex-based classifications. Commencing with the class of 2001, Virginia Military Academy becomes coeducational.

The lowest standard of equal protection scrutiny is the "rational basis" test. Under this test, a school that wishes to enforce a rule or regulation must show that the classification is "rationally related" to a legitimate government objective. It does not apply to sex- or race-based classifications.

Gender discrimination issues arise in a number of situations. They can be categorized in three major ways:

1. Men's team but no women's team.
2. Women's team but no men's team.
3. Separate teams for men and women or mixed teams.

Men's Team But No Women's Team

By far the most common equal protection claim in sports deals with women who challenge a rule that denies them the opportunity to participate in a sport where only males may play. Women may not be prohibited from playing on an all-men's team in a noncontact sport. By definition, noncontact sports do not invoke the same state or school concerns for health or safety that have historically been used to deny women the opportunity to try out. On the other hand, the courts are split on whether the Fourteenth Amendment requires a school to allow women to try out for the contact sports of football and wrestling. A school must meet the "heightened scrutiny" standard in prohibiting women from participating in these sports. Policy reasons given usually include differences in physical maturation, age (specifically to Little League where girls at the age of 8 to 12 are deemed to have similar physical characteristics as boys of the same age, thereby opening the door for girls to play), and safety concerns. Paternalistic notions of what's appropriate for women, customs, lack of protective equipment, or no locker rooms are not valid reasons for excluding women from contact sports. In 1997, Liz Heaston of Willamette College became the first female kicker in a college football game when she made two extra point kicks. Heaston is also a member of her school's women's soccer team.

Women's Team But No Men's Team

An Arizona case dismissed a lawsuit a group of boys had brought against their school when they were barred from playing on a girls-only volleyball team. The government claim for preventing boys from playing was to redress past discrimination against women in athletics. The court in *Clark* v. *Arizona Interscholastic Association*, 695 F. 2d 1126 (9th Cir. 1982), found that this was a "legitimate and important government interest." The court then examined whether the exclusion of boys is "substantially related" to this interest. By permitting boys to play varsity volleyball, the court determined because of the "average physiological differences, males would displace females to a substantial extent." The ruling was that there was a substantial relationship between excluding males from the team and the goal of redressing past discrimination and providing equal opportunities for women in athletics.

A few seasons ago, Niles Draper of Chatham, Massachusetts, wanted to play a sport that is almost solely a young women's domain: field hockey. When opposing high school teams forfeited games against his high school's team citing safety reasons, by court order his team was permitted to participate in the girls-only state tournament. NBC later ran a television special called "He Plays Hockey in a Skirt." In late 1997 this same issue arose when the Maine Human Rights Commission sought to allow a high school boy to play field hockey with high school girls.

In the late 1990s, Bill May became the only male to ever participate in synchronized swimming at the U.S. national championships. In placing third, concern was expressed because he "brought strength and power to a historically finesse sport."

Separate Teams for Men and Women/Mixed Teams

The U.S. Supreme Court, in *O'Connor* v. *Board of Education of School District 23*, 449 U.S. 1301 (1980), cert. denied, 454 U.S. 1084 (1981), let stand a lower court holding that permits separate but substantially equal men's and women's teams in contact sports. The court rejected the plea of an outstanding young female athlete who un-persuasively argued that by allowing her to play on the men's basketball team, even where there existed separate basketball teams for men and women, she could advance her skills more rapidly. U.S. Supreme Court Justice Stevens, ruling as a circuit court justice, wrote that "without a gender-based classification in competitive contact sports, there would be a substantial risk that boys would dominate the girls' programs and deny them an equal opportunity to compete in interscholastic events."

For those women who insist on the opportunity of playing with and against men in contact sports, many states have enacted equal rights amendments to their state constitution that may support a state-based, gender equity cause of action. For instance, Pennsylvania and Washington, relying upon their respective equal rights amendments, have held that relegating a woman to the girls' squad solely because of her sex might be a denial of equality under state law.[19]

For noncontact sports where a school has separate but equal teams based on gender, the concerns of health and safety in keeping teams single sex are not as strong. Many schools at the college and even high school levels are electing to provide mixed-sex teams. Track and field, cycling, cross-country running, skiing, and swimming are some of the more common mixed-gender sports.

Title IX is linked with the Fourteenth Amendment in many ways. Both require substantial parity or equality in supporting separate programs for women and men, as discussed earlier. Also, Title IX by regulation specifically permits separate teams for members of each sex when selection is based on competitive skill or the activity is a contact sport. (See 34 CFR section 106.41.) For Title IX purposes contact sports are defined as rugby, ice hockey, football, basketball, wrestling, and boxing. An important exception to the general permissiveness of separate but equal teams is noted in these regulations. When a school sponsors a team for one sex, and doesn't for members of the other sex, and athletic opportunities for the excluded sex have traditionally been limited, then the excluded sex members must be allowed to try out for the team unless it is contact sport activity. This wide-open exception opens the door for the creation of more mixed-sex teams.

Even at the professional sports level, issues of equal protection violations can arise. As commissioner of baseball, Bowie Kuhn denied a women reporter access to a locker room to interview players after a game. Kuhn cited privacy concerns for his ruling. She sued in federal court where the court ruled that barring women reporters from the players' locker room was not substantially related to the purpose of protecting the players' privacy.[20] In November 1990, the NFL determined that three New England Patriot players sexually harassed sports reporter Lisa Olson in the locker room.

Since these rulings, many professional clubs now ban locker room access to all reporters and require postgame interviews to take place in a designated press room. For an interesting historical perspective on the role of women in sports media, readers are referred to "Women Sportswriters—Business as Usual" by Mary Schmitt as printed in the *Media Studies Journal* (1997).

Key Considerations: Equal Protection
- Women may seek protection against discrimination based on gender under the equal protection clause of the Fourteenth Amendment.
- Gender-based classifications of sports teams must meet the U.S. Supreme Court's "heightened scrutiny" test.
- Distinguish between contact and noncontact sports in deciding whether single-sex teams are permissible.
- Look at the government interest at stake in determining whether women may try out or play on a men's team.
- Title IX regulations permit single-sex teams in some situations.

WOMEN'S PROFESSIONAL SPORTS

More than 25 years after Title IX the gap between female and male athletic performances is closing. Better coaching, state-of-the-art facilities, nutritional advances, weight training, heightened competition, and the opportunity to participate and feel good about playing have all contributed to unprecedented improvements in female athletic performance. Janet Evans's 1988 world swimming record in the 1,500-meter freestyle would have been better than the men's 1972 Olympic medal time for the same distance. The America3 sailing team outperformed the men's sailing team in the America's Cup. Ironwoman triathlete Karen Smyers frequently outswims, outbikes, and outruns many amateur and professional male triathletes. Former Dream Team center and current Women's National Basketball Association (WNBA) professional, Lisa Leslie, has demonstrated an ability to play-above-the-rim by dunking a basketball. ("She got game.")

From Smith College's introduction in 1892 of basketball for women to Billie Jean King's televised conquest of old tennis pro Bobby Riggs, major international corporations are now more willing to become marketing partners with a number of organized professional leagues for women. ISL Marketing AG, the marketing arm of world soccer's governing body FIFA, announced the creation of the 1999 FIFA Women's World Cup. Nine U.S. venues will participate in presenting world-class women's soccer, focusing on family entertainment and relying upon corporate sponsorship for travel, promotion, and team expenses.

Corporate sponsorship of women's sports has more than doubled over the past five years to now exceed $600 million a year. Sears discovered that women influence 70 percent of in-store and catalogue purchases, so it makes good business sense to spend more than $10 million over the 1997–2000 period sponsoring WNBA games. The WNBA completely sold all national advertising time on NBC, ESPN, and Lifetime for its initial seasons. AT&T Wireless Services paid $3 million to join marketing hands with Reebok to sponsor the new Women's Pro Fastpitch Softball League. Insurance company giant Phoenix Mutual provides sponsorship dollars to the WNBA's rival league, the American Basketball League (ABL).

In the WNBA salaries range from $15,000 to $50,000 with extra perks and money for the league stars. The eight-team league plays a 28-game schedule during the summer. The WNBA teams are all owned by the 29 NBA teams. The league's advertising slogan "We Got Next" appearing on billboards and commercials has been well received. The ABL also began play in 1997 with a 40-game schedule during the traditional fall/winter basketball season and a roster of 10 players per team. The minimum ABL player salary is $40,000 per year with an $80,000 average annual salary. The ABL, which fancies itself as the "players' league," has extended the option to own 10 percent of the league's stock to the players. Expectations are that both the WNBA and ABL will expand to international playing sites in the near future if the competing leagues don't merge first.

Both leagues rely heavily on established college and Olympic stars to promote their product. Rebecca Lobo, Cynthia Cooper, Australian Michele Timms noted for her spiked blond hair, Wilhelmina model Lisa Leslie, and mom with child-in-tow Sheryl Swoopes helped the WNBA achieve higher television ratings than the men's Major League Soccer. The ABL boasts seven 1996 U.S. Olympic gold medalists including player-coach Teresa Edwards, Katrina McClain, and sharpshooter Jennifer Azzi. The Fox Sports Network, which reaches more than 40 million households, broadcasts key ABL games.

The instant success of these two professional basketball leagues for women has led to a call for a union or players association to assist women in gaining collective bargaining rights. Already the Women's Players Association has been established to represent professional softball and soccer women players. Besides addressing issues like minimum salaries, free agency, and arbitration of disputes, the union hopes to enhance licensing and endorsement opportunities for women professional athletes.

Endorsement deals for women are expected to increase as women's sports cultivate the attention of fans and advertisers. According to a 1996 Vanderbilt University study, women receive anywhere from 7 percent to 11 percent of newspaper sports coverage. Television exposure for women sporting events is a meager 5 percent. Before today's generation of women athletes can expect to reap million-dollar endorsement pacts, the teams and leagues must get the public to pay attention. More network air time, hiring talented female sports' journalists to cover women's sporting events beyond figure skating and gymnastics in a serious and compelling fashion, building fan support through hard play and competitive games, and garnering corporate sponsorship are the initial steps to creating a lasting relationship among fans, players, and sponsors' products.

For some women athletes the tide has begun to turn. Steffi Graf through tennis (Women's Tennis Association) earnings and endorsements ranks among the 40 highest-paid athletes in the world. Tennis newcomer Venus Williams signed a $3 million, five-year deal with Reebok shoes and clothes during her first year as a professional. Former ABL most valuable player Nikki McCray signed a four-year, $1 million deal with Fila shoes after jumping the ABL ship to join the WNBA. Nike, in its deal with Sheryl Swoopes to launch Air Swoopes hopes to duplicate the magic and marketing success of its Air Jordan shoe. Gabrielle Reece earns six-figure sums from modeling but labors at well under a $100,000 a year in earnings on the pro beach volleyball circuit. Mountain biker Juliana Furtado competes thanks to the generous financial sponsorship of GT Bicycles, RockShox, and Michelin. Gold medal figure skater Tara Lipinski is expected to earn more than $15 million in endorsements.

The Ladies Professional Golf Association (LPGA) is one of the longest-standing professional athletic circuits for women. The LPGA sponsors 43 tournaments that provide a financial purse in excess of $30 million. But finding and retaining sponsors for women's golf is not always easy. Sprint elected to stop tour sponsorship of the Titleholders Championship event after 1997. A leading Canadian tobacco company has sponsored the duMaurier Classic named for one of its leading cigarette brands. Starting in 1999 this sponsorship will be lost because a new Canadian law prohibits tobacco companies from sponsoring sports and cultural events. Loss of sponsorship can lead to a loss in tournament opportunities for women.

Outstanding golfing pro, Amy Alcott, believes women's golf never gets the respect it deserves because it's unfairly compared to men's golf. Such comparisons might jeopardize the future television and sponsorship appeal of not just professional basketball for women, but also of other upstart pro leagues for women in hockey, soccer, and fastpitch softball.

The mandates of Title IX and gender equity court decisions have helped to dramatically increase the number of girls and women playing sports at locations from school playgrounds to professional arenas, and the level of play is unarguably better than ever, but for some the question remains whether or not all this is enough to attract a fan and sponsorship base. Television executives know that women watch sports. Women comprise nearly 50 percent of the NFL fan base. Women buy sports clothing and gear, and travel to sporting sites for business and pleasure. Major marketers are poised to market their wares to women and what better approach than to link women consumers to the games women play?

For many women Billy Jean King is viewed as a sports pioneer as much as Jackie Robinson. But many other modern women athletes have helped to push the envelope of opportunity. Joan Benoit in distance running, Nancy Lieberman in basketball, Martina Navratilova and Chris Evert in tennis, Picabo Street in skiing, Pat Bradley in golf, and Janet Guthrie in Indy 500 car racing are a few of the many women who have made the impossible now look almost ordinary. Women today are expected to build upon their predecessors' athletic determination, courage, and leadership.

SUMMARY

Title IX, in connection with the equal protection clause of the Fourteenth Amendment, has worked to secure equal opportunity for women in sports. Title IX prohibits gender discrimination in all programs receiving federal funds, but its role in the advancement of women's collegiate sports has been particularly significant. Compliance with Title IX demands the satisfaction of one of three requirements established by the OCR, including: (1) athletic opportunity proportionate to enrollment, (2) history of improvement, and (3) accommodation of students' needs. Several additional factors have been recently brought into consideration, and the definition of Title IX has been broadened by the Civil Rights Restoration Act to further ensure equal opportunity.

Despite impressive gains in athletic opportunities for women, significant gender gaps remain in funding for student-athletes, in salaries for coaching and administrating, and in facilities. Possibility of future progress in this area, despite the momentous decision in *Brown University* v. *Cohen*, remains uncertain, particularly at those Division I schools that play football.

The federal equal protection clause is another means of protection against gender-based discrimination in sports. Relied upon most often by women, it guarantees them positions on men's teams in noncontact sports and subjects gender-based classifications in contact sports to "heightened scrutiny." Separate but substantially equal men's and women's teams, however, are generally allowed.

Both Title IX and the equal protection clause have dramatically contributed to the advent of women's professional sports. Increased participation by women in sports has led to a significant improvement in the level of play and competition. Corporate sponsors better understand and value the purchasing power and buying decisions of women. Substantial progress has been made in obtaining corporate deals and media exposure that will be a crucial factor in the growth and survival of professional sports for women.

For Reflection

1. Should gender equity law be modified to take into account the revenue-producing nature of many Division I football and basketball programs?
2. What may explain the OCR's reluctance to terminate a college's federal funding for noncompliance with Title IX?
3. Do you think a woman who feels that her women's team does not offer the same skill and competition opportunities as the men's team should be permitted to practice and play on the men's team?
4. Is the lack of athletic opportunities for women in the past a valid reason for developing athletic team opportunities for women only?
5. Are you in favor of eliminating men's teams or capping male participation if it helps to get a school more in line with the substantial proportionality rule?
6. At present, women coaches generally receive less pay than their male counterparts. Looking back at the objective of Title IX, are there any valid explanations for this phenomenon?
7. Title IX and the equal protection clause have prompted the introduction of professional leagues for women. Given the opportunities to compete, what other factors are important to the future success of women's professional sports?
8. Should the OCR enforce Title IX beyond athletics to include gender equity enforcement in the marching band, cheerleaders, and spirit clubs?

9. Is it a denial of equal protection when men and women both play the same sport, on different teams, yet use different rules or equipment?
10. What overall changes would you recommend to Title IX in terms of program factors, enforcement, and remedies for failing to comply?

Useful Web Sites

1. http://www.arcade.uiowa.edu/proj/ge/titleIX.html
2. http://www.arcade.uiowa.edu/proj/ge/present.html
3. http://netscape.students.brown.edu/herald/librar/titleIX.html
4. http://www.ausport.gov.au/womenu.html
5. http://www.womensportswire.com

Notes

1. 524 F. Supp. 531 (E.D.Pa 1981) affirmed and renamed 688 F. 2nd 14 (3rd cir. 1982) modified by 678 F. Supp 517 (ed. Pa 1987).
2. 34 C.F.R. 106.41 (c).
3. 20 U.S.C. 1092 (1994).
4. *USA Today*, February 28, 1997, p. 1C.
5. Ibid.
6. Ibid.
7. 812 F. Supp. 578 (W.D. Pa 1993).
8. As reprinted by Kathleen Sharp, "Foul Play," *Ms. Magazine*, September/October 1993, pp. 22-26.
9. 1996 U.S. Dist. Lexis 8393 (N.D.N.Y. 1996).
10. As reported in *USA Today*, February 10, 1994, p. 6C.
11. 13 F. 3d 1313 (9th Cir. 1994).
12. www. lifetimetv.com/nosport/gereport/table 16.htm.
13. *Sports Illustrated*, June 16, 1997, p. 26.
14. *The Boston Globe*, April 22, 1997, p. A5.
15. Ibid.
16. For a good summary analysis of the equal protection clause, See Kermit Hall, ed., *The Oxford Companion to the Supreme Court of the United States*. (New York:Oxford University Press, 1992).
17. Ibid.
18. *Craig v. Boren*, 492 U.S. 190 (1976).
19. *Williams* v. *School District of Bethlehem*, PA. 998 F. 2nd 168 (3rd Cir. 1993) and *Blair* v. *Washington State University*, 740 P. 2d 1379 (Wash 1987).
20. *Ludtke and Time, Inc.* v. *Kuhn*, 461 F. Supp. 86 (1978).

CHAPTER 4

Labor and Antitrust Issues in Professional Sports

 dequate justification does not exist for baseball's special exemption from the antitrust laws.

—Special Congressional Committee, 1976

Case Study

A team owner agreed to pay $12 million a year for a free agent baseball pitcher over the next five years. The team's payroll is expected to increase by more than 25 percent. Fans can expect an increase in ticket prices and food concession costs to help build the team into a contender. Team owners lament the steady escalation of salaries paid to free agents and untested drafted players but cannot seem to stop themselves. In the next round of labor negotiations they plan to propose a cap on both salaries paid to rookies and on team payrolls. Part of the owners' rationale for the proposal is that baseball is beginning to price itself out of the entertainment market. What argument from the players' perspective would you make in favor of or in opposition to this scheme?

INTRODUCTION

Sports historians generally credit Abner Doubleday with having created the game of baseball. Thirty years later the Cincinnati Red Stockings became the sport's first professional team. By the late 1800s baseball players and owners began feuding over salaries and the free movement of players from team to team.

Owners limited players' freedom to change teams by unilaterally imposing a reserve clause in players' contracts. This condition granted teams the exclusive right to re-sign players from year to year, thereby thwarting the desire of the players to improve their financial lot by negotiating with other teams. In response, the players organized themselves into the first sports union or association in order to overturn the reserve clause and in so doing gain greater financial freedom. Although this initial attempt failed, it served as the precursor of the players associations found in all major men's professional team sports today.

Federal antitrust and labor laws have played an instrumental role in the development of the bargaining status and relationship between owners and players.[1] The by-product of these sports negotiations is what is commonly referred to as a collective bargaining agreement or CBA. After examining these developments, this chapter explores the individual collective bargaining agreements for each of the major professional sports.

ANTITRUST LAW

The seeds of baseball's recent labor discontent (which included a 1994 strike that closed the season even before the World Series could be played) can be found in a 1922 U.S. Supreme Court decision titled *Federal Baseball Club* v. *National League*.[2] Justice Oliver Wendell Holmes, writing for the Court, held that the owners and operators of professional baseball were not engaged in "trade or commerce" as defined in the federal antitrust laws. Baseball owners, alone among all organized professional sports, were held exempt from the reach of these laws and thus from scrutiny of otherwise illegal, collusive monopoly business practices. Fifty years later the Court revisited the issue of the antitrust exemption and found it an anomaly but refused to overturn the legendary Justice Holmes's opinion, under the doctrine of stare decisis in which settled principles of law are given the greatest deference.[3]

Examples of activities in other professional sports not shielded by antitrust exemption can be found in nearly every league. The National Football League (NFL) in 1960 elected Pete Rozelle as its commissioner to negotiate television agreements and oversee labor relations between players and owners. Without player approval, the NFL instituted what was known as the "Rozelle Rule." This rule was football's version of baseball's reserve clause. Under it, Rozelle was empowered to award compensation in the form of players to any team that lost players because of free agency. By this time football players had organized themselves into the National Football League Players Association (NFLPA).

The players challenged the Rozelle Rule, arguing that it constituted an illegal restraint on the mobility of players, with the intent of keeping players' salaries down. In *Mackey* v. *NFL*, it was held that the Rozelle Rule was an unreasonable restraint of trade under section 1 of the Sherman Antitrust Act.[4] This decision forced the league's owners to negotiate in good faith new rules regarding the movement of players with the players' union.

Violation of the antitrust laws can lead to treble damage awards to the prevailing party. This occurred two years after the *Mackey* case when the NFL's draft of college players into professional ranks was deemed an unreasonable "restraint . . . of trade with no purpose except stifling competition."[5] The court in *Smith* v. *Pro-Football* [6] (specifically involving the Washington Redskins) rejected the contention of the owners that the exclusive right of teams to acquire their individual draft choices (via picking players in inverse order to their winning records) is necessary to maintain competitive balance.

Former first-round draft choice James "Yazoo" Smith was awarded treble monetary damages less what he had already received. Once again the NFL was rebuffed for attempting to unilaterally impose its will on the players outside the bargaining process.

Two forces were beginning to work in favor of the players. First, courts were ruling that, apart from baseball, antitrust laws *do* apply to professional sports. Second, by virtue of having been organized in a union or professional association, players now had the benefit of federal labor laws. The National Basketball Players Association (NBAPA) and the basketball owners entered into the first professional sports collective bargaining agreement. This seminal event occurred in 1967. One year later, the National Labor Relations Board (NLRB) accepted jurisdiction over labor issues in professional sports.

This administrative body (NLRB), created by the National Labor Relations Act, oversees the right of workers (in this context, players) to form a union or association, bargain collectively through their own representatives, and engage in "concerted activities" for their collective benefit (i.e., strike when no agreement is in place). The Clayton Act and the Norris-Laguardia Act specifically exempt labor unions including players associations from antitrust laws.[7] Besides the statutory federal labor exemptions that allow players associations to enter into collective bargaining agreements with management that might otherwise eliminate competition or result in excessive market power in the hands of the union, a nonstatutory labor exemption from antitrust law exists. Application of the nonstatutory principle of law exempts any bona fide players association-management collective bargaining agreement from antitrust scrutiny.

In the aforementioned *Mackey* decision, the court noted that it will grant the by-product of the collective bargaining process precedent over antitrust laws only when the restraint on trade (here restricting a player's ability to move to another team) primarily affects the parties in the agreement; the agreement concerns the so-called "mandatory" subject; and the agreement is a product of bona fide arm's-length negotiations. The court in *Powell* v. *NFL* extended the nonstatutory labor exemption beyond the expiration of a bona fide collective bargaining agreement even after an impasse in labor negotiations occurred.[8] Interestingly, after the court's ruling in *Powell*, the NFLPA decertified itself as a union so as to remove the nonstatutory labor exemption as a barrier to the imposition of antitrust laws against NFL management.

Federal labor laws can only apply to industries "engaged in interstate commerce." The Supreme Court did a quick "two-step" in *Flood* v. *Kuhn* when it held that professional baseball is a business "engaged in interstate commerce" but refused to overrule Justice Holmes's earlier opinion that reasoned otherwise for purposes of the antitrust law.[9] Since *Flood* v. *Kuhn* was decided, there has been little dispute that labor laws apply to all professional sports, including baseball. The Curt Flood Act, expected to be passed by Congress, would allow individual players, not their union, to file antitrust suits against owners when a collective bargaining agreement has expired.

Key Considerations
- Antitrust laws apply to professional sports.
- Baseball enjoys a special judicial exemption from antitrust laws.
- A statutory labor exemption exists for professional associations to enter into collective bargaining agreements.
- A nonstatutory labor exemption generally extends the by-product of bona fide players associations-management agreements from antitrust scrutiny.
- Violators of antitrust laws are subject to treble damages.

COLLECTIVE BARGAINING IN PROFESSIONAL SPORTS

Once the NLRB has certified a players association as the exclusive bargaining agent for all players in a particular sport, the owners and the players association have a duty to bargain in good faith the basic issues pertaining to wages, hours, and working conditions.[10] These particular issues (as they apply in the context of sports—minimum salary, salary caps, pension benefits, free agency, salary arbitration, start of rookie camp, etc.) are known as *mandatory* subjects for collective bargaining. Both sides must negotiate these matters in good faith. The term *good faith* has come to mean exchanging proposals, responding to the proposals of the other side, meeting, and exchanging pertinent financial and budgetary information.

The other category of relevant subject matter that the parties may consider during collective bargaining negotiations is *permissive*. The topics are those outside the mandated subjects of wages, hours, and working conditions. No requirement exists for either party to negotiate in good faith permissive subjects as part of an industrywide labor accord.

The distinction between the mandatory and permissive categories can become confusing. Would you view a decision concerning players' uniforms (including fabric, location of team logo, and color) a mandatory or permissive subject matter? Many players complain that playing on artificial turf takes years off a player's career. Should owners be required to negotiate the playing surface in good faith? If so, can we expect a demand in the next round of collective bargaining negotiations for the three-point line in basketball to be moved forward, or backward or to require helmets in hockey, or standardize the dimensions of all baseball fields?

Earlier we discussed the court holding that the Rozelle Rule in football was a mandatory subject for collective bargaining purposes. Surprisingly, in a case involving Oscar Robertson, one of the all-time greatest players in the NBA, the reserve clause and the player draft were held not to be mandatory subjects.[11] A few years later a New York court held that minimum salaries, revenue sharing, fringe benefits, and rights of first refusal were all mandatory matters for bargaining in basketball.[12] NBA players and owners have agreed to negotiate all of these subjects in good faith in the most recent NBA collective bargaining agreements. Football, baseball, and hockey all have followed suit in agreeing that these matters are subject to mandatory collective bargaining between owners and players associations.

Key Considerations: Collective Bargaining

- Has the NLRB certified the players association?
- Owners and players associations have a duty to bargain in "good faith" on wages, hours, and working conditions.
- Distinguish between mandatory, which must be negotiated in good faith, and permissive topics for collective bargaining.

UNFAIR LABOR PRACTICES

In 1994 and 1995 the major league baseball players went out on a 232-day strike that caused the World Series to be canceled. In retaliation, the owners declared an *impasse* in collective bargaining negotiations. Unilaterally, they created their own new rules governing free agency and salary arbitration. The players successfully argued in court that the fact that the collective bargaining agreement had expired did not grant the owners the legal right to cease to bargain in good faith on these mandatory labor issues.[13]

New York Judge Sonia Sotomayer held that major league baseball owners had engaged in bad faith dealings with the players in violation of the National Labor Relations Act. The players then voted to end their strike and play ball even without a new agreement. The owners decided not to use replacement players. Both sides agreed to continue what became a nearly two-year, on-and-off negotiation process before a final four-year agreement was reached.

Baseball is not the only major league sport that has experienced labor unrest leading to charges of unfair labor practices. Former Seattle Seahawks wide receiver Sam McCullum charged his team with unfair labor practices when he alleged that he was cut because he led a "solidarity handshake" between his teammates and the opposing team's players before a preseason game.[14] McCullum had been selected as the Seahawks' union players' representative the year before and was an outspoken critic of football labor practices in general.

Despite having started for the five previous years, McCullum was cut just before the 1982 regular season began, prior to the players going out in a leaguewide strike. After almost 11 years of administrative hearings and court appeals, McCullum was awarded back pay when it was determined that he had been unjustly terminated because of his support for his union.

The 1990s were years of spectacular popular appeal and historic events in the NBA. Earvin "Magic" Johnson announced that he was HIV-positive; Michael Jordan retired from basketball to pursue a professional baseball career (only to return less than two years later); Boston Celtics captain Reggie Lewis collapsed and died during a pickup game at Brandeis University. But it was also a time when the NBA's collective bargaining expired, and leading players wanted an end to the salary cap, which they believed put too great a restraint on free agency. Meanwhile, the owners wanted a tighter salary cap and sought to eliminate or restrict the rule that enabled a team to sign its own free agent for any amount without having it count against a team's salary cap.

The salary cap has an interesting history. In the 1980s basketball was in rough financial shape. The NBA was searching for national television exposur, and the concomitant advertising revenue. Two-thirds of its teams were losing money. The owners convinced the players association that the league could not survive without some sort of curtailment of salaries.

Thus, in 1983, under the guise of protecting the jobs of NBA players, seeking payroll balance from team to team, and providing for revenue sharing between the players and the teams, a cap on the maximum and minimum amounts a team could pay its players was integrated into the new four-year agreement (for the years 1983 to 1987). The actual amount of the cap is determined from year to year. Under the 1996 agreement, players are guaranteed a minimum of 48 percent of all NBA revenues. The NBA then divides this minimum amount by the number of teams to determine the salary cap per team.

For the current season, the team salary cap is $26.9 million. In the year of the first NBA salary cap, the average player salary was $260,000. That amount is now nearly the minimum salary for NBA rookies. The average NBA player salary today is more than $2.2 million, and is scheduled to increase to an average of over $3 million per player by the year 2000.

For the years between the 1983 NBA labor agreement and the 1996 agreement (1988–1994), the NBAPA and the owners had entered into an accord that slightly modified the original salary cap agreement. By the end of this accord, the league was in much stronger financial shape, with many communities clamoring for NBA franchises.

At the time the accord expired in 1994, the players and owners as noted before (and each for their own reasons) had both come to view the salary cap negatively: The players found it to be too great a restraint on player mobility, and the owners were dissatisfied with the previously mentioned provision that allows teams to spend any amount to re-sign their own free agents to new contracts. (Note that this is the provision that the Chicago Bulls used to re-sign Michael Jordan to a contract that paid $30 million yearly—an amount that astute students have determined exceeds the Bulls' salary cap!)

In 1995 the players considered striking the NBA over the salary cap. Instead they sought judicial relief but lost when the Second U.S. Circuit Court of Appeals ruled that the expiration of the collective bargaining agreement did not free the players from their obligation to obey the NBA's salary cap, college draft, and right of first refusal.[15] The court told the players to settle their dispute at the bargaining table. As we have seen, this was the same message that Judge Sotomayer had sent to the owners when they had sought to unilaterally impose new work rules on the players.

This argument, which the NBA players lost, is critical to understanding the relationship between the labor and antitrust laws.

An exemption from antitrust laws exists for a collective bargaining agreement entered into as part of good faith negotiations between the owners and the players association. This is referred to as the labor exemption from antitrust laws. Furthermore, once a collective bargaining agreement has expired, the courts have held that these parties are not prohibited by the antitrust laws from continuing to bargain to seek a new agreement on the terms and conditions of employment. Indeed, they must engage in good faith dealings or suffer the consequences of an unfair labor practice finding. Laws related to monopoly practices or collusive activities, thus, cannot be used to subvert federal labor policies, even when collective bargaining agreements have expired.

The bottom line: *Negotiate on those mandatory" subjects for joint bargaining.* And especially for the players: *Don't expect antitrust laws to trump labor laws when you haven't even bothered to come to the bargaining table.*

A quick summary is in order. Antitrust laws seek to force owners to maintain open, competitive markets by not illegally restricting the movement of players or otherwise engaging in collusive policies that limit salaries. Labor laws are designed to encourage players to organize and negotiate collectively. If the parties bargain in good faith, then the players lose their ability to challenge owners about fixing wages and limiting player mobility. But what if the players elect to decertify their union once an ongoing CBA has expired?

This is precisely what happened in the NFL in the late 1980s and early 1990s. Led by individual free agent players like Freeman McNeil (by this time there was no longer an NFL players association) players sued on the grounds that the NFL's free agency system violated antitrust laws.[16] A 1992 jury ruled against the owners, and the league ended up paying $30 million to

235 players because clubs had illegally fixed taxi-squad wages in 1989, and another $85 million was awarded for permitting each team to freeze 37 players on its roster whether or not the players had a contract. These were treble damage awards.

Following this legal slaughter, the owners quickly granted free agency to hundreds of players. In return, the players decided to recertify their union and once again negotiate their labor differences instead of relying on antitrust challenges.

Key Considerations: Unfair Labor Practices

- Once a labor impasse is reached, management cannot unilaterally impose new workplace-related rules.
- A team that unjustly terminates a player for engaging in labor activities may be subject to an unfair labor practices charge.
- Players have a legal obligation to come to the bargaining table after expiration of a CBA to negotiate contract terms (i.e., a salary cap).

COLLECTIVE BARGAINING AGREEMENT HIGHLIGHTS

A representative look at the most recent collective bargaining agreements in the professional sports of baseball, football, basketball, and hockey is found next. The reader should recall that these agreements are all products of years of conflict, negotiation, litigation, responses to economic conditions, and market forces.

Baseball

1. A new interleague play agreement between the American and National leagues. There are up to 16 interleague games per team for the 1998 season.
2. The minimum league salary for 1998 is $170,000; and $200,000 in the years thereafter.
3. A 35 percent luxury tax is imposed on that portion of a team's payroll above $51 million for the top five salary spending teams in baseball. The money is to be given to small-market teams as a means of revenue sharing.
4. The 13 most profitable teams will be taxed on net income, which is expected to raise about $70 million for sharing with small-market teams.
5. A 2.5 percent payroll tax on player salaries is to be paid from licensing income, again, to benefit small-market teams.

6. Players may become free agents after six years of major league experience. The team losing a free agent receives a draft choice as compensation.
7. Salary arbitration for players is available after three years. Single arbitrators are eliminated and replaced with three-person panels.
8. A player with 10 or more years of major league service, the last five with one team, cannot be traded without the player's consent.
9. Any player disciplined by a fine or suspension has seven days to request a hearing.

As previously noted, baseball's latest labor agreement came after a 232-day strike.

The players refused to agree to any sort of salary cap in any of their collective bargaining negotiations with team owners. Small-market owners in Kansas, Milwaukee, Montreal, and Pittsburgh demanded financial relief from big-market teams like the New York Yankees, Cleveland Indians, and Atlanta Braves. They received help through the luxury tax, payroll tax, and revenue-sharing plan mentioned previously.

There are two special points of interest here. First, in salary arbitration the player and owner each submit a single salary figure to specially appointed arbitrators. The arbitrators then selects one or the other. This is a different procedure than most other sports, where the arbitrators have the flexibility to select a middle salary number.

Second, the public perception of baseball's ability to discipline its players was dealt a major blow during the 1996 baseball playoffs, when Baltimore Orioles second baseman Roberto Alomar was suspended for spitting at an umpire. Initially he appealed the suspension, which naturally delayed imposition of the punishment, and the whole incident led to a national debate on player accountability as opposed to a player's due process right to a hearing. Ultimately, Alomar waived his right to appeal after immense public pressure was brought on by print journalists and sports talk radio show hosts.

This incident points up the necessity for baseball to reexamine its ability to discipline its players without delay when the best interests of the game are at stake.

Many years ago the commissioner in baseball enjoyed broad authority granted to the office from the league constitution and bylaws to act in the best interests of the game. The commissioner's delegated powers may be limited by the collective bargaining agreement.

For the past few years baseball has lived without a strong commissioner. The days of Judge Kenesaw Mountain Landis, Ford Frick, Bowie Kuhn, and Peter Uberroth serving as the final arbitrator of decisions ranging from suspending a team owner to resolving disputes between clubs are probably over. However, it is worth mentioning that decisions by former commissioners Uberroth and the late Bartlet Giamatti are likely to draw public scrutiny in the near future. Cincinnati Reds manager Pete Rose was alleged to have bet on major league baseball games in violation of league rules. The commissioner at the time, Peter Uberroth, conducted a full-scale investigation and suspended Rose. First, Rose sought judicial relief alleging a violation of his right to a fair hearing by an unbiased arbitrator. Rose and Commissioner Giamatti, who succeeded Uberroth, settled the matter out of court. Rose was banned from the game of baseball for life. It is anticipated that Rose will seek to rejoin the baseball fraternity in some capacity in the near future.

Football CBA Highlights

1. The college draft consists of seven rounds. Underage college students can make themselves available for the draft, but if they do so, they lose all eligibility to play college football.
2. The minimum salaries depend on number of years in professional football, starting at $158,000 (1998) for a player on the active squad. The minimum salary for a five-year veteran player is $325,000 a year (1998) and $400,000 in 1999.
3. Every year a salary cap for team payrolls is established based on the players receiving a percentage of league revenues. For 1998 each team has about $55 million to spend on player salaries including signing and incentive bonuses. Thereafter, the players will share 64 percent of the leagues defined as gross revenue.
4. Unlikely-to-be-earned (UTBE) bonus incentives do not count against a team's salary cap. These individual player performance bonuses pay out money upon reaching "unlikely" incentives based on prior years' performance. Rookies have their own UTBE incentive scale.
5. A rookie pool of between $1.7 and $4.4 million is the maximum amount each team can pay first-year players. The actual rookie salary cap amount varies from team to team depending on the overall total of top draft picks, but cannot exceed 10 percent of the total salary cap.
6. In calculating whether or not a team exceeds the salary cap, signing bonuses are prorated over the length of the player contract, not all counted in the year they are paid.
7. Each team is permitted to designate one unrestricted free agent as a transition player and a second player as a franchise player every year. A franchise player is entitled to receive a salary equal to the average of the five largest salaries paid in the previous year to players at the franchise player's position. The same rules apply for a transition player, except that teams take the 10 largest salaries paid in the previous year, or 120 percent of the transition player's prior salary, whichever is greater.
8. Unrestricted free agency is available to any player with five or more years of service whose contract has expired. The player's current

team has a time frame in which to negotiate a new salary contract, after which the player is free to negotiate with any team.

9. Restricted free agency is available to any player with three or more years of service whose contract has expired. If a player refuses his current team's salary offer, any team he signs with afterward must give his former team a draft choice.

10. A drug violation policy can lead to a minimum one-year suspension and loss of salary for multiple substance abuse violations.

Star Dallas Cowboys defensive player Leon Lett was suspended for one year and lost $1.758 million in salary when he failed a league-imposed drug test. He joined superstar Dallas wide receiver Michael Irving, who was suspended for five games when he pleaded no contest to a criminal cocaine charge. Under football's collective bargaining agreement, both players are subject to mandatory treatment and drug testing. These suspensions, similar to baseball's disciplinary rules, may be appealed to the commissioner of football. Irving didn't bother to request a hearing. Commissioner Paul Tagliabue denied Lett's request for leniency.

The salary cap rules have led to very creative financing of player salary contracts. Many teams are granting free agents large signing bonuses, which are prorated for salary cap purposes over the length of the deal. The UTBE bonuses are an easy way around salary cap rules especially when coupled with paying out annual salaries that in some cases are barely over league minimums. Well-established stars like Deion Sanders and Hershel Walker of the Dallas Cowboys and Kevin Greene of the San Francisco 49ers all play for about the league minimum salary. Yet, they are each paid bonuses in a manner so as not to significantly add to a team's salary cap.

For instance, Greene received a signing bonus of $75,000, a workout bonus of $250,000, and $750,000 in incentives including UTBE bonuses of $550,000 even though only $350,000 actually counted against the 49ers' salary cap. Meanwhile, Sanders received a $13 million signing bonus that was for the most part prorated for salary cap purposes over the length of his seven-year contract.

Backsiding players contracts is another creative financial tool. By achieving certain defined offensive or defensive goals, players may void the final contract years and become a free agent earlier. For instance, the New Orleans Saints signed safety Chad Cota from the Carolina Panthers when Cota was offered a three-year contract for $5.4 million, where the last two years are voided if the Saints' defense is credited with 61 quarterback sacks for the season. The term "backside" came about because negotiators would flip over the last page of a player's contract and write-in bonus provisions on the back side of the paper.

The second category of players receiving league minimums are mid- to late-round draft choices who lack marketplace leverage and, in some cases, are free agents who desire to change teams but bidding teams are already at or near their salary cap maximums. The NFL is in danger of institutionally creating a two-class system of players: marquis players drafted in the first round and some veteran players who are now reaping the benefits of free agency through extraordinary signing and UTBE bonuses versus players who are not highly drafted and never achieve true market value while still contributing team members.

A new eight year, $17.6 billion NFL television contract significantly added to the coffers of the NFL teams. Annual salaries in excess of $10 million for some quarterbacks and running backs are likely.

Keep in mind that were it not for the labor exemption to antitrust law many provisions of the NFL collective bargaining agreement including the salary cap might be subject to attack on anticompetetive grounds. The same holds true for the other CBAs discussed in this chapter.

Basketball CBA Highlights

1. The college draft consists of two rounds. Underage college players may make themselves eligible for the NBA draft, and if not chosen, may return to play college basketball. High school players are also eligible.
2. The minimum salary for rookies is $220,000; for veteran players, $247,000. No signing bonuses are permitted.
3. The rookie salary cap is based on the player's draft position with a minimum three-year contract for rookies.
4. The salary cap is based on a percentage of league revenue. As noted previously, this amounts to $26.9 million per team for the current season, which is about 48 percent of all basketball-related income but because of the salary cap exemptions has led to players actually receiving around 57 percent.
5. The maximum veteran contract term is seven years, with a minimum 20 percent per year raise.
6. All long-term contracts are guaranteed except for money tied to incentives.
7. There are multiple exceptions to the salary cap rule. For instance, an injured player may be replaced by a player whose salary is half that of the injured player and not have that salary count against the cap. Any team may sign its own free agent for any amount (the Larry Bird exception).
8. Option clauses may not be for more than one year. There are no option clauses for rookies.
9. Unrestricted free agents are free to negotiate with any team. There is no compensation to teams losing a free agent player.
10. Restricted free agents are free to negotiate with other teams; however, the free agent's current team has the right to match any offer (the right of first refusal).

11. An antidrug program encourages players to come forward volun-
    tarily to seek help at team expense. Those who relapse or fail to
    admit to a known problem are subject to penalties that range from
    permanent suspension to loss of pay and mandatory drug testing.
    Ex-FBI agents are hired to keep players away from "crack" houses.

The NBA has what is known as a flexible or "soft" salary cap, unlike the
NFL, whose salary cap is more stringent, and has apparently brought some
parity to the league standings. The NBA's labor accord continues to enable
the strong teams to remain contenders for the championship by signing their
own free agents to unrestricted salaries. The re-signing of Kevin Garnett by
the Minnesota Timberwolves for about $120 million over seven years is a
representative example of this point.

Additionally, the system of compensation for loss of players in the NFL
discourages player mobility and, although major league baseball has a similar system, experience has shown that making good amateur draft choices in
baseball is harder than in football. Thus, the legacy of basketball litigation,
stemming from the *Robertson* case, has helped encourage (at a minimum) es-
calating market value for the best players because teams don't have to give
up anything when they sign another team's unrestricted free agent.

The 1996 draft marked the entry of high school students, who elected to
bypass the college experience and test the professional market. Once these
high school students make themselves eligible, under existing NCAA rules,
they lose all eligibility for college basketball.

Kobe Bryant, Jermaine O'Neal, Al Harrington, Tracy McGrady, and
Kevin Garnett are some of the most well-known high school players who
have skipped college to join the pro NBA ranks. Bryant and Harrington were
the only two of these five players who were academically qualified to play
Division I basketball under NCAA guidelines.

The rule for nonsenior college players who submit their names for draft
consideration is different. Each player must submit his or her name for draft
consideration. In such a case, the NCAA (which, as we have seen previously, has jurisdiction over its member institutions and the players who attend
those institutions) has determined that these players may return and play
college ball, providing that they were not drafted and have not signed with
an agent or accepted money to play professionally.

In the latest NBA draft, more than 30 underage college players made
themselves draft eligible. They counted for nearly 20 of the top picks in the
two round of the draft.

What would you think of a rule that prevented NBA teams from signing high school players? Before answering, would you be in favor of a rule
that said UPS or Wal-Mart or even Charles Schwabb could not hire any high
school or college student until he or she had received a diploma? Any
antitrust concerns?

On paper the NBA drug policy looks extremely stringent. In reality it is readily subject to twofold criticism. First, it excludes many so-called street drugs like marijuana from its list of prohibited drugs. Second, as illustrated by the case of Dallas Mavericks player Roy Tarpley, the rules do not mean what they say.

Tarpley was a 1986 first-round draft selection. One year later he violated the league's drug policy. The CBA rule states that after two drug violations (known as the "strike two" rule), he is to receive an indefinite suspension without pay, which is what occurred in January 1989. A few months later Tarpley was reinstated for the second half of the NBA season. Only weeks later he failed to attend his prescribed after-case drug program.

Tarpley was suspended indefinitely once again. This pattern repeated itself until October 1991 when the league banned him for life (this is the "three strikes and you're out" rule). Less than three years later, NBA commissioner, David Stern, reinstated Tarpley, who was then immediately re-signed to a six-year deal by the Mavericks.

For the third time in the past few years, in 1998 the NBA owners locked out the players. A provision in the parties CBA gave the owners the 1995 option of re-opening their CBA. After several months of unsuccessful discussions on mandatory subjects of negotiation, including eliminating guaranteed contracts and the Larry Bird exception, the owners exercised their right to bring the business of the NBA to a halt. The lockout, which is an owner's tool to force negotiations similar to a players' strike upon expiration of a CBA, prevents players from practicing, playing NBA games, and signing free agent deals.

Hockey CBA Highlights

1. The draft consists of nine rounds. Draftable players must be 19 years old, although 18-year-olds may opt in.
2. A compensatory draft exists for teams losing free agents. Draft position here is a function of salary paid to the lost player.
3. Maximum rookie salary for a drafted player under the age of 25 is $975,000 per year. However, only a player's base salary and bonuses for games played count against the rookie salary cap. Performance bonuses do not count against the cap. Signing, reporting, and other nonperformance bonuses may never exceed more than 50 percent of the cap.
4. The minimum league salary is $125,000 for the 1998 season and $150,000 thereafter.
5. Each team's player active roster size is limited to 20 players.
6. Unrestricted free agency is available in the following four categories of players:

    a. At age 32 (drops to age 31 after 1999) and the player's contract has expired.

    b. Ten or more years in NHL when the player's contract has expired and the player's salary in the last year of the contract is less than the league average. Eligible once for the category.

    c. Age 20 or older at the expiration of the contract, with three or more pro seasons and less than 80 NHL games.

    d. An undrafted player.

5. Restricted free agency is available to the following three categories of players:

    a. A player who is a defected (not unconditionally released); a player who has not completely filled previous NHL contract terms and signs a contract with another pro (may be a team that covers any period of the unfulfilled portion of the contract. Additionally, it covers a situation where a player has never signed an NFL contract but whose rights are owned by an NHL team and the player signs with any pro team. Afterward, the player becomes an NHL restricted free agent.

    b. A player who has less than three years of pro experience and whose contract has expired.

    c. A player who is not a rookie, not defected, not an unrestricted free agent, and whose contract has expired according to these situations:

        Signs first contract at ages 18 to 21 and three years pro
        Signs first contract at age 22 or 23 and two years pro
        Signs first contract at age 24 or older and one year pro

6. When a restricted free agent's contract expires, the prior team may make a qualifying offer (new contract proposal) in an amount at least 110 percent of the prior year's salary for players earning above the league minimum. The prior team has a right of first refusal to match any offer a player receives and may then keep the player at the offering price.

7. NHL and NHLPA jointly appoint eight arbitrators to hear salary arbitration. Arbitrators are selected from the national Academy of Arbitrators. Either party may remove an arbitrator.

8. Only restricted free agents are eligible for salary arbitration. The arbitrator may select any salary. The owner may decide whether a salary is for one or two years. The owner may reject an arbitrator's salary decision under certain situations, which then makes the player an unrestricted free agent who is eligible to sign with any team. Specific age and experience qualifications are required for salary arbitration.

9. The CBA runs from 1995 to 2000.

The latest NHL owners and players association labor agreement occurred after the owners exercised the right to lock out players from practicing or playing. This event happened after about two years of unsuccessful labor negotiations with no new CBA in place. The 1994–1995 hockey season opening was delayed by this lockout, causing the league to lose more than 450 games before negotiators Gary Bettman for the NHL and Bob Goodenow for the NHLPA reached an agreement on behalf of the owners and the players, respectively.

Originally, the parties had discussed imposing a salary tax on those teams with the highest payrolls, much like that now found in baseball. Ultimately, the parties settled on a rookie salary cap that has the net effect of earmarking more money for veteran players and less money for untested rookies. The average age of an NHL player is 26, and the average NHL career lasts about as long as that of an NFL player, or around five years. The years to earn the multimillion-dollar contracts landed by Wayne Gretzky of the New York Rangers, Joe Sakic of the Colorado Avalanche, Steve Yzerman of the Detroit Red Wings, and Ray Borque of the Boston Bruins are limited for most hockey players.

The NHL has experienced a spirited growth in franchises and popularity from cold climates of the northern states and Canadian provinces to the sunny weather of Florida, Texas, and California. The owners have effectively merchandised their sport to appeal to a youthful MTV audience as highlighted by the innovative use of television technology including the "halo" puck. Tie-ins with street hockey, roller blading, and in-line skating have added to hockey's appeal.

The first female NHL game referees are expected soon, following the lead of the NBA. This reflects another attempt to broaden hockey's fan base. The poor showing of the men's U.S. hockey team at the Nagano Olympics coupled with the childish behavior of a select few players who trashed the housing facility before leaving the Olympic complex has at least temporarily hurt the NHL's image.

LABOR ISSUES IN OTHER PROFESSIONAL SPORTS

This chapter has highlighted the labor and antitrust issues that have confronted North America's four major professional sports. The players of Major League Soccer (MLS) by the end of this century will have organized an association and sought NLRB certification to negotiate collectively with the league's owners. Already the owners of the MLS have imposed both a team salary cap of just under $1.5 million and a maximum player salary of around $200,000.

Abroad, the Australian Cricketers Association has threatened strike action unless the league owners substantially increase the players' share of the team revenues beyond the current 20 percent. League owners maintain that this highly popular sport loses millions annually and they cannot afford the players' outrageous demands for more pay. By now, these arguments and issues should sound familiar.

In Europe, free agency was granted to soccer players by the European Court of Justice.[17] In 1995, the court held that once a player's contract expires and the player changes teams, a transfer fee cannot be collected. The transfer fee paid by a player's new team to the former team was deemed an illegal restraint on the trade. Besides meaning more money for players because the transfer fees arguably will end up in the pockets of the players, the implications of the decision are global. Now teams ranging from Brazilian soccer clubs to NHL hockey clubs may attract European players whose contracts have expired without the added cost of transfer fees.

For the evolving professional women's sports of volleyball, basketball, soccer, and ice hockey, it is only a matter of time before antitrust challenges and allegations of bad faith labor dealings are at the forefront of player-owner concerns.

SUMMARY

Players and owners over the years have had a troubled business and legal relationship stemming from the unilateral imposition of restrictions on players' ability to change teams, called the reserve clause. The players began to organize themselves into unions or players' associations to assist in negotiating wages, hours of employment, and conditions of work.

Under federal labor law both players and management must negotiate collectively in good faith on the mandatory subjects of bargaining. Unfair labor practice charges occur when either party breaks this requirement.

More than seventy-five years ago Justice Holmes ruled that baseball enjoyed an exemption from antitrust laws. This anomaly is not shared by other professional team sports. Football, basketball, baseball, hockey, soccer, and so on are subject to triple damages whenever they engage in unlawful anticompetitive practices.

The dynamic interplay between owners and players continues to dominate the landscape. Free agency has led to more money for players. Owners who couldn't stop bidding on players demanded and received (in some collective bargaining agreements) salary caps and even a self-imposed tax on player salaries in baseball. In return, the players received more freedom to move from team to team.

The future for the astute student of sports will be as exciting in the boardrooms as on the field.

For Reflection

1. What is the only major men's professional sport studied that does not have a salary cap? Why does this sport not have a salary cap and the other leagues have salary caps?
2. What are some of the creative financing tools available in the NFL and NBA to circumvent salary caps?

3. Give examples of mandatory and permissive subjects for collective bargaining negotiations in different pro sports.
4. According to Judge Sotomayer's baseball decision, what does "good faith" dealing mean?
5. Explain the interplay between labor and antitrust rules as applied to players associations and team owners.
6. How would you change the drug policy in the NBA in light of the *Tarpley* case?
7. Define the Rozelle Rule and describe how it came into play.
8. Which pro sport had the most generous rules on free agency, and why?
9. Overall do you think players associations have served their members at the expense of the game? Provide examples.
10. Which was the last sport to experience either a lockout or a strike? What were the critical impasse issues?

Useful Web Sites

1. www.bigleaguers.com (MLB)
2. www.sportsline.com/u/NFLPlayers/
3. www.nhlpa.com (includes list of player compensation)
4. www.law.vill.edu/vls/journals/vselj
5. www.law.usm.maine.edu/iwp/caron.txt

Notes

1. Robert Berry and Glen Wong, *Law and Business of the Sports Industries* (1986) and Paul Staudohar, *Playing for Dollars: Labor Relations and the Sports Business* (1990) are both excellent texts that explain the interplay between professional sports, antitrust, and labor laws.
2. 250 U.S. 200 (1922).
3. *Flood* v. *Kuhn*, 407 U.S. 258 (1972).
4. 543 F. 2nd 606 (8th Cir. 1976), modifying 407 F. Supp. 1000 (D. Minn. 1975).
5. Ibid.
6. *Smith* v. *Pro-Football, Inc.*, 420 F. Supp. 738 (D.D.C. 1976).
7. 15 USCA 12 et. seq. (Clayton Act) and 29 U.S.C.A. 101-115 (Norris-La Guardia Act).
8. 888 F. 2nd 559 (8th Cir. 1989), cert. denied, 111 S. Ct. 711 (1991).
9. 543 F. 2nd 606 (8th Cir. 1976), modifying 407 F. Supp. 1000 (D. Minn. 1975).

10. National Labor Relations Act, Section 8(d).
11. *Robertson* v. *NBA*, 389 F. Supp. 867 (S.U.N.Y. 1975), affirmed 556 F. 2nd 682 (2nd Cir. 1977).
12. *Wood* v. *NBA*, 602 F. Supp. 525 (D.C.N.Y. 1984) affirmed 809 F. 2nd 954 (2nd Cir. 1978).
13. Larry Whiteside, "Sotomayer Passes Judgment on Owners," *The Boston Globe*, April 1, 1995, p. 70.
14. *Seattle Seahawks* v. *NFLPA and Sam McCullum*, 292 N.L.R.B. No. 110, contains the National Labor Relations Board administration hearing decision upholding the charges alleged by McCullum. It took an administrative law judge two more years to calculate his lost wages; this decision was promptly appealed by the Seahawks.
15. *National Basketball Association* v. *Williams*, 45 F. 3rd 684 (2nd Cir. 1995).
16. *McNeil* v. *National Football League*, 790 F. 871 (D. Minn. 1992).
17. Paul Gains, "In Europe, the Dawn of Free Agency Has More Athletes on the Move," *The New York Times*, April 27, 1997, p. 9.

CHAPTER 5

Player Agents

S how me the money!

> —fictional football player Rod Tidwell, speaking
> to his agent in the film *Jerry Maguire*

Case Study

Billy Bob Burton just finished his final year of football eligibility. He's slated to play in a postseason college all-star game where scouts and agents will be as plentiful as seals in a cold winter harbor. Billy Bob asked his coach for advice on selecting an agent. Coach's only advice was "don't expect to be drafted until after the fourth round." What advice would you offer Billy Bob in helping him choose an agent to represent him in this year's NFL draft?

INTRODUCTION

"Gutter brawl" is how former Dallas Cowboys owner and general manager Tex Schramm once described the solicitation of star college athletes by agents. Basketball players still in junior high school are wooed by agents to summer all-star camps by offers of free travel, sneakers, and a chance to be seen by college recruiters and professional scouts.

It hasn't always been this way. Less than 30 years ago most professional athletes negotiated their own contracts. The late Bob Woolf is acknowledged as one of the first sports agents, having begun his career in sports representation when Boston Red Sox pitcher Earl Wilson sought his advice after an automobile accident. That relationship led to Woolf negotiating Wilson's baseball contract, and so began the beginning of the player agent.

Today's player agents enjoy a prominent role in the sports business. Their tasks extend beyond signing players to top-dollar team contracts. The sports business has evolved into the entertainment business. Product endorsements,

80

sponsorships, and television appearances are all part of the daily fare on the sports agent's agenda. Michael Jordan, Tiger Woods, and former Olympic swimmer Amy Van Dyken all earn more money from agent-negotiated endorsements than from any athletic competitions.

PLAYER-TO-AGENT RELATIONSHIP

As a matter of law, an agent is someone empowered to conduct business for another person. The athlete may grant the agent broad authority (negotiate a spokesperson contract with Breathe Right, arrange a cameo appearance on a television sitcom, and manage all tax, investment and financial affairs) or limited authority (merely negotiate a one-time player-team contract). It is customary, and in many cases mandatory, that the legal relationship between a player and an agent be spelled out in written contract form. The relationship between player and agent is governed by both contract and agency law.

Typically the language of the agreement between a player and an agent contains provisions that not only spell out the services to be performed by the agent but additionally state the length of time for which the agent is permitted to act on the player's behalf, the fee arrangement, reasons for termination, and methods and procedures for dispute resolution. It should be kept in mind that all contracts between players and agents must comply with the legal requirements for a written contract in the jurisdiction where the contract is formed.

A common area of dispute that sometimes arises between a player and agent is the amount of the fee, and timing of the payment, for the agent's services rendered. The same Bob Woolf who pioneered the business of sports agency was accused of overcharging by many of his basketball player clients, including Glen Rice and Robert Parish. They argued that he illegally took his 4 percent commission from the players' deferred compensation before the players actually had received their money. They maintained that Woolf was not entitled to take his negotiated compensation until they were actually paid, not before. Woolf paid an estimated $1 million in restitution.

All agents are under a legal obligation to exercise the utmost care, loyalty, and good faith in all dealings on behalf of their clients. This obligation stems from what is known in the law as a *fiduciary relationship*.

Selecting an Agent

Many people assume that an agent must be a lawyer. This is not true. Although knowledge of the law is undoubtedly helpful in understanding the language and meaning of contracts, skills beyond familiarity with contract law are frequently needed. Today agents need schooling in the art of negotiating deals especially when sitting on the other side of the table are smart, wily, experienced, and strong-willed general managers and owners who have their own view of a player's market value.

Managing a player's investments, planning ahead for retirement years, presenting a positive image to the public, and otherwise promoting the athlete are all aspects of the work of what are called full-service sports agency firms. Mark McCormack's International Management Group (representing many outstanding professional golfers, soccer stars, and tennis players) and Donald Dell's competing Pro Serve (representing ice skating icons, tennis pros, and cyclists) are two examples of full-service sports agency firms that employ lawyers, accountants, tax experts, marketing gurus, speech writers, and investment advisors to assist players.

There are as many agents as there are professional athletes. Agents run the gamut from individuals like ex-quarterback Bernie Kosar's dentist, Rocket Ismail's mother-in-law, Olympic gold medalist Jackie Joyner-Kersee, David Falk, and former hockey player Derek Sanderson. No special training is required. Agents who are lawyers must, of course, comply with their state bar association's code of ethics. The long-standing Association of Representation of Professional Athletes and the Sports Lawyers Association are two groups that have sought to professionalize the field by providing seminars and workshop training for aspiring agents.

Personal attributes are a critical aspect of the agent-player relationship. The key element, as University of Richmond law professor Robert Shepherd has written, is trust between a player and an agent.[1]

An agent who overstates a college player's likely draft position, or who won't answer honestly how many players he or she has represented, and in what capacity he or she has represented them, is one to be avoided. Honesty and knowledge of the sport's collective bargaining agreement, team salaries, and personnel are some of the blocks used in building the trust an agent must earn, as well as regular and full disclosure of circumstances that have the potential of creating conflicts of interest.

Although the focus of this chapter is the agent's role in representing professional athletes, it should be kept in mind that many coaches, team managers, and athletic directors retain agents. Bill Parcells's acrimonious move from the Super Bowl XXXI finalist New England Patriots to the head coaching job with the New York Jets was largely orchestrated by his agent, Robert Fraley. New Jersey Nets coach John Calipari's agent negotiated his five-year, $15 million dollar deal that took him from a highly successful college program at UMASS, Amherst.

A few years ago a *Sports Illustrated* exposé on agents offered the following tips for selecting the best agent:[2]

- Keep the athlete-agent contract short term with an easy "out" for the athlete.
- Talk to different agents and compare fees.

- Don't overpay for services not needed.
- Make sure the agent has time to respond to your inquiries.
- Get a list of the agent's clients and review any actual or potential conflicts of interest.
- Be cautious about signing any sort of power of attorney.
- Inquire about postplaying days career counseling and assistance.

Agents as Subagents of Players Associations

In those team sports where the players are represented by a players association, that association is the exclusive representative of all the players under federal labor law. So how is it that superstar agent Leigh Steinberg can represent more than a dozen NFL quarterbacks (among them Steve Young, Bret Farve, Casey Weldon, Ryan Leaf, Drew Bledsoe, and Troy Aikman) and Texas-based agents, the Hendrich brothers, have a roster of outstanding baseball players (including Roger Clemons and Ricky Henderson)?

The answer lies in knowing a little sports history. Powerful individual agents existed before players decided that, through collective bargaining under the jurisdiction of federal labor laws, they could increase average salaries, expand leverage for pensions and disability pay, and generally enhance the financial position of all players.

However, according to principles of labor law that are explored more fully in the chapter on labor and antitrust, once players in a particular sport elect to collectively bargain with management on wages and working conditions, the players union becomes the sole agent for each and every player. The union, though, acceded to the wishes of key players who wanted to retain their individual agents for assistance in negotiating salaries and benefits higher than the union-negotiated minimums. This occurred, in part, because of the trusting relationship many influential agents had established with key players.

Regulation of Agents

In recent years the players associations of the men's major sports of basketball, football, hockey, and baseball have taken a much more active role in regulating and supervising the activities of agents. The primary reason for this has been because of agent misconduct and consequent cries for help from players harmed by agents who swindled clients.

In a highly publicized case, Kareem Abdul-Jabbar sued his former business manager for over $59 million in damages alleging breach of fiduciary duty, breach of contract, fraud, and negligent misrepresentation.[3] Abdul-Jabbar's 11-year relationship with agent Tom Collins came to an abrupt end after the basketball Hall of Fame player discovered he was entangled in a web of investments that left him confused and penniless.

Abdul-Jabbar granted Collins broad authority to sign checks and take out loans in his name. Allegedly, Collins never sent him the required monthly statements as to where the money was coming from and going. Abdul-Jabbar had to return to the Lakers' lineup at the age of 40 to earn money to begin to pay off his enormous debt and lawyers' fees.

Today every sport's players association requires agent certification before that agent may lawfully represent any player.[4] Each sports union has its own individual certification standards. See the appendix for a sample of agent certification requirements as provided by the National Football League Players Association (NFLPA) on behalf of its member-players.

The NFLPA refers to agents whether they are lawyers, accountants, or public relations specialists as *contract advisors* throughout the certification process. The NFLPA guidelines for certification can be found in the appendix. The reader may obtain further information on the agent certification process from the individual players associations. Commencing in 1999 all NFL contract advisors must pass a mandatory test demonstrating knowledge of the CBA and negotiation process.

The frequency of top college basketball and football players joining professional sports ranks before their eligibility has expired has led more than 20 states to enact legislation to curtail the role of the agent in encouraging players to leave school early.[5] In the eyes of many influential alumni, national championships were lost when players like Marcus Camby jumped to the NBA early from UMASS, Amherst, Deion Sanders bolted Florida State to play pro baseball and football with eligibility remaining, North Carolina's Jerry Stackhouse left Coach Dean Smith empty at guard when he turned pro after only two years, and running back Curtis Enis was banished from Penn State during his junior year. Many of these and other players fell prey to illegal inducements from agents that cost them eligibility and respectability.

Meanwhile, their schools didn't lose just star players, but in the case of UMASS, Amherst the school had to forfeit its 1996 NCAA tournament wins because Camby accepted access to cars, women, and cash from two agents. Penn State lost Enis on the eve of its 1997 bowl game because he lied about keeping a jacket given to him by an agent.

Not surprisingly, the states where college athletes are worshipped are the same states that have made it either a civil or a criminal offense for an agent to fail to register or engage in state-defined unethical conduct.

In 1981 California became the first state to regulate the role of agents. Lawyers are specifically exempted, but all other sports agents must register with the state labor commissioner, pay a licensing fee, post a surety bond, file a fee schedule, maintain records, and agree to arbitration of any player-agent disputes.[6]

The preamble to Florida's statute (adopted in 1988; partial text can be found in the appendix) clearly articulates the reason behind its regulation when it states that "dishonest or unscrupulous practices by agents who solicit representation of student athletes can cause significant harm to student athletes and the academic institutions for which they play."

Florida makes it illegal for an agent to offer anything of value to induce a player to sign an agent contract and mandates written notification to a player's athletic director or university president when such a contract is signed. Failure to comply voids the agent agreement with the athlete and may lead to civil fines or incarceration for the agent.

Many of the top intercollegiate sports programs have instituted formal educational programs dealing with sports agency. Thanks in part to enabling legislation by the NCAA, any college may establish a screening committee to help the prospective professional athlete in selecting an agent.[7] Division I schools such as Duke, Stanford, and Miami frequently call upon university law and business school professors to serve as committee members on college professional sports panels.

One of the conditions players associations impose on any certified player agent is that he or she must have signed a standard written agreement with the player. The sample document found in the appendix is an agreement for negotiation of a team-player contract. An agent and a player frequently have additional written contracts covering investment and tax management, endorsements and sponsorships, book publication, and media relations. This is especially true when the player is represented by a full-service agency firm. It is not unusual, however, for a player to hire one agent to negotiate a team contract, another agent to assist in public appearances, and a third agent to help in signing a book deal with a major publishing company.

Even the Securities and Exchange Commission has begun to examine misconduct. This federal agency has launched criminal investigations into whether agents have failed to properly register as "investment advisors" for players.

Key Considerations: Selection and Regulation of Agents
- Ask what services the agent can perform.
- Ask the agent for a client list and contact athletes on the list to gauge satisfaction.
- Ask the agent his or her qualifications and experience. Does the state where the agent conducts business regulate agents?
- Ask the agent how he or she is regulated—bar association, players' association, bonding authorities—and get copies of compliance.
- Ask the agent how much he or she charges for professional services.
- Ask to examine a sample agency contract.

Conflicts of Interest and Breach of Duties

Those states that regulate agents provide an administrative law framework for penalizing agents who violate specific statutory provisions. Texas-based agent Steve Endicott, who was accused of failing to register in Florida when he helped provide free shoes for numerous Florida State football players at a local Foot Locker store, paid a fine rather than face possible jail time. Sports agent Lance Luchnick paid $5,000 for violating Alabama's regulatory act to avoid a felony finding. Miami Hurricane booster Jim Ferraro faced five criminal charges including operating as an unlicensed agent for wining and dining three University of Miami football players. Penn State called for criminal charges against sports agent Jeff Nalley, who allegedly violated state law for offering running back Curtis Enis something of value (a sports jacket) while he still had college eligibility. Nalley pleaded no contest to unlawful activity by a sports agent and was fined $10,000 and ordered to perform 100 hours of community service.

Certified player agents may face union suspension or revocation of certification for certain prohibited conduct.[8] Penn State has asked the NFLPA that Nalley be decertified as a football sports agent. The NFLPA regulations governing agents list 18 prohibited activities.

The following items are some of the unethical or illegal acts that could cause an agent to lose certification:

- Providing or offering money to induce a player to sign with an agent.
- Engaging in fraud, deceit, misrepresentation, or, dishonesty.
- Providing misleading or materially false information in the course of recruiting or representing a player.
- Failing to comply with the stated fee provisions.
- Engaging in actual or potential conflicts of interest in regard to representing a player.

Occasionally, prospective agents are denied certification on the basis of one or more of the 18 prohibited activities. In 1993 the Major League Baseball Players Association (MLBPA) refused to certify the former general counsel to the Major League Baseball Player Relations Committee as an agent. Attorney Barry Roma had provided legal guidance to baseball's owners during a turbulent time in labor negotiations. Roma appealed the decision, denying his certification by the MLBPA, and sought an arbitration hearing. The arbitrator rejected the union's view that Roma could not be entrusted with the fiduciary responsibilities of an agent for baseball players. The MLBPA's acts of denial were deemed arbitrary and capricious.

The common law also provides grounds for punishing agents who engage in illegal activities. Former pro football player Ken Burrows authorized the Atlanta Falcons to deliver his salary checks and bonus money directly to his agents, Norman Young and Probus Management Inc. The money was properly forwarded by the Falcons; however, instead of managing his money and paying his taxes, Burrows's representatives misspent the funds. Burrows successfully sued his agents for breach of their agreement with him by dealing in bad faith. He received a court settlement for lost compensation, attorney's fees, and in order to deter repeat offenses, a substantial punitive damage award.

From time to time unethical agent practices escalate beyond civil wrongs, such as breaching the duty of loyalty and care in financial management, and into criminal conduct.

Player agents Norby Walters and Lloyd Bloom were accused of physically threatening clients who sought to change representatives. Changing agents is a fairly common practice in the business. Threatening clients who consider changing agents is rare. It was reported that the wife of one-time Notre Dame standout quarterback Tom Clements was beaten by a masked associate of Walters and Bloom as the result of his having switched to Chicago-based agent Steve Zucker.[9] Walters and Bloom also engaged in a widespread practice of inducing athletes with college eligibility remaining to sign secret agent-player contracts, which did not become effective until after the end of the season, in addition to violating NCAA rules on eligibility.[10]

Federal and state law enforcement officials were tipped off that gangland style threats were being made against any player who had second thoughts about not keeping Walters and Bloom as their agents. Based on a theory of "legal fraud," state and federal law enforcement officials held that every time a player's school unknowingly certified the player's eligibility to practice and play and mailed it to the NCAA, the Federal Mail Fraud Act was violated.

Walters pleaded guilty to mail fraud and was sentenced to jail for 18 months. Bloom received probation and community service. Charges of criminal threatening and extortion were dropped.

It should be understood that under federal mail fraud law the athletes who participated in the secret signing scheme were criminally responsible for their illegal acts. All of the Walters and Bloom athletes ended up pleading guilty to related charges. They received probation and community service sentences and were ordered to make restitution to their schools for the value of the scholarships they had received during periods of ineligibility.

According to hockey sportswriter Russ Conway, the biggest scandal in professional sports since the 1919 White Sox threw the World Series has centered around the corrupt activities of former agent and National Hockey League Players Association (NHLPA) executive director Alan Eagleson. Conway, in his Pulitzer Prize–nominated book *Game Misconduct*, alleged that Eagleson wrongly wore the dual hats of union boss and hockey agent by making unauthorized loans to his friends from NHLPA funds, profited from injured players seeking career-ending disability compensation, and used Canada Cup money for personal benefit.

The most shocking charge Conway makes is that Eagleson betrayed Bobby Orr by failing to convey a fabulous offer for Orr to re-sign with the Boston Bruins, which included a postcareer 18.5 percent ownership deal. Instead, Orr was steered to the Chicago Blackhawks, which were owned and managed by associates of Eagleson.

Eagleson was indicted in federal court in Boston, charged with racketeering, mail fraud, embezzlement, receipt of kickbacks, and obstruction of justice. Canada's investigation led to the filing of similar charges against erstwhile agent Eagleson.

In early 1998 Eagleson pleaded guilty in Boston to three federal charges of fraud including using union funds for his own benefit and taking $15,000 in insurance proceeds from former client and NHL player Glen Sharpley. Although Eagleson avoided jail time in the United States, he was sentenced to 18 months in jail in Canada and ordered to pay nearly $700,000 in restitution to defrauded clients. Civil suits against him remain.

Because Eagleson is also an attorney, he is bound to follow the rules of appropriate conduct defined by his Canadian legal society or bar association. Individual codes of professional conduct vary from state to state and country to country, but criminal fraud convictions normally lead to losing a license to practice law.

At a minimum all lawyers are duty bound to follow certain canons of ethics that require maintenance of personal integrity, honesty, and avoidance of impropriety or the appearance thereof. Disciplinary action against any attorney-agent who violates these canons ranges from public reprimand to disbarment and reimbursement for any financial loss resulting from the breach of the canons.

Key Discussions: Agent Breaches
- Players' associations certify agents.
- Unethical or illegal agent acts could lead to loss of certification.
- Some illegal acts, such as Alan Eagleson's defrauding players, may lead to criminal charges and prison time if the agent is convicted.

Endorsements and Dealing with the Media
Boston College law professor Bob Berry has written in the ABA Forum Committee on the *Entertainment and Sports Industry Newsletter* about the difficulty agents have in garnering endorsements for athletes. Yet, in an increasingly media/advertising-driven sports world, athletes are demanding that their agents identify and negotiate for their "fair share" of today's advertising, sponsorship, and personal appearance dollar.

Picture this as an agent's dream client: Minority golfer. Excelled at an early age. Strong-willed, dominant father wanting the best for his child. Compassionate housewife and mother. Left college after winning national golf championships to begin pro tour career. Won first few tournaments. Tiger Woods? Yes. And no. In 1978 this golfing phenomenon was a Mexican-American woman— Nancy Lopez. She went on to capture the hearts of the viewing public to become the leading money earner (counting winnings and endorsements) during her first year on the women's professional golf tour.

Lopez's agent was the International Management Group (IMG), the same firm that now represents golf legend in the making, Tiger Woods. Tiger's personal agent at IMG is Hughes Norton. Before Tiger even played in his first professional tournament Norton negotiated two significant endorsement deals. The first was a five-year, $40 million contract with Nike. Tiger wears Nike clothes and appears in Nike commercials. In return, he has received a $7.5 million signing bonus and the balance of $32.5 million payable in equal installments over a five-year term.

Tiger's second major endorsement was with golf club manufacturer Titleist. Norton negotiated a $3.5 million dollar per year agreement for a term of three years. Tiger agreed to play exclusively with Titleist's balls, gloves, and golf bags. In the future the company will work with him to design a line of "Tiger Woods" golf equipment.

Agent Hughes Norton frequently travels to matches with Tiger in an attempt to protect him from overzealous fans and promoters and to control media access to him.

In 1997, without his agent's knowledge, an unsuspecting Tiger Woods hitched a friendly ride with a reporter from *GQ* magazine. He told the reporter a number of off-color jokes that soon were retold in a *GQ* article (April 1997). IMG's response that Tiger had been unschooled about the motives the press was viewed by some as merely compounding the impact of the insensitive remarks.

Unfortunately, for every endorsement success story there are all too many sponsorship deals that go awry. In 1994, power-hitting golfer John Daly signed a 10-year, $30 million deal with Wilson Sporting Goods. Two divorces, allegations of spousal abuse, tournament suspension, and alcoholism (including admittance to the Betty Ford Center) led Wilson to pare down the money and length of Daly's deal.

Olympic gold medalist figure skater Oksana Baiul's passage from the rink to drunk driving charges has jeopardized her endorsement appeal. Latrell Sprewell's well-publicized choking incident against his coach cost him his sneaker contract.

One sponsorship deal was nearly ruined when NBA player-WWF grappler-film star-author Dennis Rodman kicked a courtside cameraman. This incident on January 15, 1997, occurred the day before he was to sign a $2 million endorsement contract with Converse. The shoe manufacturer's CEO began to have doubts about signing the volatile Rodman.

His agent, Dwight Manley, negotiated a quick $200,000 out-of-court settlement with the cameraman in return for dropping all charges. Rodman then inked the deal with Converse.

It is not unusual for companies sponsoring athletes to insert a morality provision into sponsorship agreements. Dallas Cowboys wide receiver Michael Irvin's 1996 plea of no contest on possession of illegal drugs, which led to court-imposed probation and a league-imposed five-game suspension, drew the wrath of a group of Dallas-based car dealers that had used Irvin in local television advertisements. They canceled their promotional deal with Irvin on the basis of his behavior and subsequently sued him for damaging their reputations.

During the 1992 summer Olympics, the entire world witnessed a clash of titans never seen before. It wasn't merely the U.S. men's basketball team battling the Russians and the Yugoslavs underneath the boards. The other duel that was just as real was taking place between heavyweight shoe and apparel rivals, Nike and Reebok.

The official shoe company of the U.S. Olympic basketball team was Reebok. Contractually U.S. team members were required to wear Reebok's warmups during the medals ceremony. Half the team including Michael Jordan, David Robinson, Scottie Pippen, Chris Mullen, and John Stockton were under contract to Nike. Their respective individual contracts required them to wear Nike's warmups. The stalemate ended when all the players wore Reebok clothing, with the Nike half of the team draping a U.S. flag over the Reebok insignia.

Nearly two-thirds of all NBA players wear Nike shoes. More than 20 percent of all NFL and major league baseball players wear the familiar Nike logo. Many of the top intercollegiate football, basketball, and baseball schools receive cash, shoes, and uniforms in return for the right to be called a "Nike school." It wasn't long before Nike elected to stretch its connection with individual athletes to include agent representation.

Miami Heat basketball standout Alonzo Mourning is a prototype Nike-managed athlete. In high school he attended Nike basketball camps and tournaments. He then went to Georgetown, a "Nike school," under legendary coach John Thompson, a Nike client and board of directors member. Drafted number two by the NBA (after Shaquille O'Neil), Mourning signed an exclusive sports-management deal with Nike. The agreement allows Nike to select an agent to conduct player-club negotiations subject to certification by the NBA Players Association (NBAPA), negotiate Mourning's marketing deals, manage his finances, plan his charitable events, and otherwise mold his public image.

Not all athletes who sign endorsement deals with Nike are fully managed like Mourning. Michael Jordan maintains an exclusive shoe-only deal that pays him more than $20 million per year. Jordan retains the "godfather of sports agents," David Falk, as his personal agent. Ken Griffey, Jr., Jerry Rice, and Tim Hardaway are marketing-only clients of Nike.

The first memorable marketing client signed by Nike was sports standout Bo Jackson. The Nike-inspired "Bo Knows" advertising campaign paid him millions and enhanced his legendary prowess as a multisport athlete.

The sheer magnitude of Nike's presence in the marketplace of sports, consumer goods, and advertising has led some agents to steer clients away from the all-too-familiar Nike "swoosh." Arnold Palmer's longtime agent and friend, Mark McCormick, once remarked to *Sports Illustrated* that "[a]gents and managers are going to be less inclined to sign athletes with Nike just to keep them away from the web."[11]

Following Nike's trend, Reebok hired a marketing M.B.A., Henry "Que" Gaskins, to serve as a full-time advisor, parent figure, and companion to basketball guard Allen Iverson. In 1997, Iverson agreed to three years of probation on concealed weapons and marijuana charges. Sports agent David Falk recommended that Reebok hire someone to assist Iverson to help prevent future problems and to protect the shoe company's $40 million investment.

Negotiating Tips

A number of well-known primers exist to help one learn how to negotiate contracts. The classic *Art of Negotiating* by Gerald Nierenberg, Donald Dell's *Minding Other People's Business*, and Harvey MacKay's *Swim with the Sharks Without Being Eaten Alive* are all recommended reading for the reader keen on viewing how practicing agents successfully negotiate deals.

Goethe wrote that "thinking is more interesting than knowing, but less interesting than looking." The "looking" part in contract negotiations begins with preparing and analyzing key sports data and information. For team sports, begin by contacting the players associations for copies of collective bargaining agreements, sample player contracts, salary caps, and salary data by team and position. Much of this information is readily available on the Internet.

Research every bit of information available on team rosters. Look for material about players including years in the league, injuries, and forthcoming free agency status.

Get to know the backgrounds of coaches, player personnel directors, and general managers. Former Buffalo Bills coach Marv Levy earned a masters degree in English from Harvard. Levy would just as soon have discussed Proust with agents as talked about signing and performance bonuses.

Find out who the player-team decision makers are for each team that might draft or sign the player. Talk to your client during this process. Communicate. Explain what you've learned. Discuss negotiating strategy in advance of contract talk. Set realistic negotiating goals. Know the client. What are his or her strengths and weaknesses as an athlete? How will the athlete fit into the "philosophy" of the organization? Character counts. Ask Christian Peters who was drafted by the New England Patriots out of Nebraska and then was released before he was signed because of "character" difficulties that became very public. Randy Moss's troubles with the law cost him millions in lost earnings when his NFL draft position fell dramatically.

Many negotiations start out awkwardly with both sides stubbornly taking positions. Help the other side solve the mutual problem—getting the player signed at a fair and reasonable salary with incentives and protections.

A few years ago an agent friend told the story of how Boston Celtics general manager Red Auerbach refused to even talk to the agent of a top draft choice, Rufus Harris, out of the University of Maine. Each party sent angry letters back and forth. The final straw came when Auerbach sent the agent a note, which read: "If I wanted to talk to you, then I would have drafted you and not Rufus!"

The agent learned that assistant coach K.C. Jones was a family friend of the player's father. K.C. agreed to talk to Auerbach and smooth over a testy agent-management relationship.

Some players will trade off salary for longer-term, full or partial guaranteed compensation. Other players coming off an injury may lack negotiating power, so they must be willing to settle for incentive-laden contracts based on future performance. Incentives clauses are discussed in another chapter; at a minimum these would include reporting bonuses for coming to camp in shape and healthy. Further bonus money can be earned for games started, innings pitched, goals scored, or minutes logged depending upon the sport.

Keep the player fully informed at all times. It's the agent's fiduciary duty!

Agent's Pay

Player agents are paid for rendering services on behalf of clients. The players associations regulate the maximum fee an agent may receive for negotiating player-team contracts. For instance, the NFL players' association caps agents' fees at 3%, while the NBA players associations cap agents' fees at 4% of the salary, bonus, and performance incentive money earned, as negotiated by the agent. Agents and players are free to agree on a lower fee.

For negotiating services outside of the traditional player-contract arrangement, the agent is paid based on the terms of the agency relationship. The standard fee for an agent negotiated publishing or recording contract is 15%. Endorsement deals frequently pay agents anywhere from 5% to 20%.

Agents who perform tax work and provide accounting and financial planning advice normally charge an hourly rate that is customary for the services rendered, which can range from $150 to $400 an hour.

SUMMARY

It is clear from the foregoing that the field of sports agency has been revolutionized in recent years from completely unregulated, uncharted territory to a situation today where many states and professional associations are safeguarding the interests of players through a certification and bonding process.

Clearly, the realization that fiduciary responsibilities apply with full force in this field, and the codification of many of these responsibilities in statute, has helped to curb some agent abuses. It is equally clear that those who seek to enter the field today must do so in the knowledge that their first responsibility is to safeguard the interests of their clients, to communicate with them at all times, and in general to treat their interests as paramount, while maintaining the highest standard of personal integrity.

For Reflection

1. What do you view as the primary responsibilities of a sports agent today? Explain.
2. If you were a player, what qualities would you regard as most important in the person you would choose to represent you?
3. What do you believe is the most serious abuse of the agent-player relationship discussed? Explain.
4. Cite three examples of illegal activities by agents?
5. How does the issue of corporate sponsorship impact the player-agent relationship?
6. What special challenges do agents face when trying to land endorsement deals for sports clients?
7. How, and how much, are sports agents paid?

Useful Web Sites

1. www.iprs.ed.ac.uk/edit/08/articles/01.html
2. www.hockey/playeragent.com
3. home.istar.ca/-simagent/faq.html
4. www.execreport.com/zine/1096.Sports.html
5. www.law.upenn.edu/bll/ulc/usas/sprtagt.html

Notes

1. Robert Shepherd, "Establishing the Contractual Relationship between the Representative and the Athlete" in *Current Issues in Professional Sports* (M. Jones, ed., University of New Hampshire Press, Durham. NH, 1980).
2. Craig Nee, "Agents: What's the Deal?" *Sports Illustrated*, October 19, 1987.
3. Ibid., p. 89.
4. Ray Yasser, James McCurdy, and C. Peter Goblerud, *Sports Law, Cases and Materials*, 3rd ed, (Anderson Publishing Co., Cincinnati, OH: 1997) pp. 557–558.
5. Ibid., pp. 579. For commentary on state laws regulating agent practices, see Athletic Agent Legislation and Regulation Update, XIV Sports Law. 4 (July/August 1996). Sports Law.1 (Fall 1995, Special ed.) lists all states regulating sports agents.

6. Cal. Labor Code 1500 et seq. (California Athlete Agents Act).

7. As reported by D. Lierman, "NCAA Leaders See Big Strides Effort to Reshape Sports," *Chron. Higher Education*, January 22, 1992, p. A39.

8. See, for instance, Section 3: Standard of Conduct for Contract Advisors (NFLPA).

9. As reported by Paul Weiler and Gary Roberts, "Agent Representation of the Athlete," *Sports and the Law*, 1st ed., pp. 316–321.

10. Ibid.

11. Donald Katz, "The Triumph of the Swoosh," *Sports Illustrated*, August 16, 1993, p. 69.

CHAPTER 6

Torts and Sports

Some restraints of civilization must accompany every athlete onto the playing field.

—Illinois Court of Appeals, *Nabozny v. Barnhill*[1]

Case Study

José Spectator is an avid sports fan who regularly attends sporting events. At a recent women's ice hockey game he was seriously hurt when an errant puck tipped off the goalie's stick over the 5' protective plexiglass into the stands. José was talking to a friend at the time of the injury, and was not paying attention to the game. Earlier José had verbally berated the goalie for her poor play. Does José have a legitimate "tort" claim against anyone or is he deemed to have assumed the risk of his injury by voluntarily attending the game?

INTRODUCTION

Outrageous conduct has become an unfortunate part of the landscape of the sports world both on and off the playing field. Recent notable examples include Golden State Warrior Latrell Sprewell attacking coach P.J. Carlesimo; Dennis Rodman kicking a photographer in the groin during a Chicago Bulls game; Colorado Avalanche defenseman Claude Lemieux breaking Red Wing Chris Drapier's nose, jaw, and cheekbone with a crushing check; and Dallas Cowboys Michael Irvin and Eric Williams wrongfully accused of forcing a woman to perform sexual acts. This list is clearly not exhaustive. Athletes at every level of competition suffer injuries at the hands of their opponents, coaches, medical providers, and from defective equipment. Players sometimes suffer harm to their reputations when either false or personal information is the subject of a news story. In addition, spectators suffer injuries from flying pucks, balls, players, cleats, skis, race car parts, and just about anything else imaginable.

It is not surprising, given the physical nature of sports and the public's fascination with athletes, that the same rules that apply to society at large do not

95

always apply to athletics. For example, holding a football player liable for tackling an opposing player would be ludicrous. Although such behavior may incur liability off the field, tough, physical play is not only accepted, it is also a required part of football. Similarly, professional athletes should expect that although their popularity may bring them fame and fortune, it exposes them up to more criticism and scrutiny than the average person is expected to tolerate.

The most commonly occurring tort claims in the sports setting involve one or more of the following: physical harm to a player engaged in athletic competition; harm to a spectator; harm to a player or spectator because of a dangerously defective product; defamation, meaning harm to a player's reputation; and invasion of right to publicity. In the following sections, we will examine these areas in detail and outline the elements of each tort and consider how the law of torts has adapted to the aggressive, and sometimes violent nature of sports.

INTRODUCTORY LEGAL PRINCIPLES

Although scholars agree that there is no single definition that comprehensively defines tort law, most agree that a common element of all torts is one person's unreasonable interference with the interests of another.[2] As Justice Oliver Wendell Holmes put it, "The business of torts is to fix the dividing lines between those cases in which [a person] is liable for harm which he has done and those in which he has not."[3]

Tort law allows individuals to seek compensation for losses that they have suffered within the scope of their legally recognized interests.[4] Unlike a crime, which is an offense against the public and is prosecuted by the government, a tort is an offense against an individual for which the injured party may seek recourse by filing a lawsuit in civil court. The opposing sides or *parties* are the *plaintiff*, the person filing the suit, and the *defendant*, the party against whom claims are made. The purpose of the suit is to compensate the plaintiff for the damage suffered.

In general, a court will not hold a defendant responsible for his or her acts unless the plaintiff can prove the defendant is at fault for the plaintiff's damages. A defendant is said to be at fault if he or she intended his or her acts or was negligent. An exception to the general rule that there is no liability without fault is strict liability. As a result, torts generally fall within one of three categories: intentional torts, negligence, and strict liability.

Intentional Torts	*Forms of Negligence*	*Strict Liability*
Assault	Medical Malpractice	Products Liability
Battery	Failure to Protect Spectators	Hazardous Activities
	Negligent Supervision	
	Negligent Hiring	

An actor's intent means his or her desire to cause the consequences of an act or that he or she believes that the consequences of his act are substantially certain to follow from what he does.[5] A negligent actor, however, does not desire to cause the consequences of an act nor does he or she believe that such consequences are substantially certain to follow. Rather, the actor has created a foreseeable risk of harm against which a reasonable person in the same or similar circumstances would protect.[6] Consider the following examples:

- Diane Driver, who is late for her afternoon tee time, bumps into Sam Slowpoke because Sam is driving too slowly. Diane's act is intentional because she desires to cause the consequence (bumping into Sam) of her act (bumping into the other driver's vehicle).
- Suppose that Diane engages in a high-speed pursuit of Crazy Chris, who cut Diane off. In her pursuit, however, Diane loses control of her car and she strikes Paul Pedestrian. Diane would be liable in negligence because Diane's conduct fell below the standard established by law for the protection of others against unreasonable risk of harm.

NEGLIGENCE

Most tort claims in sports are based in negligence. In its simplest form, *negligence* is defined as conduct that creates an undue or unreasonable risk of harm to others.[7] In an ordinary negligence claim, the defendant must first establish that the plaintiff owed the defendant a *duty of care*. The plaintiff must show that he or she was in the defendant's "range of apprehension" and that the plaintiff is part of the class of people to whom the defendant *owes a duty* of reasonable care in the same and similar circumstances.[8] The plaintiff must then show that the defendant *breached* his or her duty, proving that the defendant failed to do what a reasonable person would do under the same or similar circumstances. The plaintiff must then demonstrate that the defendant's breach caused *harm* to the plaintiff and the plaintiff has suffered *damages* as a result.[9]

Reckless disregard of safety, also called *recklessness*, is, as one scholar described it, "negligence plus."[10] In proving a claim for recklessness, the plaintiff must demonstrate that the actor knew or should have known that his or her conduct involved an even greater risk than that which is necessary to make his or her conduct negligent.[11] As you will see in the section concerning player-to-player liability, in the majority of jurisdictions, recklessness is the standard that courts apply to player-to-player liability cases.

Defenses to Negligence

When a plaintiff files a civil lawsuit based in tort, he or she is required to notify the defendant by providing the defendant with a document called a *complaint.* The complaint officially commences the suit, and it provides the name of the defendant(s), as well as the basis of the suit. The law requires the defendant to answer the plaintiff's complaint in a document called the *answer.* In his or her answer, the defendant, among other things, may assert his or her *defenses* to the plaintiff's claims. Defenses are explanations of why the plaintiff's claims against the particular defendant are either incorrect or legally insufficient to impose liability on the defendant. In sports related cases, contributory negligence and assumption of the risk are commonly asserted defenses. Contributory negligence focuses on the conduct of the plaintiff and determines whether the plaintiff's conduct fell below the standard to which the plaintiff should conform for his or her own protection. Assumption of the risk focuses on the plaintiff's knowledge and whether the plaintiff expressly or impliedly assumed the risk of harm arising from the negligent or reckless conduct of the defendant. In the following sections, we will examine each of these defenses and how they appear in sports-related cases.

Player-to-Player Liability

In sports arenas across the world, two events are guaranteed to get spectators up off their seats: outstanding play and excessive physical contact. Because fans demand such action, sports media outlets compete to air the day's best collisions, checks, fights, and brawls.

To hold players liable for aggressive, on-the-field play would undermine the purpose of sports at all levels. It would be absurd to hold a boxer liable for knocking out an opponent or to hold a hockey player liable for a clean hip check, despite the potentially dangerous consequences of these acts. The law recognizes that "taking part in a game manifests a willingness to such bodily contact or restriction of liberty as are permitted by its rules or usages."[12] As a result, a boxer is not liable for punching his opponent during a match nor is a lacrosse player held liable for accidentally striking an opponent with his stick. Yellow cards, free throws, and in some cases player ejection illustrate examples of how some sports punish their players for rules violations. However, at some point, when the rule does not adequately compensate for the harm done to another, the injured party may seek recourse in the law.

Before 1975, courts nationwide summarily denied participants' claims for injuries arising out of another's negligence during a sporting event. In denying participants' negligence claims, courts held athletic participants immune from liability to other players for all conduct, no matter how egregious, reasoning that all participants in contact sports have implied consent to harmful contact and assume the risk of injury. As a result, the defendant had no legal duty to the plaintiff and was thus not liable regardless of whether the conduct caused the plaintiff's damages.

In 1975, however, the appeals court of Illinois broke away from this line of thought in its decision in the case of *Nabozny* v. *Barnhill*.[13] In this case, the court held a soccer player liable for kicking an opposing team's goalie in the head. The defendant, a forward, ran into the penalty area and as the goalie was bent over picking up the ball, kicked him in the head. The kick resulted in damage to the goalie's skull and brain. Although the lower court had found that the defendant was not liable, the appeals court reversed, holding that "a player is liable for injury in a tort action if his or her conduct is such that it is either deliberate, willful or with a reckless disregard for the safety of the other player so as to cause injury to that player."[14]

This decision created a "grey area" between the traditional negligence standard and the court's customary refusal to punish sports-related negligence. After *Nabozny*, although an injured participant may seek some recourse, the standard of conduct that other participants owe to him or her is only to refrain from the utter disregard for the physical well-being of others. This is obviously a much less stringent standard than the one applicable to all other types of negligence.

Although a minority of courts, including the Supreme Court of Wisconsin, have applied the traditional negligence standard in cases involving an injury to a player, most courts have followed the principle established in *Nabozny*.[15] In applying the *Nabozny* standard courts have denied recovery to a college hockey player whose spleen was ruptured as a result of a being butt-ended with a hockey stick, a softball player injured in a home plate collision, and most recently, a woman injured while participating in a coed soccer game.[16] In each case, the question of liability turned on the defendant's duty and whether the defendant's conduct rose to the level of recklessness as opposed to the carelessness necessary to ordinary negligence.

Most courts provide that participants in noncontact sports owe a greater duty of care to fellow participants and apply an ordinary negligence standard. The query thus becomes whether the particular sport is a contact sport or noncontact sport. Most courts agree that golf and tennis are noncontact sports and thus require participants to exercise a duty of reasonable care to fellow participants. However, courts have ruled that kick the can, touch football, and pickup baseball are contact sports and thus applied the Nabozny standard.[17]

Key Considerations: Player-to-Player Liability
- Determine what duty of care one player owes to another player.
- Check to determine if the Nabozny standards apply.
- Determine if the defendant's breach of duty proximately caused damage to the plaintiff.
- Examine the customs and rules of the sport.

- Distinguish between a contact or noncontact sport.
- Players frequently raise contributing negligence or assumption of risk as defenses to negligence actions.

Spectator Liability

Regardless of the level of competition, spectators suffer injuries at sporting events. Although a front row seat to a ball game promises an up-close and personal experience, it also increases the chance that the ticket holder will be injured in the course of the game. Whereas baseballs and hockey pucks are the sources of the majority of spectator injuries, other potential sources of spectator injuries include facility defects and poisonous food.

The majority of spectator injury cases arise out of the facility owner's negligence. In these cases, the court's primary task is to determine what duty the facility owner owes to the game-watching visitors. Applying a traditional negligence analysis, a facility owner owes spectators a duty of reasonable care to protect the spectators from harm. In determining the standard of care, the courts focus on the facility owner's knowledge of unsafe conditions and whether the dangerous conditions are foreseeable. For example, it is reasonably foreseeable that in the course of a baseball game, foul balls will deflect into the stands. It is also known that foul balls pose a substantial risk of serious harm to those sitting behind or close to home plate. As a result, in executing a duty of reasonable care to protect spectators from harm, the facility is obliged to take protective measures, which in the baseball scenario may include installing a screen or posting warnings to spectators.

Under what is often referred to as the "no-duty" rule of baseball, baseball stadium owners are not liable for injuries to spectators hit by a ball, provided the owner has exercised reasonable care to protect spectators from harm.[18] Courts have held that the extent of the baseball park owner's duty includes furnishing screening for the area of the field where the danger of spectator injury is greatest, which is usually the area behind home plate. Classic reasoning is provided in *Brown* v. *San Francisco Baseball Club* where the court held that spectators subject themselves "to certain risks necessarily and usually incident to the game. This does not mean he assumes the risk of being injured by the proprietor's negligence but that by voluntarily entering into the sport as a spectator he knowingly accepts the reasonable risks inherent in incident to the game."[19]

The "no duty" rule is not absolute. The case of *Jones* v. *Three Rivers Management Corporation* illustrates a situation in which, despite the established rule of nonliability in baseball induced injury cases and the plaintiff's knowledge of baseball, the Supreme Court of Pennsylvania upheld a lower court's award to the plaintiff.[20] Evelyn Jones, a long-time Pittsburgh Pirates fan, was part of the Pirates' inaugural game at Three Rivers Stadium. While standing in a right field walkway, Evelyn, unaware that players were engaged in batting practice, was hit in the eye with a ball. The court upheld the lower court's ruling that "the no-duty rule applies only to risks which are common, frequent and expected." In the court's view, a person who attends a baseball game as a spectator cannot be properly expected to anticipate as inherent to baseball the risk of being struck by a baseball while properly using a walkway.

This reasoning is not limited to baseball. The case of *Silva* v. *Woodhouse* illustrates a case in which the "deadly projectile" was no less than a 290-pound wrestler.[21] In Silva, an amateur wrestler was pushed out of the ring by his opponent. The falling wrestler landed on a spectator, seriously injuring the spectator's knee. The court held the owner of the arena liable for failing to warn the plaintiff of the danger of being struck by the wrestler and for failing to place the front row seat at a safer distance from the ring. In reaching its decision, the court determined that although the plaintiff had previously attended wrestling matches at the defendant's arena, he was not aware of the risk of a wrestler being thrown from the ring and thus could not have assumed such a risk. Conversely, the court held that the defendant was aware of this fact and should have either posted a warning or arranged the seating to avoid the risk of injury.

A final issue, and often a most difficult issue, is determining exactly who is responsible for the plaintiff's injury. Given the astronomical expense of professional franchise ownership, few teams actually hold legal title to their own facilities. Similarly, collegiate and amateur teams, and to a lesser extent, high school teams often play in arenas owned by another party. To further complicate matters, municipalities frequently have a total or partial ownership right in the facility and regulations and limitations are generally imposed on a citizen's right to sue the government in tort.

The case of *Riley* v. *Chicago Cougars Hockey Club, Inc.* illustrates just how important this issue can be.[22] In that case, the plaintiff was struck by a deflected puck, knocked unconscious, and suffered serious head injuries. When filing suit, instead of guessing who was responsible, the plaintiff's attorney filed suit against the Chicago Cougars Hockey Club, International Amphitheater, and the World Hockey Association. The court ultimately focused on the language of the lease which provided that the Cougars would be responsible for crowd protection and absolved the arena owner and the World Hockey Association of liability. One final thought where there are multiple defendants: Although determining who is responsible may prove a difficult analysis, the defendant(s) will quickly point the finger at others in an effort to avoid liability.

Finally, courts tend not to view favorably language in tickets that seek to absolve stadium or arena operators or owners of all liability for spectator harm.

Key Considerations: Spectator Liability
- Ask if the plaintiff knew about the sport and the risks of attending the event.
- What did the defendant know regarding the forseeability of injury to the plaintiff?

- Identify who owns, manages, and uses the arena.
- If a municipality is party to the litigation, then there may be limits on liability, depending on the jurisdiction.

Medical Malpractice

A 1995 study conducted by the National Athletic Trainers' Association found that of the 441,000 girl's high school basketball players surveyed, 23 percent had experienced injuries that forced them to temporarily stop playing.[23] In addition, 37 percent of the roughly 1 million boys who played high school football sustained injuries that required them to stop playing for at least a few days. The study found that among football and basketball players of both sexes, 15 percent to 20 percent of the injuries were recurring injuries. At the professional level, the statistics are no better. For example, the National Football League reports that the average career span of an NFL player is 3.6 years. Although attributed to other factors, including performance and competition, injury is a key factor in that determination.[24]

Given the frequency of sports-related injury, medical professionals, including doctors, nurses, therapists, and trainers, are an integral part of any sports team. Most professional teams have a full medical staff, and most amateur and high school teams have at least a working relationship with a medical professional. Despite such a demand, however, medical professionals are expected to "have and use the knowledge, skill, and care ordinarily possessed and employed by members of the profession."[25] Athletes injured by a medical professional's failure to uphold his or her duty can bring a medical malpractice suit.

In professional athletics, team doctors face a difficult dilemma. On the one hand, they have an obligation to follow the directions of the team, their employer, which in many cases is to do whatever is necessary to get an injured player back on the field. In some cases, the issue becomes more complicated because the doctor may have a financial stake in the team. On the other hand, doctors owe the same professional duty to the player-patient as to anyone whom they treat. A breach of that duty is actionable negligence in the eyes of the law.

Though clearly a difficult dilemma, juries in recent athlete-team doctor cases have not been sympathetic to doctors. Where the juries have found that doctors failed to act with a reasonable level of skill or judgment which led to additional medical problems and interfered with the careers of their athlete-patients, they have awarded the athletes substantial awards. One example involves former major league baseball infielder Marty Barrett.[26]

Shortly after signing a three year contract extension with the Boston Red Sox, Barrett was injured while running to first base. Two days later, team doctor Arthur Pappas, who at the time was a partial owner of the Red Sox, performed arthroscopic surgery on Barrett's knee. Pappas told Barrett that he had suffered some torn cartilage and had stretched a ligament but that he should be able to return to the lineup within six weeks of his injury following physical therapy and rehabilitation. When Barrett's knee problems persisted, he was evaluated by another doctor who informed him that he had suffered a more serious injury, a torn anterior cruciate ligament.

In his suit against Pappas, Barrett alleged that Pappas had failed to alert him to the more serious damage, which would have required more extensive reconstruction surgery and which would, presumably, have kept Barrett on the injured list and off the field. Barrett's attorney argued that Pappas, motivated by his interests in the Red Sox, intentionally misinformed Barrett to get him back into the lineup as quickly as possible to help the Red Sox in their pennant hunt. Barrett also alleged that Pappas knew that Barrett was not part of the Red Sox's long term plans because the Red Sox had prospects who could replace Barrett. As a result, Pappas had no interest in preserving Barrett's knee beyond the 1989 pennant race. The jury awarded Barrett $1.7 million in damages.[27]

In similar cases, juries have given significant awards to athletes. Recent medical malpractice claims by athletes netted a number of substantial verdicts including former Chicago Bears wide receiver Ron Morris who won a $5.3 million verdict and Philadelphia Flyer hot-prospect Glen Seabrooke who was awarded $5.5 million.[28]

Careless or improper medical care is not the only problematic aspect of the athlete-team doctor relationship. Teams and team doctors face a recurring dilemma when they become aware that a player has a health problem that could be aggravated by the player's participation in sports. On the one hand, if the team prohibits the player from participation, the team may face a lawsuit for either breach of contract, in professional sports, or in high school or college sports may face a constitutional challenge for unfairly excluding the player. Consider the case of Long Beach State wide receiver Mark Seay.[29] On October 30, 1988, Seay was shot by gang members in a drive-by shooting while he was attending a children's Halloween party at his sister's home in Long Beach, California. Seay was shot in his right kidney, which he lost as a result. Seay's hopes to return to football were dashed when Long Beach State informed Seay that they would not permit him to return as a player to football because of the risk of injury to his remaining kidney. Seay filed suit against Long Beach and after over a year of litigation, he was allowed to play, provided he signed a waiver absolving Long Beach State of any liability.

On the other hand, if a team allows a player to play, despite knowledge of a potentially harmful medical condition, it exposes itself to potential liability in the event that playing worsens or triggers ill effects related to that condition. College basketball fans have seen this played out in the tragic death of Loyola Marymount star Hank Gathers, who collapsed and died while playing basketball as a result of a heart condition.[30]

Gathers, the NCAA's leading scorer and rebounder in the 1988–1989 season, was primed for the NBA, confident he would be one of the country's top draft picks. However, Hank Gathers's life took a tragic turn in December

1989, when he collapsed while playing in a Loyola game. Gathers was quickly diagnosed with a cardiac arrhythmia or an irregular heartbeat and underwent a course of treatment that included medications and weekly treadmill testing. Gathers returned to basketball that season, but on March 4, 1990, Hank Gathers collapsed during a game. Despite the efforts of doctors who performed cardiopulmonary resuscitation in front of a stunned crowd, which tragically included Gathers' mother and brothers, he died later that day.

The events leading up to Gathers's death raise a number of unresolved questions regarding the motivations and intention of Gathers, Loyola Marymount, and the medical professionals charged with Gathers's care. Would the outcome have been different if the university had taken a more active role in Gathers's care? Following Gathers's first collapse the university reportedly kept a defibrillator by its bench. Did the university really believe that Hank Gathers was well enough to play basketball? Reports claim that doctors had privately told Gathers that by playing basketball he was putting himself at risk. Should doctors and university officials have more aggressively appealed to Gathers to give up playing basketball? And what about Gathers himself? Reports indicate that he was so concerned that his draft value had dropped that he altered his medication, ranging from pleading with his doctors to reduce his dosage to Gathers not taking any medication at all. How much is he to blame?

Key Considerations: Medical Malpractice
- The medical provider's care must not fall below the accepted standard in the community.
- Each jurisdiction has specific statutes outlining the requirements of commencing a medical malpractice action.
- Look at the medical professional's relationship with the organization.
- Determine whether or not the medical provider's judgment was impaired by his or her responsibility to the organization.

PRODUCTS LIABILITY

A consumer who has been injured by a defective product may sue a manufacturer or seller of a product on a product liability claim. This type of case can proceed under a number of theories, including negligence, breach of warranty, and strict liability. In a strict liability claim a manufacturer or seller of a product in defective condition unreasonably dangerous to the user is liable for physical harm or property damage regardless of negligence. Under a breach of warranty theory, a consumer can argue that express and implied warranties were breached. A consumer may bring a products liability action regardless of whether he or she bought or owned the product that caused injury and may also bring a products liability action for used goods, provided the goods have not been modified or changed after purchase.

Negligence actions arise out of negligent design, manufacture, or negligent warning of potential danger. Although each state has its own statutes for strict liability and warranty based claims, most states have adopted the rules suggested in the Restatement (Second) of Torts 402A and have in some form adopted Article Two of the Uniform Commercial Code.

Consumers injured by an unreasonably dangerous sports-related product can proceed under the same product liability theories available to the users of other types of products. *Hauter* v. *Zogarts* is an example of how product liability claims came into play in sports.[31] In that case, Louise Hauter purchased the "Golfing Gizmo" as a Christmas present for her 13-year-old son, Fred. The court described the Golfing Gizmo as two pegs placed approximately two feet apart. An elastic cord was looped over the pegs, and a cotton cord with a golf ball attached to the end was attached to the middle of the elastic cord, leaving a final "T" configuration. Using his seven iron, Fred hit the ball. Unfortunately, the Golfing Gizmo did not respond as promised; instead of returning to the place of impact, as the directions described, the ball struck Fred in the head, leaving him brain damaged.

Ironically, the packaging of the Golfing Gizmo displayed the message, "Completely Safe—Ball Will Not Hit Player." The Supreme Court of California held that the words on the package were more than just decorative "sales talk," and held that the language on the Gizmo's box amounted to an express warranty. After deciding that the injured boy's mother had relied on the warranty when purchasing the Gizmo, the court held the manufacturer liable for breaching its warranty. The court also found the manufacturer liable for false representation, breach of implied warranties, and strict liability in tort based on defective design. Incidents like this are thankfully rare, likely due in part to manufacturers' interests in ensuring the safety of their products in order to avoid the cost in dollars and bad publicity of a products liability judgment against them.

Perhaps the most common subject matter—and perhaps the most controversial—of product liability actions in sports-related cases concerns protective helmets. These cases involve both situations in which helmets fail to prevent particular injuries and cases in which the helmet itself is alleged to have caused a particular injury. Although a defect is clear in cases like *Rawlings Sporting Goods Co.* v. *Daniels*, where the plaintiff's helmet "caved in" on impact, claiming that the helmet failed to provide the protection it was supposed to offer is more problematic.[32] The case of James R. Arnold ("J.R."), who was severely injured in 1987 while quarterbacking the Ashland High School football team, is one of these more difficult cases.[33]

On October 28, 1988, J.R. was injured when he collided with an opposing player while trying to recover a fumble. J.R.'s spine fractured, rendering him a quadriplegic and leaving him dependent on a respirator. At the time of the accident, J.R. was wearing a PAC-3 helmet manufactured by the defendant, Riddell, Inc.

J.R.'s parents bought a products liability claim on J.R.'s behalf against Riddell. They argued that the helmet was defective because it was not designed to minimize forces to the neck despite Riddell's knowledge that quadriplegic injuries were occurring and its awareness that other helmet designs, including another Riddell model, provided more protection to the neck. J.R.'s parents alleged that if Riddell had properly designed the PAC-3, J.R. would not have sustained a quadriplegic injury.

In response, Riddell argued that no helmet could prevent a cervical spine injury. It was Riddell's position that playing technique and not equipment design was the critical factor in preventing injuries like J.R.'s. In addition, Riddell presented an expert to give the opinion that no helmet would have prevented his injury. The jury rejected Riddell's arguments and awarded J.R. millions of dollars in damages.

Key Considerations: Products Liability
- Products liability claims may proceed under negligence, breach of warranty, and strict liability theories.
- Negligence claims occur when there are defects in design, manufacture, or warning labels.
- Warranty claims arise from a breach of implied or express warranties.
- Strict liability claims happen only when a defective piece of equipment or condition is unreasonably dangerous.

DEFAMATION AND ATHLETES

Newspapers, television newscasts, talk shows, and most recently the Internet are chock-full of "inside" information on athletes, which often has little to do with their on-the-field performance. Media outlets compete to get the public's attention by reporting sensational stories concerning the private lives of professional athletes.

Whereas tort law is generally used to seek compensation for damages suffered as a result of an athlete's physical injury, the law of defamation deals with injury to a less tangible, nebulous aspect of an athlete's makeup: one's reputation. A communication is defamatory "if it tends so to harm the reputation of another as to lower him in the estimation of the community or to deter third persons from associating or dealing with him."[34] Often referred to as "twin torts," libel refers to the publication of defamatory written words whereas slander is defamation by spoken words.

In a defamation case, a plaintiff must show (1) the defendant's communication was of a defamatory nature, (2) the communication was published, and (3) the communication applied to plaintiff.[35] In addition, the plaintiff must demonstrate that the recipients understood the defamatory meaning of the defendant's communication and its application to the plaintiff, and the plaintiff suffered special harm resulting from the publication.

In *New York Times Co.* v. *Sullivan*, the United States Supreme Court held that comments and criticism of a public officer relating to his public conduct were protected under the constitutional guarantee of freedom of speech and freedom of the press, provided they were not made with "actual malice." The Court defined actual malice as "knowledge that it was false or with reckless disregard of whether it was false or not."[36]

In *Curtis Publishing* v. *Butts*, the Supreme Court extended the malice standard to public figures. In that case, then University of Georgia athletic director, Wally Butts, sued Curtis for a story published in Curtis's *Saturday Evening Post (The Post)* which asserted that Butts conspired with University of Alabama football coach Paul "Bear" Bryant to fix a 1962 football game between the two teams.[37] The article, entitled "The Story of a College Football Fix," alleged that Butts gave Bryant Georgia's "secrets," including offensive and defensive plays and information about particular players. The source of the article was George Burnett, an Atlanta insurance salesman, who allegedly overheard Bryant and Butts's telephone conversation. The article reported that as a result of the conversation, "the Georgia players, their moves analyzed and forecasted like those of rats in a maze, took a frightful physical beating."[38] Butts was forced to retire from his position as a result of the controversy and subsequently filed a libel suit against Curtis.

Evidence at the trial revealed that although Burnett had indeed overheard a telephone conversation between Butts and Bryant, the content of the conversation was "hotly disputed." Butts contended, in sharp contrast to the article, that he and Bryant had a general "football talk" in which he had not divulged any valuable information to the opposing coach.[39]

Shortly after the verdict, the Supreme Court handed down the *New York Times* decision. Curtis appealed on the basis that under the *New York Times* standard, it could not be held liable for its article. Among other things, the Supreme Court held that Butts was a public figure and set forth the test that "a public figure who is not a public official may also recover damages for a defamatory falsehood whose substance makes substantial danger to reputation apparent, on a showing of highly unreasonable conduct constituting an extreme departure from the standards of investigation and reporting ordinarily adhered to by responsible publishers."[40]

In determining whether the article met the malice standard, the Court considered specific facts contained in the trial record. Specifically, the Court provided that because the Butts story was not "hot news," *The Post* should have conducted a thorough investigation.[41] The Court listed specific examples of *The Post's* failure to conduct a thorough investigation, including the fact that *The Post* writer was not a football expert and made no attempt to check the story with someone knowledgeable in the sport nor did the writer compare Burnett's notes of his conversations with the actual film of the game.[42] In addition, the Court pointed out that at the time of the article, The Post was actively trying to change its image to "sophisticated muckraking."[43] As a result, the Supreme Court upheld the lower court's ruling, holding that although *The Post* had no preexisting animosity toward Butts, the investigation was "grossly inadequate in the circumstances" and met the malice standard expressed in *New York Times*.[44]

Since *Butts*, courts have consistently ruled that athletes (professional baseball players, race car drivers, horse jockeys, and amateurs, for instance) are public figures;[45] however, in general, courts have been reluctant to hold that public figure athletes were defamed because in most cases the plaintiff has been unable to demonstrate that the communication was malicious or published with a reckless disregard for the truth.

Key Considerations: Defamation
- Is the athlete a public figure or a nonpublic figure?
- The law of defamation protects one's reputation.
- Actual malice or reckless disregard for the truth in the publication must be proven for a public figure to win a defamation case.
- Truth is a complete defense.

THE ATHLETE'S RIGHT TO PUBLICITY

Product endorsements can be a considerable source of income for well-known athletes. Given the substantial revenue associated with endorsements, athletes clearly have considerable interest in discouraging the unauthorized commercial use of their image.

One way athletes have protected themselves against unauthorized appropriations of their names and faces has been to argue that such appropriations constitute violations of the athlete's *right to publicity*. Ironically, in making such claims, athletes and other celebrities have relied on the law of *privacy*. Any one of the following four acts qualifies as an invasion of the right to privacy: (1) intrusion on the seclusion of another person; (2) public disclosure of embarrassing private facts about another person; (3) publicly depicting another person in a false light; or (4) appropriating another person's name or likeness.[46] Whereas the first three of these categories might be said to be violations of a right to be left alone, the last category might be described as violation of a person's right to determine how to *avoid* being left alone. This last category of acts defines the athlete's right to publicity. In order to show a violation of this right, the athlete must prove that (1) another person (the defendant) used the athlete's identity to his or her advantage; (2) the athlete did not authorize that use; and (3) the athlete suffered harm as a result of the defendant's unauthorized action. The intersection of these theoretical rights with the practical commercial world in which they must be applied has required careful regulation by the judicial system.

The courts have recognized that the importance of protecting athletes' right to publicity cannot in all cases take priority over other, competing concerns, like the public interest in the free flow of information. For this reason, although the media's regular and for-profit dissemination of athletes' images in magazines, newspapers, on television, and over the Internet technically violates the athletes' right to publicity, the courts have declined to take steps to prohibit the media from broadcasting those images. The courts have weighed the athletes' intertests in maintaining control over their images against the strong right of the media to report on newsworthy matters in the public interest, and have determined that the public's interest in being informed outweighs the athletes' risk of harm as a result. To avoid an unconstitutional interference with the freedom of the press, the courts have held that publication of an athlete's name or image for a newsworthy purpose is *not* a violation of an athlete's right to publicity.

Although it is clear that the unauthorized use of an athlete's name or picture is a violation or his or her right to publicity, the alleged misappropriation often presents itself in varying forms, which has required courts to expand the athlete's identity beyond the athlete's name and photograph. In *Motschenbacher* v. *R.J. Reynolds Tobacco Co.*, R.J. Reynolds used the race car of Lothar Motschenbacher, a well-known driver, in a Winston cigarette commerical.[47] Although R.J. Reynolds had altered the image of Motschenbacher's car, the Ninth Circuit Court of Appeals found that the commercial created the appearance that Motschenbacher endorsed Winston cigarettes and, because the race car represented a symbol of the driver's identity, misappropriation had occurred.

Another case where the issue concerned the plaintiff's identity was *Hirsch* v. *S.C. Johnson & Son*, Inc.[48] In that case, Johnson used the name "Crazylegs" to to promote a shaving gel for women. Elroy Hirsch, a famous football player nicknamed Crazylegs, brought an action on the grounds that the use of Crazylegs was an appropriation of his image. The trial court found in favor of Johnson, and Hirsch appealed. On appeal, Johnson argued, among other things, that Crazylegs was a nickname and was not an appropriation of Hirsch's image. The Wisconsin Supreme Court disagreed and ordered a new trial. Specifically, the Court stated the fact that Crazylegs was a nickname "did not preclude a cause of action . . . and that all that is required is that the name clearly identify the wronged person."[49]

More recently, former baseball player Bernie Carbo sued Major League Baseball for using his likeness in an MCI commercial without his authorization. Carbo charged that the advertisement suggested he endorsed MCI, when he was never even asked.

TRADEMARK LAW

A *trademark* is a word, phrase, symbol, or other indicator that distinctly identifies the source of a product. Team names, team logos, and catch phrases such as Pat Riley's "Three-Peat" and John Calipari's "Refuse to Lose," are commonly the subject of trademarks in the sports setting. A trademark owner may seek legal recourse against others whose use of the trademark gives rise to a likelihood of confusion in the market. For example, Nike places their famous "swoosh" symbol on its merchandise to indicate that the product is a Nike product. Consumers purchasing sneakers or clothing can rely on the "swoosh" symbol to indicate that Nike manufactured the product, and consumers can have expectations of quality based on their perception of Nike. If another sneaker manufacturer were to use the same or substantially similar mark, there might be confusion in the market and both the consumer and Nike might suffer as a result.

Athletes often couple publicity claims with trademark infringement claims. For example, in June 1997, Tiger Woods sued the Frankin Mint Co. for trademark infringement and violation of Woods's right to publicity, seeking to stop the marketing of an unauthorized "Tiger Woods Eyewitness Commemorative Medal," a $37.50 item bearing Wood's likeness.[50] Woods's suit claimed that he has carefully managed sponsosrship deals using his name or likeness to prevent overexposure or cheapening or tarnishing of his image. The Franklin Mint responded that the issuance of medals commemorating a newsworthy event is protected by the First Amendment, and that they did not need Woods's permission or authorization. Tiger Woods did, however, lend his name and likeness via Nike to the video game maker Electronic Arts. The video company has created a Tiger Woods golf game for portable computers and Sony PlayStation systems.

Key Considerations
- Courts have recognized an athlete's right to publicity.
- An athlete's interest in protecting his or her name or likeness is balanced against the media's right to report on newsworthy matters.
- Trademarks are another means for athletes and teams to protect team names, logos, and catch phrases.

SUMMARY

Tort claims arise in numerous ways in the sports world. Players who harm other players or spectators can be charged with acting negligently. A facility owner who has knowledge of unsafe or dangerous conditions at a ballpark may be deemed to have breached his or her duty of protecting the fan from harm.

Special issues of liability arise when professional athletes are treated by team physicians. Pressures on the medical doctor or team trainer to do whatever is necessary to help the player quickly return to the playing field can lead to medical malpractice charges.

Consumers who are injured by unreasonably dangerous equipment or games may sue under a variety of different legal theories. Helmets are one of the most frequent subject of products liability suits.

The media has a protected, compelling interst in reporting on the public and private lives of professional athletes. However, they must publish articles in a manner that does not recklessly disregard the truth for those athletes that are deemed public figures.

Professional athletes enjoy a right to publicity. This right protects the athlete from unauthorized appropriations of her or her name or likeness. Increasingly, trademark rights are utilized to protect team names, logos, and slogans.

For Reflection

1. Have professional sports taken on a "WWF-like" atmosphere? And if they have, should the standard of liability be a pre-*Nabozny* standard, that is, that the playing field is essentially free from liability?

2. Given the gruesome nature of some of the plays featured in highlight films, why do you suppose so few professional player-to-player tort cases are filed?

3. Would you be in favor of a rule that states spectators assume all risks of attending a sporting event? Why or why not?

4. In a football helmet lawsuit, the helmet manufacturer argued that the parents of an injured athlete were negligent for allowing him to participate in high school football. The jury assessed 12 percent of the blame on the parents. Do you think the jury meant that parents who allow their children to play football are negligent? What do you think?

5. Although product liability jury verdicts provide injured athletes with much-needed finances for their basic necessities of living, manufacturers claim to be suffering as a result of such large verdicts. Proponents of tort reform seek to limit awards in product liability cases. They point out that because of the high potential for injury in sports, equipment manufacturing companies have pulled out of the helmet manufacturing area to avoid the risk of big product liability suits. Reports estimate that the number of football helmet manufacturers has declined from twenty to four and in some estimates only two. What do you think? Can any helmet be made to prevent injury?

6. At what point should the decision to play be taken from injured high school, college, and professional athletes? How likely is an athlete to admit he or she has a physical problem? Hank Gathers was considered a lock for the NBA's first round. Yet, is it reasonable for

Gathers or anyone else in his position to make an objective decision regarding his health and his ability to perform?

7. Has the public come to believe that the public's personal interactions with athletes are also subject to a relaxed standard? Athletes argue that they and their family members are frequently confronted in public by irate fans. Although a player should expect jeering fans in the stands, should they expect such conduct when they are in a restaurant, night club, or shopping mall?

Useful Web Sites

1. www.findlaw.com/01topics/12entertainsport/publications.html
2. www.ljx.com/practice/negligence/index.html
3. www.nando.neet/newsroom/sport.html
4. www.law.vill.edu/vls/journals/vslej.htm
5. http://www.law.cornell.edu/topics/torts.html
6. http://www.ll.georgetown.edu/lr/rs/sports.html
7. vls.law.vill.edu/students/orgs/sports/
8. http://www.abanet.org/forums/entsports/e&sl.html
9. http://www.law.tulane.edu/journals/slj/frame.htm

Notes

1. *Nabozny* v. *Barnhill*, Ill. App. 3d 212, 334 N.E. 2d 258 (1975).
2. W. Page Keeton et al., *Prosser and Keeton on the Law of Torts*, 5th ed. (West Publishing, St. Paul, MN: 1984), 82 at 6.
3. Oliver Wendell Holmes, *The Common Law* (Cambridge, MA: The Belk Napp Press of Harvard University Press, 1967).
4. Keeton et al., *Prosser and Keeton on the Law of Torts*, p. §2.
5. Ibid. p. §8 at 35.
6. Ibid. pp. §3 at 169–170.
7. Ibid. p. §65 at 453.
8. *Palsgraf* v. *Long Island R. Co.*, 148 N.Y. 339, 162 N.E. 99 (1928).
9. Keeton et al., *Prosser and Keeton on the Law of Torts*, §30 at pp. 164–165.
10. Distinguished Professor Thomas F. Lambert, Suffolk University Law School, Boston, MA.
11. Keeton et al., *Prosser and Keeton on the Law of Torts*, §8 at p. 36.
12. Restatement (Second) of Torts section 50(b).
13. *Nabozny* v. *Barnhill*, Ill. App. 3d 212, 334 N.E. 2d 258 (1975).
14. Ibid. p. 215.

15. See *Lestina* v. *West Bend Mutual Insurance Co.*, 174 Wis. 2d 901, 501 NW. 2d 28 (1993) (Wisconsin Supreme Court applying ordinary negligence standard to determine liability of injury sustained during recreational soccer game).

16. *Gauvin* v. *Clark*, 404 Mass. 450, 537 N.E.2d 94 (1989)(denying recovery to college hockey player injured by an opponent's stick's "butt-end"); *Keller* v. *Mols*, Ill. App. 3d 235, 509 N.E. 2nd 235 (1987) (denying recovery to player injured in collision); *Jaworksi* v. *Kiernan*, 696 A. 2d 332 (Conn. 1991) (denying recovery to player injured in recreational soccer game).

17. See *Pfister* v. *Shusta*, 167 Ill. 2d 417, 657 N.E. 2d 1013 (1995) (holding that a college dormitory game of kick-the-can was a contact sport, and that a voluntary participant was not allowed recovery for injuries caused by negligence); *Knight* v. *Jewett*, 3 Cal. 4th 296, 834 P. 2d 696 (1992) (holding that touch football was a contact sport); *Dotzler* v. *Tuttle*, 234 Neb. 176, 449 N.W. 2d 774 (1990) (holding that pickup baseball was a contact sport).

18. See *Brown* v. *San Francisco Ball Club*, 99 Cal. App. 2d 484, 222 P. 2d 19 (1950).

19. Ibid.

20. *Jones* v. *Three Rivers Management Corporation et al.*, 483 Pa. 75, 394 A. 2d 546 (1978).

21. *Silva* v. *Woodhouse*, 356 Mass. 119 (1969).

22. *Riley* v. *Chicago Cougars Hockey Club, Inc.* 100 Ill. App. 3d 664, 427 N.E. 2d 290 (1981).

23. Steven Findlay, "Breaks of the Game," 103 *U.S. News & World Report* 75 (October 5, 1987).

24. Bob Glauber, "Life After Football," newsday.com (January 13, 1997).

25. Keeton et al., *Prosser and Keeton on the Law of Torts*, §32 at p. 187.

26. "Bitter Medicine," 83 *Sports Illustrated* 20 (November 6, 1995).

27. *The Boston Globe*, October 26, 1995, p. 69.

28. "Bitter Medicine," 83 *Sports Illustrated* 20 (November 6, 1995).

29. Stefanie Krasnow, "A Hero Returns," 72 *Sports Illustrated* 14 (May 7, 1990); Shelly Smith, "Not What the Doctor Ordered," 72 *Sports Illustrated* 24 (June 11, 1990).

30. Shelley Smith, "Hank Gathers," 72 *Sports Illustrated* 16 (March 12, 1990); Philip Elmer-DeWitt, "Death on the Basketball Court," 135 TIME 56 (March 19, 1990).

31. *Hauter* v. *Zogarts*, 14 Cal. 3d 104, 534 P. 2d 377 (1975).

32. *Rawlings Sporting Goods Co.* v. *Daniels*, 619 S.W. 2d 435 (1981).

33. *Arnold* v. *Riddell, Inc. et. al.*, 882 F. Supp 979 (1995).

34. Keeton et al., *Prosser and Keeton on the Law of Torts*, §111 at p. 774.

35. Keeton et al., *Prosser and Keeton on the Law of Torts*, §113 at p. 802 (5th ed. 1984).

36. *New York Times* v. *Sullivan*, 367 U.S. 254, 279–280 (1964).
37. *Curtis Publishing Co.* v. *Butts*, 388 U.S. 130, 87 S. Ct. (1975).
38. Ibid. p. 12.
39. Ibid. p. 14.
40. Ibid. p. 155.
41. Ibid. p. 157.
42. Ibid. p. 158.
43. Ibid. p. 158.
44. Ibid. p. 156.
45. See *Chuy* v. *Philadelphia Eagles Football Club*, 595 F2d 1265 (1975) (holding that a professional football player was a public figure, but that a statement made by the team physician to a newspaper sports columnist was not defamatory); *Johnson* v. *Time, Inc.*, 321 F. Supp. 837 (1971) (holding that a former professional basketball player was a public figure because he remained involved in basketball, but was not defamed by an article in which Red Auerbach stated that Bill Russell "destroyed" him).
46. W. Page Keeton et al., *Prosser and Keeton on the Law of Torts*, §117 (5th ed., 1984).
47. 489 F. 2d 821 (9th Cir. 1974).
48. 90 N.W. 2d 379 (Wis. 1979).
49. Ibid. at 397.
50. "Tiger Woods Sues Franklin Mint over 'Unauthorized' Medal," *Andrews Sports & Entertainment Litigation Reports*, July 1997.

CHAPTER 7

The Business of Sports: Leagues, Teams, Relocations, and Building Stadiums

T *he market no longer functions. We have cartel behavior from the leagues and corporate welfare from the cities and states.*

—David Swindell, urban affairs expert commenting
on the plight of cities bidding for pro sports teams

Case Study

The Jackson Jacks team makes about **40 percent** of its revenue from ticket sales, another **40 percent** from television and radio licensing fees, and the remainder from advertising sales. The team sells out nearly every home game but believes it could increase team revenue substantially if additional "skybox" seats were built. The team announced it is considering the issuance of public stock to fund the skybox project subject to league approval. Recently, though, a major international pay-per-view company offered to acquire the team and build a new arena in a warmer-climate city. The new investors plan to purchase the team through the sale of advance rights to purchase season tickets and build the arena through a publicly funded lottery as a part of a new corporate entertainment theme park. What advice would you give to the current team owners as to the different options? What value do you place on fan loyalty and team tradition? What price should taxpayers be required to pay to fund a private activity? What role should the league play in determining whether to approve or disapprove the stock issue or team transfer?

INTRODUCTION

The preceding chapters focus on the legal relationship between various parties in amateur and professional sports. This chapter looks at the business and legal aspects of teams and leagues specifically as they affect communities that are either vying for new sports teams or in danger of losing a team. The analysis includes a discussion of the economic aspects of what some have referred to as the "stadium shell game" where owners seek public funding for private arenas and stadiums. Finally, the chapter reviews prospective congressional responses to fan outcry when one city loses a team to another community and the antitrust concerns of leagues and team owners surrounding trying to stop franchise movement.

LEAGUE CONSTITUTIONS AND BYLAWS

Not too many years ago ownership of professional sports teams was the exclusive province of wealthy individuals. The Galbraiths owned the Pittsburgh Pirates, the Wrigleys owned the Chicago Cubs, and the O'Malley family for nearly half a century owned the Los Angeles Dodgers. In the wake of rising salaries, labor uneasiness, and attendance worries private, family owners have sold out to media and entertainment conglomerates.

Today almost one-half of all sports franchises are owned by public companies. Only the National Football League restricts the legal form of team ownership to corporations engaged solely in the operation of a professional football franchise, but this exclusionary rule is not expected to last for long. More and more financial pressure is brought to bear on owners to put competitive teams on the field and either turn a profit or enhance the team's asset value. To meet these objectives team owners may need the financial resources and marketing strengths of a larger enterprise.

According to many owners, making money in the sports ownership business is not always an easy proposition. The Dodgers earned a little over $13 million in 1997 on revenue of about $75 million.[1] Major league baseball as a whole lost around $250 million.[2] About half the teams in the National Basketball Association lost money.[3] Deep-pocket corporations that view sports ownership as merely one "product" that can blend with other corporate assets (e.g., interactive toy games, cable television broadcast of games, and cartoon characters featuring sports figures) can take a longer view than owners whose livelihood rests on the financial success of the team from year to year.

The legal relationship between leagues, teams, and owners is a complex one. Every sports league enters into a contractual relationship with its member teams. This relationship is in the form of a league constitution. The owner of each individual team is granted a nonassignable *franchise* to operate the team within an exclusive geographic region. The team or franchise owner is also granted the right to vote on league-related matters including issues related to the number of teams in the league, expansion of teams, relocation of a team from one geographic territory to another, approval of broadcasting agreements, sharing of revenue, licensing of league trademarks, and the collective bargaining agreement with the players association. These rights are usually formulated via the league bylaws.

Each league constitution grants its members the power to vote on a commissioner or chief executive officer for the league. The commissioner's job is essentially threefold: act in the "best interests of the game" on matters ranging from resolving disputes between owners to disciplining players who, for instance, breach the "good moral character or good citizenship" player contract clause; establish game schedules, employ referees, and negotiate broadcasting deals; and serve as chief public spokesperson for the sport.[4]

The commissioner's powers in a particular sport are not absolute, as addressed in an earlier chapter. These powers may be subject to judicial review, albeit reluctantly, as seen in the case of *Pete Rose* v. *Bart Giamatti*, where the court asked: "To what extent should public law speaking through judges, venture to overturn decisions made by private leagues, speaking through their commissioners?"[5] The NBA's collective bargaining agreement permits a challenge to the commissioner's disciplinary action of fining or suspending a player on grounds that it is "arbitrary and capricious." Latrell Sprewell's arbitration hearing where he successfully sought to overrule Commissioner Stern's one-year suspension as being "unduly excessive" is an instance of an arbitrator reviewing, and thereby "limiting," the power of a commissioner to act in the best interest of the game.

On two occasions during the past 25 years soccer has sought to become recognized as a major professional league sport in North America. A few years ago the United States served as the host country for the World Cup soccer finals. By hosting this international spectacle, the opportunity was viewed as ripe to start a new professional league. The Major League Soccer (MLS) loaded with franchises in major U.S. cities was born. Before the start of the MLS, the North American Soccer League (NASL) sought to gain admission and acceptance as a professional league on a par with basketball, baseball, and football.

The founders of the NASL sought franchise owners among the existing elite group of sports owners including those in football. At the time the National Football League (NFL) barred its team owners, including club officers and families of owners or officers, from acquiring a financial interest in the NASL. The NASL sued the NFL on grounds that the league's bylaw provision against cross-ownership of sports franchises in different leagues violated section 1 of the Sherman Act's prohibition on illegal restraint of trade.

The NASL initially lost its case against the NFL. On appeal the federal court held that the anticompetitive effects of the cross-ownership ban did not outweigh the ban's clear restraint on competition in violation of the antitrust provisions of the Sherman Act.[6] The court embraced a "rule of reason" test in analyzing the NFL's restrictive policies. The traditional "rule of reason" test applied here requires inquiry as to whether the restraint imposed is justified by legitimate business purposes and is not any more restrictive than necessary. Significantly, the court was not willing to accept the NFL's characterization of itself as a group of teams operating as "a single economic entity." Nor did the court tolerate the NFL's argument that by acting as a "single economic entity" it was exempt from antitrust scrutiny.

Whereas the court's decision opened the way for football owners to acquire a financial stake in pro soccer teams [and even in a rival football league—the United States Football League (USFL)], then the NASL and now the MLS, the case also served as the forerunner of a more contemporary issue that will be explored later, that is, antitrust issues facing a league that wishes to deny a franchise owner's desire to relocate.

Before addressing these issues, a legislative event took place in 1966 that dramatically altered the economic landscape of pro sports. It was then that Congress permitted two financially successful, rival football leagues to merge. The NFL and the American Football League (AFL) that had fought for broadcasting rights and expansion of teams into each other's territory sought and received permission to unite as one league free from antitrust fear.

Prior to this merger the AFL had sued and lost its antitrust suit against the NFL. The federal court held that the AFL failed to prove that the NFL possessed monopoly power and the NFL's actions prevented or excluded competition in violation of section 2 of the Sherman Act.[7] Part of the antitrust inquiry in section 2 deals with defining the "relevant product market" in which the monopoly is occurring. The court defined the market in question as the "sport of professional football" as opposed to a broader definition encompassing the entire "entertainment" market, which might have led to a different finding.

After these decisions, the rival American Basketball Association merged with the National Basketball Association (NBA) and the World Hockey Association became one with the National Hockey League (NHL). Both events occurred after numerous antitrust complaints. The mergers were permitted under federal statute, 15 U.S.C. section 1291, enacted in November 1966, which exempts merger of sports leagues from antitrust scrutiny.

Key Considerations: League Constitutions and Bylaws
- Team ownership is shifting to public corporate ownership especially by media and entertainment companies.
- Team owners acquire a franchise from the sports league.
- League constitutions grant owners the right to vote on matters such as sharing revenue, the number of teams in the league, licensing on logos, and election of a commissioner or executive officer.
- Congress granted antitrust immunity for sports teams to merge.

ADMISSION INTO THE LEAGUE

Each pro sports league has separate requirements for admission. Membership traditionally has been restricted to ensure that team owners are sufficiently capitalized, can meet the team payroll, and are of good moral character. Occasionally personality issues arise when voting in new team owners.

In 1972 two businessmen acquired the right to purchase the Boston Celtics subject to the NBA's standard three-fourths of the owners voting approval, which has since been changed to a simple majority vote. The three-fourths of team owners approving new ownership is a standard league constitution requirement throughout most pro sports, except for when the transfer of ownership is to another family member. The votes were cast and the team owners rejected the new hopeful owner. They sued alleging their friendship with the owner of the Seattle SuperSonics, who was not universally liked by other team owners, as the real reason for the negative vote. The court sided with the league in agreeing that it was the business relationship between Seattle's owner and the two prospective team owners of a rival franchise that violated the constitution's "conflict of interest" rule.[8]

Team ownership can take many legal forms: sole proprietorship, partnership, business association, or corporation. The NFL further restricts corporate ownership to a business purpose limited solely to operating a professional football franchise.

The ownership arrangement of the Green Bay Packers is an anomaly that could serve as a blueprint for other communities that are fearful of losing their "home" teams if the NFL were willing to change its bylaws. The Packers are a community-owned nonprofit corporation that pays no dividend to its shareholders. Since the inception of the team in 1923, the residents of Green Bay have repeatedly aided the team when money was needed to starve off bankruptcy or if the stadium needed refurbishing.

According to Green Bay's mayor "the bond was strengthened" each time the NFL's smallest television market community rescued the team.[9] Today the "cheeseheads," as the Packer fans are nicknamed, run the refreshment stands and claim 45 members on the corporate board of directors. The team generates $60 million a year in direct economic benefits to the community.[10]

The league's bylaws grandfathered Green Bay's public stockholder ownership. Normally the NFL requires that one person own at least 51 percent of the stock of any corporate entity franchise.

The average NFL franchise is conservatively worth $200 million.[11] The new Cleveland Browns football franchise is expected to cost investors well in excess of $450 million; included in the franchise fee is the right to share national broadcast revenue. The most recent hockey franchise for sale including cable television rights has an offering price of around $160 million. In 1992 Wayne Huizenga paid $50 million to purchase the Florida Panthers hockey team. Huizenga recently sold 58 percent of the team to the public in the form of corporate stock for $10 per share. The team owner of the Edmonton Oilers plans to sell part ownership in the form of shares to help raise money.

In 1986 the Boston Celtics became the first NBA team to claim public ownership when the for-profit team established a limited partnership, which owns and operates the team. The nonvoting shares of the public limited partnership are traded on the New York Stock Exchange.

Renowned Stanford University economist Roger Noll estimates that pro sports revenues have increased on the average about 12 percent for year over the last 20 years.[12] Revenue isn't the sole reason sports franchises are changing hands at a near record pace.

Walt Disney Company, the home of the Magic Kingdom, saw "vertical integration" and "cross-promotion" opportunities when it acquired an expansion hockey team for $50 million and a 25 percent ownership in baseball's Anaheim Angels for $30 million.[13]

Disney's Mighty Ducks NHL franchise represents what *Insight* magazine refers to as the "most synergistic sports story" in the world. The hockey team was named after Disney's wildly successful motion picture *Mighty Ducks*. Merchandise tie-ins between movie characters and sports figures have rocketed Mighty Ducks apparel sales into third place trailing the Chicago Bulls and Dallas Cowboys. The $100 million Wide World of Sports resort and athletic complex opened in Orlando to enthusiastic reviews. Disney owns part of ABC and ESPN, ESPN2, and ESPNNEWS, all of which broadcast sporting news and events.

Australian-based News Corporation followed Disney's lead by spending $350 million to purchase baseball's "crown jewel," the Los Angeles Dodgers. News Corporation owner Rupert Murdoch, whose empire includes the Fox television network and newspapers, sees profits in integrating sports and media as part of a worldwide entertainment conglomerate.

Media mogul Ted Turner acquired the NBA's Atlanta Hawks and MLB's Atlanta Braves more than 20 years ago. He expanded his reach by establishing the Turner Broadcasting network to run both sports enterprises and broadcast their games on cable's "superstation." CNN, another Turner television network, broadcasts sports and news worldwide. Turner even added professional wrestling to his entertainment package by broadcasting World Championship Wrestling bouts, many on a pay-per-view basis.

Many sports purists criticize Disney's acquiring of sports teams, the Tribune Company buying the Chicago Cubs, and Paramount Communications owning the New York Knicks. The fear is that corporations are obligated to answer to shareholders, not fans. Some of the older team owners profess fear that the league loses control over franchise ownership when conglomerates larger than the league itself buy teams as part of a global marketing strategy.

Restricted public ownership of individual teams, although a novel way for the team owner to make money, has limited appeal because the local stock purchasers have no voting rights, if the pattern as seen in the the Panthers and Celtics is followed. The Packers' community-based ownership is unique, but little insider impetus exists to duplicate this model. The demand for a limited number of sports franchises and the enormous investment required to acquire and maintain a competitive team naturally give rise to corporate giants buying sports teams as part of an overall corporate strategy to extend and expand brand identity or product lines.

Key Considerations: Admission to the League

- Owners must vote on new team owners.
- The prospective team owner must be sufficiently capitalized.
- Different leagues permit different legal forms of ownership.
- Teams have escalated in value.

TERRITORIAL RESTRICTIONS

NFL commissioner Paul Tagliabue recently appeared before the U.S. Senate Judiciary Subcommittee on Antitrust, Business Rights, and Competition.[14] There he described the restrictive nature of an NFL franchise as "a license to serve the league's fans and to play league games in a prescribed geographic area. A franchise was the means by which the league created a stable, continuous relationship with a community, subject to change only by league decision, ordinarily through a super-majority vote." This definition, he went on to testify, was valid prior to Al Davis and the Oakland Raiders suing the NFL in the 1980s.

The litigation surrounding the Oakland Raiders suing the league for refusing to approve the franchise's relocation to Los Angeles is expansive.[15] In brief, a federal court ruled that the NFL's bylaw, Article 4.3 requiring three-quarters approval of all teams in the league whenever one team wants to move into the home territory of another team, violated section 1 of the Sherman Act. More specifically, the bylaw restriction was deemed an unreasonable and unlawful restraint on trade.

The Raiders wanted to move from Oakland to Los Angeles to play at the Coliseum. The Los Angeles Rams had just moved from the Coliseum to Anaheim. The Coliseum was within the geographic franchise territory of the Rams. The league owners voted 22–0 against the Raiders relocation with five abstentions.

Once more the court concluded the league was not a "single entity" for antitrust purposes. The Raiders and the Coliseum owners won. Triple damages amounting to in excess of $45 million were awarded but later reduced. The court advised the league to look to Congress for help.

RELOCATION OF FRANCHISES

Commissioner Taglibeau cites the Raiders' lawsuits as a contributing cause for why teams so swiftly leave one community for stadium perks found in another. Ironically, in 1994 the Raiders sued the league for holding it "hostage" in Los Angeles and delaying the team's desire to move back to Oakland.

In both the latest Raiders' suit and former New England Patriots' owner the late Billy Sullivan's antitrust action against the NFL, the league was never asked to vote on the proposed moves.[16] Sullivan's suit, which was settled out of court, alleged that the league diminished the value of his franchise by preventing him from relocating outside of New England. Sullivan claimed he never sought a league vote because he was "told" it wouldn't have been approved.

In 1995 the Rams sought to relocate to St. Louis, which had lost its football franchise to Phoenix. Initially the league disapproved the Rams' request for failing to satisfy the league's guidelines. Upon reconsideration, and after threats of antitrust action by the Rams and St. Louis, the league approved the franchise transfer. Two years later St. Louis sued the league on antitrust grounds for $130 million. St. Louis alleges the city overpaid for the Rams because Commissioner Tagliabue didn't permit other teams to negotiate a franchise transfer.

There is no more definitive example of the problems associated with franchise relocation than the move of the Cleveland Browns football team to Baltimore. The Browns were a part of the city of Cleveland for more than 50 years. Fans turned out in record numbers game after game. Household television ratings were consistently first or second in the league. The community voted by a margin of 72 percent to tax itself to build a new stadium. Still Browns' owner Art Modell left Cleveland for a better offer from Baltimore.

In 1984 the Baltimore Colts fled Memorial Stadium for a new home in Indianapolis. Baltimore was hungry for a replacement NFL franchise. The offer to the first taker: $50 million to agree to relocate; a brand-new 70,000-seat stadium built at a cost of $200 million; 108 skyboxes and 7,500 club seats; $80 million from the sale of "personal seat licenses," which merely assures the license holder the right to buy season tickets; complete profits from parking, in-house advertising and concessions; and state reimbursement for any relocation fee to be shared by the other owners charged by the NFL.[17] Twelve years after Baltimore lost the Colts the city now had a new team from Cleveland renamed the Baltimore Ravens, after the league reluctantly approved the transfer.

Critics of Baltimore's use of a new sports lottery and revenue bonds to fund the stadium's construction point out that nearly 1,400 jobs were created, $123 million in new total economic activity is generated each year from the presence of an NFL team, and $17 million in new state and local tax revenues are paid annually.[18] Cleveland's consolation prize included keeping the "Browns" name and a guarantee of either an expansion or relocation team by 1999. Cleveland, of course, had to agree to build a new stadium.

Commentator Curtis Stock of *The Edmonton Journal* doesn't know whether to call franchise relocation in hockey "blackmail" or "hostage taking." The owners of the Quebec Nordiques, who had paid just under $15 million for their franchise in 1990, accepted $75 million from COMSAT Video as part of a package deal to move the team to Colorado. The Nordique owners had demanded that the city of Quebec build a new stadium and absorb all future team losses. Quebec nixed the request. The Nordiques moved and became the Colorado Avalanche. The team plays in a brand-new, 19,000-seat hockey complex named the Pepsi Centre.

The Raiders' Al Davis nets an extra $7.6 million a year from the lease of luxury skybox suites in Oakland that were unavailable at the L.A. Coliseum. Under NFL rules team owners do not have to share luxury and club box revenues with other teams. The Rams' new stadium in St. Louis contains 120 luxury suites, each leasing for thousands of dollars a year, where stadium-related revenue increased by 25 percent the first season.

The second, fourth, and twelfth largest markets in the United States, Los Angeles, Houston, and Cleveland, respectively, currently have no NFL franchise because of recent franchise relocation decisions. Nearly 40 pro sports teams are contemplating building new facilities. By the year 2000 U.S. communities will have committed more than $12 billion to build new sports arenas and stadiums.[19] Taxpayers' indebtedness will total more than $7 billion.[20]

Key Considerations: Territorial Restrictions and Team Relocation

- Team owners are fearful of restricting a team from moving because of antitrust concerns.
- The Oakland Raiders lawsuits have encouraged team owners to seek Congressional protection from triple damage suits.
- The move of the Cleveland Browns football team to Baltimore serves as the definitive example of why teams move from one franchise location to another.

ECONOMIC COSTS

There is a paradox to the public stampede to build stadiums using public funds. The owners of many pro clubs are some of the wealthiest corporations and individuals in the world. Yet, communities willingly line up to build new facilities or contribute to infrastructure costs. The current monopoly system almost encourages team owners to "extort" communities into bidding wars, leaving behind loyal and betrayed fans.

Economist Andrew Zimbalist in testimony before the U.S. House of Representatives Judiciary Committee on February 6, 1996 remarked:

Professional sports teams move for two very simple reasons: to augment their profits and to increase their franchise value. The fact that the NFL, the NBA, the NHL and MLB are monopoly sports leagues enables them to limit the supply of teams in their leagues below the effective demand for such teams from economically viable cities. This excess demand to host a professional sports team leads U.S. cities to compete against each other.

The economic costs involved are not just those associated with construction costs, moving expenses, and franchise relocation fees paid to the league. Debt service on funding and infrastructural costs to build roads and lay cable can often double the cost of the project. The stadium lease arrangements between the community and team frequently grant the team exclusive rights to all concessions, stadium advertising, and parking fees. This extra revenue flows into the coffers of club owners for higher profits and more money to spend on player salaries instead of servicing any public debt service.

In earlier chapters baseball was singled out as the sole professional sports league that enjoys exemption from antitrust scrutiny. In reality, football, basketball, and hockey also enjoy their own form of antitrust exemption. The Sports Broadcasting Act of 1966 granted these four major pro sports leagues a limited right to join their separate television, radio, cable, and Internet rights for sale to a single buyer.

This *limited* antitrust exemption, for instance, makes it possible for the NFL to negotiate broadcast rights on behalf of the individual franchises and then divide the revenue in equal shares to each club. The NFL also shares equally per team all league licensing and marketing revenues. Regarding live ticket sales, home teams keep 60 percent of the game revenue and give 40 percent to visiting teams. Stadium revenue from luxury and club box rentals, personal seat licenses (PSL), in-stadium advertising including putting a corporate name on the stadium, concessions, interactive games, and parking is not shared.

The division of revenue in the NFL acts as a "powerful incentive" in the words of Zimbalist to maximize stadium revenue. What better way for an NFL owner to leverage the value of the franchise and enhance profits than to enter into a bidding war for the team between different communities by demanding a new stadium at public expense?

Eli Jacobs experienced the rewards from playing the stadium game when he acquired the Baltimore Orioles for $70 million in 1989. Right after the public agreed to spend $200 million to build Oriole Park at Camden Yards in Baltimore, Jacobs sold the team for $173 million for a 150 percent appreciation in four years of ownership.

Baseball's George Steinbrenner and shoe and apparel giant adidas dropped a suit against the league for allegedly infringing on a 10-year, $95 million sponsorship deal. The league successfully convinced Steinbrenner that it has the right to block local franchise sponsorship arrangements that interfere with the league's merchandising contracts. In this case, Steinbrenner wanted the adidas logo to adorn his players' uniforms. The league struck back, arguing that what goes on players' uniforms is a league-wide decision. Adidas agreed to become a general apparel merchandise supplier to the league.

Not all owners look to the public to build a new sports facility. Jerry Richardson, CEO of Flagstar, which owns the Carolina Panthers expansion NFL franchise, told *Forbes* magazine, "I don't think it's the obligation of the taxpayers to build facilities for professional sports franchises."[21] The owners of the revered Fenway Park home of the Boston Red Sox baseball team are not looking for public subsidy of any stadium renovations.

Clearly, the imbalance between the number of teams and leagues (supply) and the demand for sports franchises when coupled with Congress permitting the mergers of leagues and pooling of broadcasting rights creates a situation that encourages bidding wars at the public's expense. A number of thoughtful solutions have been proposed.

LEGISLATIVE RESPONSES

In the wake of Modell's relocating the Cleveland NFL team to Baltimore even when Cleveland was prepared to build a new stadium, many legislative members of Ohio's delegation called for an equitable legislative response to the costly and painful disputes related to franchise movement. The Fans Rights Act grants a limited antitrust exemption for league decisions relating to franchise relocation.[22] This proposed legislation would give immunity from antitrust suits for reasonable restraints the league internally enacts to prevent teams from transferring unless certain specified criteria are met. Academics, legislative leaders, mayors, and league commissioners proffered diverse testimony as to both the wisdom of Congress intervening and the language of the criteria for stopping franchise relocation and avoiding "Raiders-style" antitrust lawsuits.

The most recent legislative response, the "Professional Sports Franchise Relocation Act of 1998," was filed by Democratic Congressman Meehan of Massachusetts and Republican Congressman Bryant of Tennessee.[23]

The bill is aimed at professional teams, specifically football, basketball, hockey, and soccer franchises. The object of this bill is to exempt professional sports leagues from liability under the antitrust laws for certain conduct relating to the relocation of their respective member teams. In essence, it prevents professional sports teams from relocating at will and, when rejected by their leagues, it prevents the leagues from being sued under the antitrust laws.

The highlights of the bill are as follows:

- Each owner requesting to relocate the team must notify the local news media and interested parties within 30 days of a team's official request to relocate, with reasons and a detailed description of the issues.

- The pro leagues must consider fan loyalty as a factor in approving or disapproving relocation.
- A hearing will be conducted with all interested parties given the opportunity to submit written testimony and exhibits.
- The relocation decision by the leagues must be provided to interested parties and local media, with descriptions and any legal remedies.

If a dispute arises from a team relocation denial or approval, and a plaintiff wins in court, the relief is not monetary. Instead, under section 5, subsection (c) of the bill titled "Judical Review," relief will come in the form of vacating the decision of such league to approve or disapprove the request by the member team involved to change its home territory and not to approve or disapprove such request until such league complies with section 4 of the bill. Section 4 of the bill entails the procedural requirements for the request for approval for relocation.

It is worth noting that baseball's overall antitrust exemption has contributed to the lack of movement of franchises, because the league can effectively block a move free from antitrust scrutiny. The last baseball team to relocate was the Washington Senators in 1972.

Another legislative proposal, the Sports Heritage Act, permits communities to retain the sports franchise's name after a team relocation.[24] This legislation does not address any antitrust concerns; it merely grants the home team a right to the club's name so long as the team was in town for 10 or more years.

A host of alternative legislative responses have been proposed: denying the use of tax-exempt bonds as a means of financing the construction of stadiums and arenas; requiring leagues to award a new franchise to every community that loses a team; encouraging community-based ownership similar to the public ownership of the Green Bay Packers; repealing all antitrust exemptions including the Sports Broadcasting Act and the 1966 act allowing the merger of competing leagues; demanding all stadium-related revenue be shared equally by all league members; and splitting the existing leagues into competing leagues. All of these proposed solutions seek to end what former NFL Commissioner Pete Rozelle referred to as "franchise free agency" in light of the research of economists like Robert Baade of Lake Forest College who argues new stadiums produce few economic benefits. [25]

Perhaps not surprisingly, new stadiums, although initially leading to increased attendance at higher ticket prices, do not ensure better-performing teams on the playing field. For instance, the New Jersey Devils hockey team and the Atlanta Braves baseball team both won their respective league championships playing in older buildings against teams hosted by new facilities.

Key Considerations: Economic Costs and Legislative Responses

- Pro sports leagues operate as a monopoly in many ways.
- Taxpayers are underwriting many of the costs associated with building new stadiums.
- Cities are bidding against each other to acquire sports teams.
- Legislative proposals seek to protect fans and host cities from losing their sports teams.

SUMMARY

The clear trend in professional sports is toward corporate ownership of league franchises. Media and entertainment companies are adding pro sports teams to their brand mix. Increasingly, these same billion-dollar businesses are not merely asking local taxpayers to pay for new stadiums and arenas but are actively seeking taxpayer-subsidized deals from cities willing to pay for teams to relocate. The leagues, although required to vote on any team move, are fearful of losing "Raiders-style" antitrust lawsuits. NFL Commissioner Taglibeau and leading economists and political figures have pleaded before Congress to bring a halt to franchise free agency by enacting legislation to insulate leagues from lawsuits and make it easier for communities to retain their "home" teams.

For Reflection

1. Although the move from Cleveland to Baltimore is one of the most lucrative deals in sports history for the team owner, what steps should be taken to protect the loyal fans of Cleveland, if any?
2. The Green Bay Packers operate in the smallest city in the United States with a pro sports team. The NFL's policy of sharing its television revenue when combined with community-based ownership has enabled the Packers to thrive on the field and financially. Is this a model for ownership that other NFL teams might follow? Why or why not?
3. Research indicates that taxpayers pay more than teams pay to finance stadiums. New stadiums lead to higher ticket prices. The owners and players get richer. Would you be in favor of Congress granting pro sports leagues limited antitrust immunity on issues related to franchise relocation to prevent this "madness"?
4. Some economists point to the direct benefit of jobs and taxes from building new arenas and stadiums. Yet, other economists state that

these jobs come at too high a cost by diverting money from more useful public projects like schools and law enforcement. What are the economic gains and losses to a community from a franchise relocation?

5. The supply and demand mismatch for professional sports teams and leagues contributes to communities raising the bar on stadium deals. What steps could the league take to solve this problem?

6. For many years team owners were satisfied with television and gate revenue sharing. Now owners seek to tap into lucrative stadium deals ranging from the licensing of the stadium's name to building non-revenue sharing luxury boxes. Is there a legitimate worry that this trend will lead to major imbalances in money available to spend on players to build a winning team?

7. Congress has been asked to prohibit tax-exempt financing of sports facilities. So far it has refused to close this loophole. How would you vote, and why?

Useful Web Sites

1. www.heartland.org/stadps
2. www.house.gov/judiciary/126.htm
3. www.newsday.com/sports/specials/stad 18a.htm
4. www.metropolismag.com/june97/greenbay
5. www.usnews.com/usnews/issue/stad.htm

Notes

1. Roy Johnson, "Take Me Out to the Boardroom," *Fortune*, July 21, 1997, v. 136, 42.
2. Ibid.
3. Ibid.
4. See Paul Weiler and Gary Roberts, *Sports Law* (St. Paul, MN: West Publication, 1993), pp. 1–2, for a chapter discussion on the legal rights and responsibilities of the office of the commissioner and the "best interests of the game."
5. 721 F. Supp. 906 (S.D. Ohio 1989).
6. 670 F. 2nd 1249 (2nd Cir. 1982).
7. 323 F. 2nd 124 (4th Cir. 1963).
8. *Levin* v. *National Basketball Association*, 385 F. Supp. 149 (S.D. N.Y. 1974).
9. http://www.metrolismag.com/june 97/ greenbay.html.

10. Ibid.
11. Based on the most recent reprinted sales of NFL franchises. See Johnson, "Take Me Out to the Boardroom." *Financial Worth* magazine annually publishes valuations of all the major sports teams in North America. See Barbara Murray, "Game Over" *US News and World Report*, February 16, 1998, p. 17, discussing author Tom Clancey's $205 million bid for the Minnesota Vikings, which eventually sold for $250 million.
12. Jason Vest, "Uproot for the Home Team: Can public ownership save cities from sports owners?" *US News and World Report*, March 10, 1997, v. 122, p. 53(3). See Roger Noll, "The Economics of the Sports Leagues," in *Law of Amateur Sports*, ch. 17 (Uberstine ed., Clark Boardman and Callaghan, New York: 1995).
13. Karen Goldberg, "Disney Wants to be Sports' MVP-Most Valuable Player," *Insight*, June 20, 1997, p. 40.
14. Hearing before the Subcommittee on Antitrust, Business Rights, and Competition, Senate Committee on the Judiciary, November 29, 1995. Topic: "Should Congress Stop the Bidding War for Sports Franchises?"
15. There are nearly a dozen court rulings relating to the battle between the NFL represented by Commissioner Pete Roselle and the owner of the Oakland Raiders, Al Davis. Current NFL Commissioner Tagliabue summarizes the case law in his testimony before the Senate subcommittee on November 25, 1995; for a more extensive reading of the case law, see Robert Berry and Glen Wong, *Law and Business of the Sports Industries* (Westport, CT: Greenwood Publication, 1986).
16. *Sullivan* v. *NFL*, 34 F. 3rd 1091 (1st Cir. 1994).
17. Mike Gollust, "This Means War: Why Art Modell Will Destroy the NFL," http:www.netspace.org/indy/issues/11-16-95/sports1/html.
18. John Riley, "Where the Grass Is Always . . . Greener" http: www.newsday.com/sports/speeches/stad18a.html.
19. "Franchises," http://www.heartland.org/stadps4.html.
20. Ibid.
21. Randall Love, "Bread and Circuses (Sports Stadiums)," *Forbes*, June 6, 1994, Vol. 153, November 12, p. 62.
22. "Should Congress Stop the Bidding Wars for Sports Franchises?" Hearing before the Subcommittee on the Antitrust, Business Rights, and Competition, Senate Committee on the Judiciary, November 29, 1995.
23. H. R. 3817, 105th Congress, 2d session submitted May 7, 1998.
24. Proposed by Senator Glenn (D-OH), found in his testimony before the Subcommittee on Antitrust Business Rights and Competition, Senate Committee on the Judiciary, November 29, 1995.
25. Ibid. as part of the heartland executive summary involving academic responses to stop bidding wars for sports franchises at http://www.heartland.org/stadiumm.htm.

CHAPTER 8

Criminal, Racial, and Social Issues

Don't feel sorry for me. I've had a great life, great friends. Please think of the real O.J. and not this lost person.

—O.J. Simpson

Case Study

Sally Fitness doesn't like her coach. Sally feels her coach singles her out for unfair public criticism. Occasionally, her coach even points her finger at her. Once the player and coach even exchanged pushes after a play Sally messed up that cost the team a game. Finally, Sally told herself she couldn't take the verbal abuse and physical intimidation anymore. Sally confronted her coach who went "ballistic" and threw Sally to the ground and began choking her in front of other players at the end of another team loss. Should criminal charges be brought against Sally's coach for assault and battery, or is this a matter better left to the team or league?

INTRODUCTION

For years television brought O.J. Simpson into our living rooms on Saturdays as a star running back for the University of Southern California, and thereafter, on Sundays and on Monday nights as one of the premier tailbacks in professional football. His smiling, bubbling personality led to commercial success. The image of O.J.—and perhaps all sports heroes—was forever altered as millions of prime-time television viewers watched his slow ride in the back of a Ford Bronco with a gun pointed to his head on a Los Angeles freeway trying to escape from the horrors of his murdered ex-wife Nicole Brown Simpson and Ron Goldman.

The same medium, television, that helped O.J. achieve the American Dream of colorblind fame and fortune from the depths of Oakland's worst neighborhood ultimately aided in bringing him down. Television networks devoted daily coverage to his criminal trial. Although acquitted of the killings, his image today is that of wife-beater and murderer, a celebrity turned killer who got away with it by trumping the state and society with the "race" card.

Through it all people watched, and talked, and learned about *domestic violence* by sports figures. Beating a spouse at home no longer would be treated as a family spat even when committed by a celebrity. Using the derogatory "N-word" by police and others should cause a storm of protest. DNA evidence is becoming more widely understood and accepted by the judicial system. Judge Ito's apparent intimidation by the lawyers and media celebrities was vividly contrasted with Judge Fujisaki's textbook demonstration of control in the nontelevised civil trial that led to a more than $33 million civil verdict against O.J.

Media attention focuses now on incidents of violence both inside and outside the playing arena. Following sports once meant keeping track of team standings and box scores. This then evolved into knowing about salary caps, free agency, and long-term contracts. Player misconduct, fan violence, and "hooliganism" at soccer matches now are a part of the daily fare of the sports law student.

ATHLETES AS ROLE MODELS

Professor Sharon Stoll, and other members of the Center for Ethics at the University of Idaho, conducted a survey of more than 40,000 student-athletes regarding making moral judgments.[1] Stoll's studies led her to conclude that athletes invariably score lower than nonathletes in moral reasoning.

Athletes learn early in life that society values success on the playing field rather than the ethics of playing hard and honestly regardless of outcome. Institutionally coaches and athletic administrators direct the lives of star athletes by treating those who do succeed in the system as coddled and privileged members of the team.

Contrasting the notion that personal privilege does not lead to personal responsibility is Karl Malone. This NBA standout maintains that society does not have to expect its athletes to behave perfectly all the time. By virtue of athletes' public prominence Malone argues that whether they like it or not star athletes are viewed as heroes and role models by the public and they have a duty to accept that responsibility. Why else, Malone states, do players receive lucrative endorsement deals other than to hope others will follow their lead and buy a certain cereal, shoe, or thirst-quenching drink?

Malone's viewpoint runs counter to a former U.S. Olympic basketball dream teammate of his, Charles Barkley. In a well-known Nike ad, Barkley advises viewers that "I am not a role model." Malone and a number of esteemed psychologists respond that society chooses who its role models are, not the other way around.

The off-the-field behavior of prominent athletes ranging from Michael Tyson's rape of a former beauty queen while at the same time exclaiming to women who refused his advances, "Don't you know who I am? I'm the heavyweight champion of the world!" to Dallas Cowboy receiver Michael Irvin at the center of an attempted solicitation by a police officer to kill Irvin for allegedly threatening the officer's common-law wife for her testimony during a grand jury drug charge involving Irvin certainly draws into question the wisdom of lionizing athletes. Even the public revelations of NBA players who have fathered children out of wedlock, including Shawn Kemp, Gary Payton, and Jason Kidd, contribute to a sense of more irresponsible behavior by athletes. If nothing else, athletes need to have an awareness that they are being watched by fans on and off the playing fields.

Whether or not they accept the responsibility to behave in an appropriate manner is more often than not a function of their home, neighborhood, school, and environment which helps mold a sense of personal responsibility and dignity. For every Mike Tyson there exists an Alan Page, who after retiring from professional football earned a law degree, established a charitable foundation to help minority children, and was elected the first African-American to the Minnesota Supreme Court.

VIOLENCE IN SPORTS

Fan Violence

Soccer is the most widely played and watched sport in the world. Not surprisingly, given the loyalty fans express for their home teams, it has provided the largest number of incidents of fan violence including riots. Disgruntled, passionate fans became angry at a referee's call, causing the deaths of hundreds of spectators caught in a brawl in Lima, Peru. After a particularly distasteful incident where British Leeds soccer fans literally destroyed a soccer stadium in France after their team lost a European Cup match to Bayern of Munich, Germany, the following description of the typical Leeds soccer fan was written by a newspaper columnist: "a foul-mouthed, crude, drunken, intolerable oaf, bereft of reason, poisoned by prejudice, grotesque with self-invested arrogance, bent on the destruction of property and intent on abusing anyone who speaks a foreign tongue."[2] English fans behaved no better at the 1998 World Cup in France as hundreds battled French riot police outside the site of matches.

Over the last eight years more than 40 deaths due to soccer violence have occurred in Argentina alone. Europe's governing soccer body recently announced that all soccer games abroad will be deemed high risk because of violent and threatening fan behavior. Following a World Cup loss in the United States in which Colombian star Andres Escobar accidentally deflected a ball into his own net, he was found dead in the streets after returning home.

European and South American soccer fans, unfortunately, are not alone in destroying personal property and harming one another. The city of Philadelphia during the most recent professional football season established a satellite courthouse at the stadium to handle criminal arraignments immediately after rowdy fans were arrested for public intoxication and fighting.

"I didn't want to kill her. I just wanted to hurt her slightly so that Monica wouldn't be able to play for a couple of weeks." So testified the unemployed lathe operator who plunged a knife into the back of Monica Seles during a tennis changeover. His motivation was to disable Seles so that Steffi Graf, the object of his obsession, could retain her status as number one in women's tennis.

The stalker and attacker received a suspended sentence for his premeditated crime of grievous bodily harm. Seles suffered a half-inch deep wound in her back and missed months of tournament play. The tennis community was shocked by the German court's lenient sentence and the negative message conveyed.

Player Violence

Undoubtedly, violence is a part of some sports. Fans and players expect a certain amount of "violent" hits in many team sports. Rugby, hockey, and football stand out as examples. Traditionally, as long as the player collisions, checks and tackles are nonflagrant, these violations are merely subject to penalties and fines imposed by referees and league officials.

The critical question is: When violence on the playing field or in the arena escalates to an unacceptable level during the course of play, should society step in and impose criminal law principles and penalties? Mike Tyson biting the ear of Evander Holyfield during their heavyweight championship fight stands out for inspection as one situation. Arguably Holyfield did not expect nor consent to the unforseeable biting that occurred while engaging in a violent activity by definition. *Consent* by the harmed athlete to a reasonably forseeable hazard is a common defense to criminal charges.

Society has not yet drawn the bright lines for determining when criminal law applies to sports violence. *Battery* or the unlawful application of force to another person that results in bodily harm is the most common criminal offense imaginable in a sports setting. Intentionally bringing about unlawful force against another player by a hockey stick or baseball bat or foot or fist are also ways for battery to occur. Engaging in criminally negligent conduct, which amounts to something more than ordinary tort negligence that results in a high degree of risk or harm to another, is a second form of battery. Biting or choking an opponent could clearly fall within this category. Bodily injury caused by acting in *self-defense* when threatened by physical harm normally does not constitute a criminal act.

U.S. prosecutors have demonstrated an unwillingness to pursue criminal charges that occur on the ice, arena, or playing field. Consent to any unprivileged contact or self-defense in response to the offensive action of another makes a conviction difficult.

More than 20 years ago Boston Bruin hockey player Dave Forbes was criminally charged for hitting Minnesota player Henry Boucha with his stick and fist during a game, requiring more than 25 stitches and surgery to repair a fractured eye socket.[3] The alleged battery occurred after two players engaged in a fight that left both players landing in the penalty box for seven minutes. A jury refused to criminally convict Forbes.

A year later in a heralded case, David Maloney, a Detroit Red Wing, viciously attacked the Toronto Maple Leafs player, Brian Glennie. Maloney rushed Glennie from behind during a game, throwing him down on the ice repeatedly while punching him in the face area. A Canadian jury acquitted Maloney of criminal charges in *Regina v. Maloney*, 28 C.C.C. 2nd 323, Ont. Co.Ct. 1976.

The first known case where a hockey player was sentenced to jail for an on-ice assault happened in the late 1980s.[4] Dino Cicarelli, the all-time leading goal scorer for the Minnesota (now Dallas) North Stars, hammered Luke Richardson of the Toronto Maple Leafs during a game. Richardson's helmet shielded him from harm so Cicarelli repeatedly punched him in the mouth. A Canadian judge found him guilty of criminal assault or intentionally placing another player in reasonable apprehension of bodily harm. Cicarelli was sentenced to one day in jail to serve as an example that "violence in a hockey game or in any other circumstance is not acceptable in our society," as stated by the judge.[5]

A good example of the use of the self-defense argument in hockey prosecutions is found in the case of *Regina v. Maki* [(14 D.L.R. 3rd 164 (1970)] and *Regina v. Green* [(16 D.L.R. 3rd 137 (1970)]. During an exhibition game between the Boston Bruins and the St. Louis Blues in Ottawa two opposing players, Ted Green and Wayne Maki, engaged in a series of shoving, punching, and hitting matches, which led to two serious fights. Testimony was disputed as to whether Green raised his hockey stick above his shoulders, which is a violation of official game rules, in an attempt to strike Maki. Testimony was clear that Maki swung at Green, hitting Green's stick. Maki's stick then glanced off Green's stick, landing on Green's head causing bodily injury. On criminal assault leading to bodily harm against each player, the court held that the players were engaged in self-defense. No criminal conviction resulted for either athlete.

Almost every contact sport carries the risk of violent collisions or hits. Most player-to-player contact is a foreseeable aspect of the game. It's the vicious, unprovoked attacks that raise the specter of criminal liability. Kermit Washington's unexpected punch of peacemaker Rudy Tomjanovich, shattering his facial bones, during a 1977 NBA ball game stands out as a fact pattern where criminal charges might hold. A baseball pitcher who threatens to bean an opposing hitter before a game, and then follows through, might find himself appearing before a local magistrate. Football linebacker Bryan Cox's "stark raving mad" game behavior that includes spitting at fans, fighting players, and verbally abusing game officials while costing Cox fines in excess of $100,000 borders on criminal behavior.

In one of the more bizarre foul plays involving a professional athlete, Latrell Sprewell of the Golden State Warriors was first suspended and then saw his four-year, $32 million contract terminated after threatening to kill his coach and then choking him before he went to the locker room only to come back 15 minutes later to strike him again. Prior to this attack, coach P.J. Carlesimo had repeatedly criticized Sprewell's lazy and selfish practice and play habits. Many players complained about the severity of Sprewell's punishment that initially included a one-year suspension; however, few players defended his "mistake," as Sprewell referred to it.

Sprewell's conduct prompted the NBA to exclaim: "A sports league does not have to accept or condone behavior that would not be tolerated in any other segment of society." [6] Yet, no local district attorney sought a criminal indictment or brought criminal assault and battery charges against Sprewell. If this same incident between a boss and employee had occurred almost anywhere but during a practice or a game involving an athlete, does anyone realistically doubt criminal charges would not have been filed? The distinction of athlete versus nonathlete during a game or practice, especially given the premeditated nature of Sprewell's second attack, does not seem remarkable enough to circumvent the application of criminal law principles.

Sprewell became the first player ever suspended for a year by the NBA for other than drug violations. The president of the NBA Players Association, Patrick Ewing, seized the opportunity to claim that the league's "stern" reaction disregarded Sprewell's due process rights. [7] For many sports fans Sprewell's ugly attack wasn't about contract rights but rather reflected a loss of any sense of sportsmanship, self control, and respect by professional athletes whom society once expected to behave like champions. Ironically, Sprewell sued the league and the Golden State Warriors for $30 million, alleging a violation of contract rights, labor, and antitrust laws stemming from his 68 game suspension, then dropped his civil complaint.

Beyond the individual acts of malfeasance by players and fans, many experts argue that acts of violence both on the field and in the stands merely reflect the inherent violence in our society. Unfortunately, acts of mayhem have crossed over gender lines. This newspaper headline appeared in an Associated Press story: "Women's Team Was 'Validated' by Fracas." The all-women's Colorado Silver Bullets professional baseball team engaged in a brawl against an all-star boys' high school baseball team in Georgia. The fight included punching, body slamming, and hair pulling between members of the two opposing teams. After the combat, attendance skyrocketed to a high of 30,000 fans in Denver as the Bullets continued to play out their final season against all-star teams throughout the country.

Finally, an Italian prosecutor sought criminal manslaughter charges when three-time Formula One champion Ayrton Senna of Brazil crashed and died at the San Marino Grand Prix.[8] Charged were race car owner Frank Williams, the car designer, and track officials. Italian officials alleged Senna's death in 1994 occurred because of poor track maintenance and faulty welding on the steering column by crew members. The court refused to find that the charged parties had engaged in criminal or reckless negligence in the course of an unlawful act.

Mentors in Violence Prevention and Public Pressure

Incidents of player and fan violence have encouraged greater public awareness of the need to change people's attitudes about violence.

At the college level in 1993 Northeastern University established the Mentors in Violence Prevention Project to institutionalize greater male participation in university-based efforts to *prevent* violence against women. Specifically, the program has sought to not merely raise men's awareness of women's issues like sexual violence, harassment, and abuse, but also encourage men to assume an active role in prevention.

A few years after the program was started, it was expanded to help train and empower women to work with men and other women to eliminate gender violence and abuse. Northeastern has developed a training module that utilizes training teams of college personnel to implement a violence prevention program at over 100 campuses, ranging from the University of Alberta, Edmonton to the University of Portland, Oregon. Students who participate in the program are expected to assume leadership roles.

Recently, a federal court upheld the Federal Violence Against Women Act, which imposes civil liability for any person who commits a crime motivated by gender, as being constitutional under the Commerce Clause. In *Brozonkia v. Virginia Polytechnical Institute and State University* (66 U.S.L.W 1387), a freshman student sued her university after alleging being raped by the football players in a dormitory within an hour after meeting them.

Outside the college ranks much civic work still needs to be done. The well-publicized domestic violence case of 25-year-old outfielder Wilfredo Cordero, who pleaded guilty to choking, beating, and threatening to kill his wife after a bad game, led to his release by the Boston Red Sox. Part of his court punishment for the misdemeanor conviction includes counseling on alcoholism and battering.

Keep in mind, though, that a professional athlete is protected by contract and union rules that generally limit unilateral responses against players by even well-meaning general managers. The contract rule exception that permits clubs to terminate a player's contract occurs when the player fails to adhere to "standards of good citizenship, good moral character . . . and good sportsmanship," a clause found in nearly all professional sports' player contracts.

Of course, even managers can engage in violent behavior. Atlanta Braves baseball manager Bobby Cox was jailed and charged with simple battery after police broke up a domestic dispute between Cox and his wife. As a first-time offender, Cox was ordered to attend violence counseling.

One other recent national incident involving a celebrity is worth describing. After long-time NBA announcer Marv Albert assured his employer, NBC, that "there was no basis whatsoever for the charges," he pleaded guilty to assault and battery charges against a female friend.[9] The victim charged that Albert repeatedly bit her on the back and forced her to have oral sex in a hotel. Albert, who regularly appeared in movie cameos and was seen on *The David Letterman Show* more than 100 times, had hoped to introduce into evidence the victim's past sexual behavior and earlier threats against prior boyfriends. Citing Virginia's rape shield law, the judge barred the introduction of this evidence. When another woman came forward ready to claim the same crime against Albert, he hastily retreated and admitted his guilt.

In the aftermath of the Albert conviction, questions arose regarding the stigma a guilty plea would have on his broadcasting career. CBS fired golf announcer Ben Wright after he made some disparaging remarks about women golfers and lesbians. ABC stood by former football great, and *Monday Night Football* broadcaster Frank Gifford, after published reports of his adulterous relationship. Both of these situations can be distinguished from Marv Albert because they did not lead to criminal charges.

Perhaps David Kindred, a contributing editor for *The Sporting News*, stated it best when he wrote, "Could anyone again hear Albert's voice without hearing a woman's pain?"[10] Yet, both Albert and Wright recently returned to the broadcast booth.

Are these public outcries, and even criminal abuse convictions, enough to stop the violence by sports figures against women? Probably not, but at least public attention and disapproval have shifted from the victim to the accused.

And in the "Apocalypse Is Upon Us Now" category the "Badsport Homepage" chronicles on a weekly basis the police blotter for professional and college athletes. The American Civil Liberties Union (ACLU) offers a detailed list of alleged hate crimes against women in its "Sports Hall of Shame!" home page.

BRIBERY AND FORGERY

Shortly before the United States was about to play El Salvador in a World Cup qualifying match in early November 1997, a hotel phone message was left for team captain John Harkes. The message asked Harkes to contact the caller because "(y)ou understand what this game means."[11] The caller indicated he represented El Salvador, which was desperate for a win to qualify for the World Cup Soccer Championships, whereas the United States had already earned its way.

Although rumors of soccer skullduggery have dogged this sport for years, perhaps the greatest bribery scandal to hit sports in the United States occurred in the late 1940s and early 1950s. A total of 86 games involving seven top teams and 32 players were scandalized by a nationwide fix of college basketball orchestrated by organized gambling.

Another kind of organized ring surfaced in the late 1990s in Chicago. Six individuals received federal prison terms of over 18 months for conspiring to sell fake sports memorabilia. The bogus goods included apparel, bats, balls, and photographs bearing false autographs of celebrity athletes. The most commonly forged signature was that of Michael Jordan, who has a reputation for rarely signing photos or balls. Frank Thomas of the Chicago White Sox and Shawn Kemp of the Seattle SuperSonics were two other prominent athletes whose signatures were frequently forged.

The FBI agents who investigated the counterfeiting operation estimated that the total annual sports memorabilia fraud business is around $100 million out of a $3 billion a year industry,[12] all from an industry that began for many fans as a childhood hobby collecting baseball cards from the Topps Chewing Gum company.

Allegations of fraud and deceit at the highest levels of corporate finance took place when John Spano was arrested and charged with bank and wire fraud.[13] In 1997 Spano had attempted to purchase the New York Islanders for around $165 million, while allegedly misrepresenting his net worth on the order of nearly $250 million. Embarrassed NHL officials apparently failed to conduct the proper financial due diligence required of a prospective team buyer. Spano pleaded guilty to federal charges of forging bank and broker documents in his ill-fated attempt to buy the Islanders with no real assets.

The Spano affair bears some similarity to the criminal convictions based on two counts of bank fraud and one count of wire fraud of former Los Angeles Kings hockey owner Bruce McNall. Six banks, Merrill Lynch, Wayne Gretzky, and the Kings were all duped by the fast-talking McNall who received a 5-year federal prison sentence.[14]

Key Considerations: Crime
- Player-on-player violence traditionally has not led to criminal charges.
- Should society impose criminal law principles on athletic participation?
- Is it fair to ask: do athletes who participate in sports consent to all harm or only to reasonably foreseeable harm?
- Unsportsmanlike conduct by players against other players or coaches may demand stricter punishment.
- The Mentors in Violence Program seeks to halt the assault against women on college campuses.
- Criminal fraud has occured at the highest level of team ownership.

Race

Few societal issues befuddle whites and exhaust blacks more than *racism*. Race in numerous ways has scarred the souls of all Americans. Recent court decisions have scaled back affirmative action programs for minorities. Former

Los Angeles Dodgers executive Al Campanis's infamous television comment that blacks "may not have some of the necessities" to coach a professional team set off a storm of protest. Many black leaders point to the lack of progress, since Campanis's 1987 remark, by colleges and pro teams in hiring minorities to head coaching and major administrative positions.

In 1997 baseball celebrated five decades of integration after Jackie Robinson became the first black major league player. At present there are no minority owners in baseball and about 15 percent of all baseball executives are Latino or African-American.[15] Bill White became the first African-American to head a professional sports league when in 1989 he was named president of the National League. Baseball's 30 major league teams have fewer than five minority head coaches. In 1996 Bob Watson became the first minority general manager to lead his team (the New York Yankees) to a World Series championship.

The commissioners of the established sports leagues have sought to exercise an active role on race relations. The NBA leads the way in minority hiring by a substantial margin. Approximately 30 percent of all executive positions are held by blacks.[16] Women constitute nearly 40 percent of all league managerial positions.[17] Minority referees are more common in the NBA than in any other sport. The first African-American to play in the NBA was Nat "Sweetwater" Clifton, who joined the New York Knicks in 1950 when his contract was purchased from the Harlem Globetrotters.

Starting in the fall of 1997, the NBA began diversity training for all its league employees. Individual teams have been encouraged to follow suit. Part of the impetus for the NBA's most recent attention to racial issues stems from New Jersey Nets coach John Calipari's intemperate racial ethnic slurs to a Hispanic beat reporter.

Today African-Americans constitute about 18 percent of all major league players in baseball.[18] Hispanics make up 22 percent of all major league baseball players.[19] Approximately 69 percent of the NFL players and roughly 80 percent of the NBA players are minorities.[20] Beyond these figures critics argue that certain positions are played nearly exclusively by white athletes whereas other positions remain the province of black athletes at the pro level. Almost all defensive backs and wide receivers in the NFL are black. Over 80 percent of all major league baseball pitchers and catchers are white.[21]

Several theories exist as to why "stacking" of players of color for certain positions occurs. A study conducted by professors at Eastern Michigan University found that the college coaches surveyed have developed stereotypes about skills and personality traits required at each position.[22] Coaches also have developed stereotypes about psychological, physical, and personality characteristics of white and black players. Match the two stereotypes and it's easy to see how players get placed at certain positions based on skin color. Through time, education, and experience, these stereotypes can be overcome.

A 1997 special report by *Sports Illustrated* asked, and attempted to answer, if there are reasons beyond "racial stereotyping by position" that might explain the overall domination of male African-Americans in track, football, baseball, basketball, and boxing. The magazine's December 8, 1997 cover story entitled "What Ever Happened to the White Athlete" drew as much criticism as praise for pondering whether black males are genetically athletically superior to white males.

One of the leading experts on race and athletic performance, David W. Hunter of Hampton University, recently published a survey of reported quantitative physiological athletic differences between racial groups in the Fall 1996/Winter 1997 issue of the *Journal of African American Men.* Hunter's research was heavily cited by *Sports Illustrated.* He concluded that "(t)he available scientifically based physiological data do not seem to support the observed performance differences among racial groups—certainly not to the magnitude that would be needed to account for the disproportionate representations and successes."[23] Hunter concedes "anatomical and physiological differences ha(ve) not yet been exhaustively studied."[24]

Thoughtful observers caution others against making statements like that of Dr. Roger Bannister, the first person to break the 4-minute-mile barrier, who claimed that black sprinters have "certain natural advantages" over white sprinters in the absence of sound, empirical studies.[25] Despite these cautionary remarks, the "logic of the obvious" as noted by numerous coaches, players, and fans concede that male African-Americans appear to run faster and jump higher than their white male counterparts. The unanswered question is whether these differences are biological, cultural, social, psychological, or a combination of genetic and environmental factors? The conclusion is that we don't fully know, that more research is needed, and further testing should include women.

Although the world heralded the arrival of golf's first male minority supertalent, Tiger Woods, the professional tennis establishment is not sure how to deal with a young, black, female prodigy who promises to shake up the U.S. Tennis Association establishment in more than one way. The tall, occasionally arrogant Venus Williams lost the finals of the 1997 U.S. Open to teenage sensation Martina Hingis at the Arthur Ashe Stadium at Flushing Meadows. When an opposing player purposely collided with Williams on a changeover, Williams's father charged the bumping was "racially motivated."[26] His remark that the opposing player, Irina Spirlea, was "a big, tall, white turkey" cast a pall over an otherwise emotionally energizing coming-out tennis party for Williams.[27]

In many ways this partly physical and partly verbal exchange on the tennis court symbolizes the present debate on race in sports. Williams and her family are seeking to become tennis trailblazers in a sport that hasn't experienced a top woman African-American player since Althea Gibson broke the color barrier in 1950. (Gibson also broke the color barrier in women's pro golf.) Williams's behavior, although acceptable when exhibited by male players like John McEnroe and Jimmy Connors, is seen as too brash and divisive for women. Toss in controversial racial comments by a father trying to protect his daughter and we are back to the beginning. Whites cannot understand why she needs to act unfriendly and hostile. Blacks claim she is being singled out for being herself, which means she is not white and not a product of the rigorous junior tennis circuit.

The United States is not the only country that has experienced racial sports difficulties. Australia's 400-meter Olympic gold medal contender, Cathy Freeman, was told by an Aboriginal chief not to compete in the 2000 Sydney Olympics because it is the "white man's Olympics." Freeman, who is Aborigine, quickly announced she had no intention of boycotting the Olympics for political purposes.

Freeman has also been counseled against performing any victory lap at the Olympics carrying the Aboriginal flag, as opposed to the Australian flag. The Olympic Charter rules decry political or racial demonstrations in the Olympic area, and she has been forewarned that disqualification may occur.[28] John Carlos and Tommie Smith were disqualified by the IOC in 1968 when they raised their clenched fists on the medal stand in a display of black power at the Mexico Olympics.

In Europe, black soccer players are sometimes targets of racial baiting. Racial graffiti was recently found on the walls of the Italian soccer club headquarters, Padova, when word got out the team was going to sign Nigerian players.

Hockey has had its share of racial disharmony recently. During the 1997–1998 NHL season, two Washington Capitals players received suspensions for derogatory racial remarks in two separate games. Craig Berube called Florida's Peter Worrel, who is African-American, a "monkey" during a game scuffle. Chris Simmons, a Native American, called Edmonton's Mike Grier, whose father is player personnel director for the New England Patriots, a racial slur.

The sport of baseball has taken the lead in looking for international talent. Players from Spanish-speaking countries are having a profound effect on the game. For most Hispanic ballplayers Roberto Clemente is regarded as the break-through Latin star. Clemente who died tragically in 1972, while assisting in relief efforts in Nicaragua, garnered his 3,000 and final hit in his last at-bat of the season for the Pittsburgh Pirates. Clemente is one of five Latinos elected to baseball's Hall of Fame.

In the late 1990s the 1997 World Series Champion Florida Marlins, Texas Rangers, and Los Angeles Dodgers all commenced specific marketing campaigns geared toward wooing Hispanic fans.[29] Bill Robertson of Anaheim Sports, a subsidiary of the Disney-owned Anaheim Angels, commented that "(g)etting more Hispanic fans to our ballpark and getting more Hispanic ballplayers is a hot button for our organization."[30] Baseball teams located in areas populated by large numbers of Hispanic fans are now broadcasting games in Spanish.

The early Latin ball players had to overcome many of the same racial barriers that blocked the entry of Negro League players into the major leagues. In 1911 two Cuban players, Rafael Almeida and Armando Marsans, were permitted to play for the Cincinnati Reds because they were deemed "white" and a local paper assured fans that they were "two of the purest bars of Castillian soap ever to wash upon our shores."[31] By the mid-1930s dark-skinned Latin ball players began to join the "big leagues."[32] They were allowed to play because they were Latino, noncitizens despite not always being light skinned, whereas domestic blacks in baseball still found the doors closed until Jackie Robinson opened them.

Today Alex Rodriguez of the Seattle Mariners and Pudge Rodriguez of the Texas Rangers are viewed as two of baseball's hottest marketing commodities, notwithstanding their Latino backgrounds. Both Rodriguezs have signed multiyear, multimillion-dollar endorsement deals with Nike. The future of major league baseball may hinge on the game's ability to market itself to the Hispanic community while continuing to reach out to its traditional marketing base of fans.

Key Considerations: Race

- In 1947 Jackie Robinson integrated major league baseball.
- Although African-American players constitute the majority of the rosters of the NFL and NBA, there are no African-American owners in any major professional sport.
- Players in team sports are still subject to racial stereotyping by position.
- Incidents of racism exist in sports today.
- Latino players have had to overcome barriers in baseball similar to those experienced by African-American players.

THE AMERICANS WITH DISABILITIES ACT OF 1990

The Americans with Disabilities Act of 1990 (ADA) is the most comprehensive federal civil rights law passed to protect individuals with disabilities.[33] The reach of the ADA is broad, for instance, extending to ensure access to sports arenas and stadiums for the disabled fan.[34]

Publicly and privately owned sports facilities as places of exhibition or entertainment are covered by the ADA. Two different standards of compliance apply depending on whether a facility is new or old.

Existing facilities, such as Fenway Park in Boston or the Rose Bowl in Pasadena, must remove architectural barriers where such removal is "readily achievable." Factors such as the cost and nature of the modification are considered. Lowering a drinking fountain, refitting restrooms for wheelchairs, and adding seats throughout a facility for the handicapped are all examples of modifications that have been required because the cost is relatively modest in light of the advantages gained.

The ADA demands that new stadiums must be "readily accessible to and usable by" the disabled. The Department of Justice has prepared very specific guidelines regarding the design of entrances, parking, restrooms, concessions, signs, and seats for the wheelchair bound. For instance, wheelchair seating locations must be available throughout the facility including luxury boxes. The disabled must also have access to seats and views at prices comparable to those available to the general public.

The newly opened MCI arena in Washington, D.C., home to the Wizards NBA team, was subject to charges of violating the ADA by not constructing all wheelchair seating locations in a fashion that a line of sight to the field is provided over standing spectators. The court denied the owners' request to eliminate the sightline guidelines imposed by the Justice Department, and held that "substantial compliance" was sufficient. The court approved a design plan that provided 78 percent of the wheelchair seating with sight-lines over standing spectators.

A different application of the ADA occurred in 1998 when Casey Martin, a 25-year-old pro golfer suffering from a rare, painful circulatory ailment in his legs that makes walking an 18-hole course nearly impossible, successfully challenged for the first time under the ADA a sports organization's playing rules.

In granting Martin a permanent injunction to use a cart while playing on the Professional Golfers Association (PGA) Tour, the federal court determined the following:

- A golf course during a tournament meets the ADA's definition of a place of public accommodation.
- Martin is disabled and entitled to reasonable accommodation to participate in tournament golf.
- Reasonable accommodation includes riding a cart.
- The PGA failed to meet its burden of proof that allowing Martin to use a cart would alter competitive golf fundamentally.
- Walking 18 holes over five hours is not fundamentally taxing.[35]

The long-term implications of this decision in the world of professional sports are unknown. It is known that Casey Martin just wanted a chance to play tournament golf, and by pressing his claim against the PGA he sent a message that people with disabilities are entitled to a meaningful opportunity to try.

DEATH OF A MARKETING MARRIAGE

In the early 1970s the National Association of Stock Car Racing (NASCAR) was searching for a major sponsor. At the same time R.J. Reynolds was looking for an advertising hook to attach to the marketing of its Winston brand of cigarettes.

Their nearly 30-year marriage may end. While Congress has not voted to approve a nearly $400 billion class-action tobacco industry settlement, many experts believe Congress in time may ban any tobacco related advertising in ball parks and arenas, ending T-shirt and other promotional giveaways and ceasing tobacco-brand sponsorship of sporting events.[36] Nearly 95 percent of tobacco firms' $195 million sports sponsorship budget went directly to car racing sports.[37] R.J. Reynolds spent $30 million promoting the Winston Cup and other NASCAR events.[38]

The proposed class-action settlement has a provision that helps compensate teams or sporting events that aren't able to immediately find substitute sponsors. Consumer goods companies like McDonald's and Coca-Cola are expected to expand their sponsorship budgets and jump in where R.J. Reynolds and Phillip Morris might bow out. The tobacco deal proposal is expected to reverberate throughout the global sports world as other countries seek to impose similar negotiated bans on tobacco advertising in sports venues.

The tobacco industry does not stand out alone for public scrutiny. Liquor advertisements in popular sport magazines, newspapers, and on televised sports shows may become the next targeted product for policing. Special interest groups including the National Organization for Women (NOW) have earmarked Nike for allegedly exploiting Asian factory workers. Reebok, adidas, and Nike have conceded problems in past efforts to avoid producing shoes and soccer balls manufactured by child laborers. Thirty sporting goods companies have joined together to develop uniform standards and monitoring practices.

SUMMARY

Like it or not, today's professional athletes serve as role models. The conduct and behavior of some recognizable players both on and off the field have raised concern about a growing lack of sportsmanship and civility that is increasingly translating into criminal behavior. For now the courts have been unwilling to impose the same criminal legal standards to on-the-court activities that outside the playing field would lead to charges of assault and battery and worse.

Issues of race surface in different ways in sports. For years, black athletes suffered under racial barriers that denied them entrance into professional sports. Today the black athlete has begun to dominate some sports in both numbers and star status. Scientists are unsure of the reasons for this dramatic alteration in the color composition of team rosters. Hispanic ball players, especially in the sport of baseball, have gained nationwide popularity. At the managerial and operational levels blacks and Hispanics still lag whites in positions of responsibility.

The sports industry is subject to increasing public pressure. Special-interest groups have begun to monitor and speak out against the use of child labor to make sporting equipment. Congress might require the tobacco industry to sever all promotional connections to sports.

For Reflection

1. Are professional athletes role models for children? What responsibility, if any, do they have to society to behave appropriately?
2. Is it time for prosecutors to rigorously impose criminal law statutes to on-the-field acts of player-to-player or player-to-coach violence?
3. In a recent poll, half those surveyed responded that African-Americans bring more natural ability to sports than whites. Do you agree or disagree? On what basis?
4. Do you agree or disagree with the statement that there is no abiding sense of right or wrong among today's professional athletes? List three examples to support your view.
5. Does racism still exist in professional sports? Examples?
6. Paula Pitcher is a one-armed softball player who wants to pitch for the Women's Professional Softball League. Paula is perfectly able to pitch and field. Assuming Paula is a good enough pitcher to pitch for this league, does the ADA require the league to alter its competitive rules to allow a designated hitter to bat solely for Paula, as a means of reasonably accommodating her disability?
7. Would you be in favor of extending any proposed ban on tobacco advertisements to include magazines that publish articles on sports and health?

Useful Web Sites

1. cag-www.les.mit.edu/frankkim/sports/si/violence.html
2. www.usatoday.com/sports/sfront.htm
3. www.epnet.com/bin/epwgargoyl...ext/session
4. www.latinolink.com/opinion/opinion97/1026orog.htm
5. www.bestware.net/spreng/dodgers/index.html

Notes

1. The Center for Ethics Web page that contains the full report of its more than ten years of research is: http://www.ets.vidaho.edu//center/for/ethics. See also: Jay Benedict, *Public Heroes and Private Felons* (Cornell Univ. Press, Ithaca, N.Y.: 1997).
2. James Michner, *Sports in America* (New York: Random House, 1976), p. 532.
3. *State* v. *Forbes* (no 63280 Minn. Dist. Ct., 4th Cir., 4th Jud. Dist.).

4. For a report on the Cicarelli incident see Austin Murphy, "North Star on Ice," *Sports Illustrated*, September 5, 1988, p. 34.
5. Ibid.
6. Found in numerous sources including: *The Boston Globe*, December 5 1997, p. 2c in an Associated Press story titled "All-Star Guard Suspended for a Year by NBA."
7. As reported by Gary Boek, "Players Stunned by Severity of Penalty Against Sprewell," *USA Today,* December 5, 1997, p. 26C.
8. See Liz Clarke, "Racing Officials Cleared in '94 Death of Senna," *USA Today*, December 17, 1997, p. 5C.
9. As reprinted by Michael Hiestand, "Plea, Firing Raise Marketability Doubts," *USA Today*, September 26, 1997, p. 3C.
10. Dave Kindred, "The Truth Hurts," *The Sporting News*, October 6, 1997, p. 5.
11. *Sports Illustrated*, November 24, 1997, p. 22.
12. David Seideman, "Caught in the Act of Forgery," *Sports Illustrated*, October 20, 1997, p. 7.
13. "Spano Agrees to Plea," *The Atlanta Constitution*, October 8, 1997. p. F10.
14. "Scorecards: NHL Owners and the Feds, Another McNall?" *Sports Illustrated*, August 4, 1997, p. 20.
15. Center for the Study of Sports in Society, Northeastern University. Note: Richard Lapchick, director of the center, has published a number of reports related to the opportunities existing for minorities in sports. 1997 Racial Report Card.
16. Ibid.
17. Ibid.
18. Ibid.
19. Ibid.
20. Ibid.
21. Ibid.
22. As reported in "Is Discrimination Against Minorities a Serious Problem in Sports," Opposing Viewpoints Pamphlets (1994), pp. 137–138.
23. David Hunter, "Race and Athletic Performance: A Physiological Review," *Journal of African American Men*, Fall 1996/Winter 1997, Vol. 2, Issues 2/3, p. 36.
24. Ibid.
25. S.L. Price, "Is It in the Genes?" *Sports Illustrated*, December 8, 1997, p. 54.
26. S.L. Price, "Venus Envy," *Sports Illustrated*, September 15, 1997, p. 35.
27. Ibid.
28. Louise Evans, "Freeman Warned: Don't Fly the Flag," *Sydney Morning Herald*, July 20, 1996.
29. Bill Meyers, "Teams Woo Hispanic Fans," *USA Today*, September 29, 1997, p. 8C.

30. Ibid.
31. From "A Short History of Latino Baseball," *USA Today*, September 29, 1997, p. 8C.
32. Ibid.
33. 42 U.S.C.A. 12101 et seq. (1990).
34. Much of the material on stadiums and the ADA is drawn from a law review article "A Hot Dog at the Ballgame: Looking at the Physical Accessibility of Professional Baseball Stadiums in Northern New England," by Lee A. Perselary, *N.H. Bar Journal*, December 1997, p. 73.
35. Harry Blauvelt, "Martin Now Ready to Compete," *USA Today*, February 12, 1998, p. 6C.
36. Bill Meyers and Liz Clarke, "No Trouble Foreseen in Finding Sponsors," *USA Today*, June 23, 1997, p. 3B.
37. Ibid.
38. Ibid.

APPENDIXES

Text of NCAA Drug Testing Consent Form

FOR: STUDENT ATHLETES
ACTION: SIGN AND RETURN TO YOUR DIRECTOR
OF ATHLETICS
DUE DATE: In sports in which the Association does not conduct year-round drug testing, before the institution's first scheduled intercollegiate competition.

A nonrecruited student athlete in sports other than those sports involved in the Association's year round drug testing program may participate in pre-season practice activities before the team's first contest or date of competition without signing the drug-testing consent.

REQUIRED BY: NCAA Constitution 3.2.4.6 and Bylaws 14.1.4 and
 30.5
PURPOSE: To assist in certifying eligibility.

TO STUDENT ATHLETE

Name of your institution _____

You must sign this form to participate (i.e. practice or compete) in intercollegiate athletics.

The requirement that you sign this form is spelled out in the following articles of the NCAA Division Manual:

- Constitution 3.2.4.6
- Bylaws 14.1.4 and 30.5

If you have any questions, you should discuss them with your director of athletics.

Drug-Testing Consent

By signing this form, you affirm that you are aware of the NCAA drug-testing program, which provides:

A student-athlete who is found to have utilized a substance on the list of banned drugs, as set forth as set forth in Bylaw 31.2.3.1, shall be declared IN-ELIGIBLE for further participation in regular-season and postseason competition in all sports in accordance with the provisions in Bylaw 18.4.1.5.1. The certifying institution may appeal to the NCAA Eligibility Committee for restoration of the student-athlete's eligibility if the institution concludes that circumstances warrant restoration. (Bylaw 18.4.1.5)

A student-athlete who tests positive outside the sports season (in accordance with the testing methods authorized by the NCAA Executive Committee) shall be INELIGIBLE to participate in regular-season and postseason competition during the time period of one calendar year (i.e., 365 days) after the positive drug test, and shall be charged with the loss of a minimum of one season of competition in all sports. A student-athlete who tests positive during the playing season (in accordance with the testing methods authorized by the NCAA Executive Committee) shall be INELIGIBLE to participate in regular-season and postseason competition during the time period ending one calendar year after the positive drug test. The student-athlete also will lose all remaining eligibility during the season in which he or she tested positive, and, in addition, shall be charged with the loss of a minimum of one season of competition in all sports.

The student-athlete shall remain INELIGIBLE for all regular-season and postseason competition during the time period ending one calendar year after the student-athlete's positive drug test, and until the student-athlete retests negative (in accordance with the testing methods authorized by the NCAA Executive Committee) and the student-athlete's eligibility is restored by the Eligibility Committee.

If the student-athlete tests positive a second time for the use of any drug, other than a "street drug" as defined in Bylaw 31.2.3.1, he or she shall lose all remaining regular-season and postseason eligibility in all sports. In addition, the penalty for missing a scheduled drug test is the same as the penalty for testing positive for the use of a banned drug.

If the student-athlete tests positive for the use of a "street drug" after being restored to eligibility, he or she shall be charged with the loss of a minimum of one additional season of competition in all sports and also shall remain INELIGIBLE for regular-season and postseason competition at least through the next calendar year. (Bylaw 18.4.1.5.1)

The Executive Committee shall adopt a list of banned drugs, and shall authorize methods for drug testing of student-athletes on a year-round basis. This list of banned drugs and the procedure for informing member institutions about authorized methods for drug testing are set forth in Bylaws 31.2.3.1and 31.2.3.3, respectively. (Bylaw 18.4.1.5.2)

You agree to allow the NCAA to test you in relation to any participation by you in any NCAA championship or in any postseason football game certified by the NCAA for the banned drugs listed in Bylaw 31.2.3.1. Additionally, if you participate in Division II football, you also agree to be tested on a year-round basis for anabolic agents, diuretics and urine manipulators.

You were provided an opportunity to review the procedures for NCAA drug testing that are described in the NCAA Drug-Testing program brochure.

You understand that this consent and the results of your drug tests, if any, will only be disclosed in accordance with the provisions of the Buckley Amendment consent.

You agree to disclose your drug-testing results only for purposes related to your eligibility for participation in regular-season and postseason competition.

You affirm that you understand that if you sign this statement falsely or erroneously you violate NCAA legislation on ethical conduct and you will further jeopardize your eligibility.

Date	Signature of Student-Athlete
Date	Signature of Parent (if student-athlete is a minor)
Name (please print)	Date of birth
Home Address	
Sport(s)	

The Amateur Sports Act of 1978—Excerpts: Olympic Committee

36 U.S.C. § 373. Definitions

As used in this chapter, the term—

(1) "amateur athlete" means any athlete who meets the eligibility standards established by the national governing body for the sport in which the athlete competes;

(2) "amateur athletic competition" means a contest, game, meet, match, tournament, regatta, or other event in which amateur athletes compete;

(3) "amateur sports organization" means a not-for-profit corporation, club, federation, union, association, or other group organized in the United States which sponsors or arranges any amateur athletic competition;

(4) "Corporation" means the United States Olympic Committee;

(5) "international amateur athletic competition" means any amateur athletic competition between any athlete or athletes representing the United States, either individually or as part of a team, and any athlete or athletes representing any foreign country;

(6) "national governing body" means an amateur sports organization which is recognized by the Corporation in accordance with section 391 of this title; and

(7) "sanction" means a certificate of approval issued by a national governing body.

36 U.S.C. § 374. Objects and purposes of Corporation

The objects and purposes of the Corporation shall be to—

(1) establish national goals for amateur athletic activities and encourage the attainment of those goals;

(2) coordinate and develop amateur athletic activity in the United States directly relating to international amateur athletic competition, so as

to foster productive working relationships among sports-related organizations;

(3) exercise exclusive jurisdiction, either directly or through its constituent members or committees, over all matters pertaining to the participation of the United States in the Olympic Games and in the Pan-American Games, including the representation of the United States in such games, and over the organization of the Olympic Games and the Pan-American Games when held in the United States;

(4) obtain for the United States, either directly or by delegation to the appropriate national governing body, the most competent amateur representation possible in each competition and event of the Olympic Games and of the Pan-American Games;

(5) promote and support amateur athletic activities involving the United States and foreign nations;

(8) provide for the swift resolution of conflicts and disputes involving amateur athletes, national governing bodies, and amateur sports organizations, and protect the opportunity of any amateur athlete, coach, trainer, manager administrator, or official to participate in amateur athletic competition * * *.

36 U.S.C. § 375.   Powers of Corporation

(a) The Corporation shall have perpetual succession and power to—

(1) serve as the coordinating body for amateur athletic activity in the United States directly relating to international amateur athletic competition;

(2) represent the United States as its national Olympic committee in relations with the International Olympic Committee and the Pan-American Sports Organization;

(3) organize, finance, and control the representation of the United States in the competitions and events of the Olympic Games and of the Pan-American Games, and obtain, either directly or by delegation to the appropriate national governing body, amateur representation for such games;

(4) recognize eligible amateur sports organizations as national governing bodies for any sport which is included on the program of the Olympic Games or the Pan-American Games;

(5) facilitate, through orderly and effective administrative procedures, the resolution of conflicts or disputes which involve any of its members and any amateur athlete, coach, trainer, manager, administrator, official, national governing body, or amateur sports organization and which arise in connection with their eligibility for and participation in the Olympic Games, the Pan-American world championship competition, or other protected competition as defined in the constitution and bylaws of the Corporation;

(16) do any and all acts and things necessary and proper to carry out the purposes of the Corporation.

36 U.S.C. § 377.   Nonpolitical nature of Corporation

The Corporation shall be nonpolitical and, as an organization, shall not promote the candidacy of any person seeking public office.

36 U.S.C. § 391.   Recognition of amateur sports organizations

(a) **National governing body; application; notice and hearing**—For any sport which is included on the program of the Olympic Games or the Pan-American Games, the Corporation is authorized to recognize as a national governing body an amateur sports organization which files an application and is eligible for such recognition, in accordance with the provisions of subsection (b) of this section. The Corporation shall recognize only one national governing body for each sport for which application is made and approved. * * *

(d) **Recommendation of national governing body as United States representative to appropriate international sports federation**—Within 61 days after recognizing an amateur sports organization as a national governing body, * * * the Corporation shall recommend and support in any appropriate manner such national governing body to the appropriate international sports federation as the representative of the United States for that sport.

36 U.S.C. § 392.   Duties of national governing bodies

(a) For the sport which it governs, a national governing body is under a duty to—

(1) develop interest and participation throughout the United States and be responsible to the persons and amateur sports organizations it represents;

(2) minimize, through coordination with other amateur sports organizations, conflicts in the scheduling of all practices and competitions;

(3) keep amateur athletes informed of policy matters and reasonably reflect the views of such athletes in its policy decisions;

(4) promptly review every request submitted by an amateur sports organization or person for a sanction (A) to hold an international amateur athletic competition in the United States; or (B) to sponsor United States amateur athletes to compete in international amateur athletic competition held outside the United States, and determine whether to grant such sanction, in accordance with the provisions of subsection (b) of this section;

(5) allow an amateur athlete to compete in any international amateur athletic competition conducted under its auspices or that of any other amateur sports organization or person, unless it establishes that its denial was based on evidence that the organization or person conducting the competition did not meet the requirements stated in subsection (b) of this section;

36 U.S.C. § 393.   Authority of national governing bodies

For the sport which it governs, a national governing body is authorized to—

(1) represent the United States in the appropriate international sports federation;

(2) establish national goals and encourage the attainment of those goals;

(3) serve as the coordinating body for amateur athletic activity in the United States;

(4) exercise jurisdiction over international amateur athletic activities and sanction international amateur athletic competition held in the United States and sanction the sponsorship of international amateur athletic competition held outside the United States;

(5) conduct amateur athletic competition, including national championships and international amateur athletic competition in the United States, and establish procedures for the determination of eligibility standards for participation in such competitions * * *;

(6) recommend to the Corporation individuals and teams to represent the United States in the Olympic Games and the Pan-American Games; and

(7) designate individuals and teams to represent the United States in international amateur athletic competition (other than the Olympic Games and the Pan-American Games) and certify, in accordance with applicable international rules, the amateur eligibility of such individuals and teams.

36 U.S.C. § 395.   Compelling compliance with eligibility requirements and performance of duties by national governing bodies

(c) *Arbitration of Corporation determinations*

(1) The right to review by any party aggrieved by a determination of the Corporation under the requirements of this section or section 391(c) of this title shall be to any regional office of the American Arbitration Association. Such demand for arbitration shall be submitted within 30 days of the determination of the Corporation.

(5) Final decision of the arbitrators shall be binding upon the involved parties, if such award is not inconsistent with the constitution and bylaws of the Corporation.

The Olympic Charter (Excerpts)

CHAPTER I—THE OLYMPIC MOVEMENT

1. Supreme Authority

1–The IOC is the supreme authority of the Olympic Movement.

2–Any person or organization belonging in any capacity whatsoever to the Olympic Movement is bound by the provisions of the Olympic Charter and shall abide by the decisions of the IOC.

3. Belonging to the Olympic Movement

1–In addition to the IOC, the Olympic Movement includes the International Federations (IF's), the National Olympic Committees (NOC's), the Organizing Committees of the Olympic Games (OCOG's), the national associations, clubs and persons belonging to them, particularly the athletes. Furthermore, the Olympic Movement includes other organizations and institutions as recognized by the IOC.

9. Olympic Games

1–The Olympic Games are competitions between athletes in individual or team events and not between countries. They bring together the athletes designated for such purpose by their respective NOCs, whose entries have been accepted by the IOC, and who compete under the technical direction of the IFs concerned.

2–The authority of last resort on any question concerning the Olympic Games rests in the IOC.

3–The Olympic Games consist of the Games of the Olympiad and the Olympic Winter Games. Both take place every four years under the provisions of Paragraph 4 below.

4–The first Olympic Winter Games were celebrated in 1924. Starting from that date, they are numbered in the order in which they are held, the XVII Olympic Winter Games being however held in 1994. Those sports which are practiced on snow and ice are considered as winter sports.

CHAPTER II—THE INTERNATIONAL OLYMPIC COMMITTEE

19. Legal Status

1–The IOC is an international non-governmental non-profit organization, of unlimited duration, in the form of an association with the status of a legal person, recognized by decree of the Swiss Federal Council of September 17, 1981.

4–The decisions of the IOC, taken on the basis of the provisions of the Olympic Charter, are final. Any dispute relating to their application or interpretation may be resolved solely by the IOC Executive Board and, in certain cases, by arbitration before the Court of Arbitration for Sport (CAS).

28. IOC Resources

1–The IOC may accept gifts or bequests and seek all other resources enabling it to fulfill its tasks. It collects revenues from the exploitation of rights, including television rights, as well as from the celebration of the Olympic Games.

2–The IOC may grant part of the revenues derived from the exploitation of television rights to the IFs, NOCs including Olympic Solidarity and the OCOGs.

CHAPTER III—THE INTERNATIONAL FEDERATIONS

30. Role—1-The role of the IFs is to:

1.1 establish and enforce the rules concerning the practice of their respective sports and to ensure their application;

1.2 ensure the development of their sports throughout the world;

1.3 contribute to the achievement of the goals set out in the Olympic Charter;

1.4 establish their criteria of eligibility to enter the competitions of the Olympic Games in conformity with the Olympic Charter, and to submit these to the IOC for approval;

1.5 assume the responsibility for the technical control and direction of their sports at the Olympic Games and at Games under the patronage of the IOC;

1.6 provide technical assistance in the practical implementation of the Olympic Solidarity program.

CHAPTER IV–THE NATIONAL OLYMPIC COMMITTEES

1–The mission of the NOCs is to develop and protect the Olympic Movement in their respective countries, in accordance with the Olympic Charter.

33. The National Federations—To be recognized by an NOC and accepted as a member of such NOC, a national federation must be affiliated to an IF recognized by the IOC and conduct its activities in compliance with both the Olympic Charter and the rules of its IF.

CHAPTER V—THE OLYMPIC GAMES

39. Organizing Committee

1–The organization of the Olympic Games is entrusted by the IOC to the NOC of the country of the host city as well as to the host city itself. The NOC shall form, for that purpose, an Organizing Committee (OCOG) which, from the time it is constituted, communicates directly with IOC, from which it receives instruction.

45. Eligibility Code— To be eligible for the participation in the Olympic Games a competitor must comply with the Olympic Charter as well as with the rules of the IF concerned as approved by the IOC, and must be entered by his NOC.

BYLAW TO RULE 45

1–Each IF establishes its sport's own eligibility criteria in accordance with the Olympic Charter. Such criteria must be submitted to the IOC Executive Board for approval.

4–No competitor who participates in the Olympic Games allow his person, name, picture, or sports performances to be used for advertising purposes during the Olympic Games.

49. Entries

1–Only NOCs recognized by the IOC may enter competitors in the Olympic Games. The right of final acceptance of entries rests with the IOC Executive Board.

Text of Court of Arbitration for Sports Waiver Form

I, the undersigned, accept that any dispute arising from decisions of the International Triathlon Union (ITU), which cannot be settled by its appeal procedures, shall be settled by the Court of Arbitration for Sport (CAS), Lausanne, Switzerland, to the exclusion of ordinary courts. Upon participating in activities/events sponsored by ITU and/or its affiliated associations, I agree to abide by the rules of ITU as currently published. I understand and appreciate that participation or observation of the sport constitutes a risk to me of serious injury, including permanent paralysis or death. I voluntarily and knowingly recognize, accept and assume the risk and release ITU, its Associates, their Sponsors, Event Organizers and Officials from any liability therefrom.

I grant ITU a license to use my name, likeness, signature, image and any similar or associated trademarks (the "image") in connection with any promotions, public relations, publicity or advertisement produced, broadcast and published either for, by, or on behalf of ITU including without limitation; a) television (including dialogue) whether broadcast free to air or on cable television or satellite; b) cinema (including dialogue); c) video (including dialogue); d) radio; e) public video screens; f) press and materials; g) point of sale materials; h) public relations including documentary material; i) billboards and outdoor advertising; j) merchandise material; k) sales contest materials; l) community service announcements and broadcasts. I grant ITU the right to sub-license this license. I warrant that I have the capacity to grant this license.

Name (Block Capitals) _____
Address _____
Country Representing _____
Signature

_____

NFL Player Contract

THIS CONTRACT is between _____, hereinafter "Player," and _____, a _____ corporation (a limited partnership), hereinafter "Club," operating under the name of the _____ as a member of the National Football League, hereinafter "League." In consideration of the promises made by each to the other, Player and Club agree as follows:

1. TERM. This contract covers one football season, and will begin on the date of execution or April 1, _____, unless extended, terminated, or renewed as specified elsewhere in this contract.

2. EMPLOYMENT AND SERVICES. Club employs Player as a skilled football player. Player accepts such employment. He agrees to give his best efforts and loyalty to the Club, and to conduct himself on and off the field with appropriate recognition of the fact that the success of professional football depends largely on public respect for and approval of those associated with the game. Player will report promptly for and participate fully in Club's official pre-season training camp, all Club meetings and practice sessions, and all pre-season, regular-season and post-season football games scheduled for or by Club. If invited, Player will practice for and play in any all-star football game sponsored by the League. Player will not participate in any football game not sponsored by the League unless the game is first approved by the League.

3. OTHER ACTIVITIES. Without prior written consent of Club, Player will not play football or engage in activities related to football otherwise than for Club or engage in any activity other than football which may involve a significant risk of personal injury. Player represents that he has special, exceptional and unique knowledge, skill, ability, and experience as a football player, the loss of which cannot be estimated with any certainty and cannot be fairly or adequately compensated by damages. Player therefore agrees that Club will have the right, in addition to any other right which Club may possess, to enjoin Player by appropriate proceedings from playing football or engaging in football-related activities other than for Club or from engaging in any activity other than football which may involve a significant risk of personal injury.

4. PUBLICITY. Player grants to Club and League, separately and together, the authority to use his name and picture for publicity and promotional purposes in newspapers, magazines, motion pictures, game programs and roster manuals, broadcasts and telecasts, and all other publicity and advertising media, provided such publicity and promotion does not in itself constitute an endorsement by Player of a commercial product. Player will cooperate with the news media, and will participate upon request in reasonable promotional activities of Club and the League.

5. COMPENSATION. For performance of Player's services and all other promises of Player, Club will pay Player a yearly salary of $_____, payable as provided in Paragraph 6; such earned performance bonuses as may be called for in paragraph 24 of or any attachment to this contract; Player's necessary traveling expenses from his residence to training camp; Player's reasonable board and lodging expenses during pre-season training and in connection with playing pre-season, regular-season, and post-season football games outside Club's home city; Player's necessary traveling expenses to his residence if this contract is terminated by Club; and such additional compensation, benefits and reimbursement of expenses as may be called for in any collective bargaining agreement in existence during the term of this contract. (For purposes of this contract, a collective bargaining agreement will be deemed to be "in existence" during its stated term or during any period for which the parties to that agreement agree to extend it.)

6. PAYMENT. Unless this contract or any collective bargaining agreement in existence during the term of this contract specifically provides otherwise, Player will be paid as follows: If Player has not previously reported to any NFL club's official pre-season training camp in any year, he will be paid 100% of his yearly salary under this contract in equal weekly or bi-weekly installments over the course of the regular season period, commencing with the first regular season game played by Club. If Player has previously reported to any NFL club's official pre-season training camp in any year, he will be paid 10% of his yearly salary under this contract in equal weekly installments over the course of the pre-season period, commencing with the end of the first week of Club's official pre-season training camp as designated for Player and ending one week prior to the first regular season game played by Club, and 90% of his yearly salary in equal weekly or bi-weekly installments over the course of the regular season period, commencing with the first regular season game played by Club. If this contract is executed or Player is activated after the start of Club's official pre-season training camp, the yearly salary will be reduced proportionately and Player will be paid the weekly or bi-weekly portions of his weekly salary becoming due and payable after he is activated. If this contract is terminated after the start of Club's official pre-season training camp, the yearly salary payable to Player will be reduced proportionately and Player will be paid the weekly or bi-weekly portions of his yearly salary becoming due and payable up to the time of termination (prorated daily if termination occurs before one week prior to the first regular season game played by Club).

7. DEDUCTIONS. Any advance made to Player will be repaid to Club, and any properly levied Club fine or Commissioner fine against Player will be paid, in cash on demand or by means of deductions from payments coming due to the Player under this contract, the amount of such deductions to be determined by Club unless this contract specifically provides otherwise.

8. PHYSICAL CONDITION. Player represents to Club that he is and will maintain himself in excellent physical condition. Player will undergo a complete physical examination by the Club physician upon Club request, during which physical examination Player agrees to make full and complete disclosure of any physical or mental condition known to him which might impair his performance under this contract and to respond fully and in good faith when questioned by the Club physician about such condition. If Player fails to establish or maintain his excellent physical condition to the satisfaction of the Club physician, or make the required full and complete disclosure and good faith responses to the Club physician, then Club may terminate this contract.

9. INJURY. If Player is injured in the performance of his services under this contract and promptly reports such injury to the Club physician or trainer, then Player will receive such medical and hospital care during the term of this contract as the Club physician may deem necessary, and, in accordance with Club's practice, will continue to receive his yearly salary for so long, during the season of injury only and for no subsequent period, as Player is physically unable to perform the services required of him by this contract because of such injury. If Player's injury in the performance of his services under this contract results in his death, the unpaid balance of his yearly salary for the season of injury will be paid to his stated beneficiary, or, in the absence of a stated beneficiary, to his estate.

10. WORKMEN'S COMPENSATION. Any compensation paid to Player under this contract or under any collective bargaining agreement in existence during the term of this contract for a period during which he is entitled to workmen's compensation benefits by reason of temporary total, permanent total, temporary partial, or permanent partial disability will be deemed an advance payment of workmen's compensation benefits due Player, and Club will be entitled to be reimbursed the amount of such payment out of any award of workmen's compensation.

11. SKILL, PERFORMANCE AND CONDUCT. Player understands that he is competing with other players for a position on Club's roster within the applicable player limits. If at any time, in the sole judgment of Club, Player's skill or performance has been unsatisfactory as compared with that of other players competing for positions on Club's roster, or if Player has engaged in personal conduct reasonably judged by Club to adversely affect or reflect on Club, then Club may terminate this contract.

12. TERMINATION. The rights of termination set forth in this contract will be in addition to any other rights of termination allowed either party by law. Termination will be effective upon the giving of written notice, except that Player's death, other than as a result of injury incurred in the performance of his services under this contract, will automatically terminate this contract. If this contract is terminated by Club and either Player or Club so requests, Player will promptly undergo a complete physical examination by the Club physician.

13. INJURY GRIEVANCE. Unless a collective bargaining agreement in existence at the time of the termination of this contract by Club provides otherwise, the following injury grievance procedure will apply: If Player believes that at the time of termination of this contract by Club he was physically unable to perform the services required of him by this contract because of an injury incurred in the performance of his services under this contract, Player may, within a reasonably brief time after examination by the Club physician, submit at his own expense to examination by a physician of his choice. If the opinion of Player's physician with respect to his physical ability to perform the services required of him by this contract is contrary to that of the Club's physician, the dispute will be submitted within a reasonable time to final and binding arbitration by an arbitrator selected by Club and Player or, if they are unable to agree, one selected by the League Commissioner on application by either party.

14. RULES. Player will comply with and be bound by all reasonable Club rules and regulations in effect during the term of this contract which are not inconsistent with the provisions of this contract or of any collective bargaining agreement in existence during the term of this contract. Player's attention is also called to the fact that the League functions with certain rules and procedures expressive of its operation as a joint venture among its member clubs and that these rules and practices may affect Player's relationship to the League and its member clubs independently of the provisions of this contract.

15. INTEGRITY OF GAME. Player recognizes the detriment to the League and professional football that would result from impairment of public confidence in the honest and orderly conduct of NFL games or the integrity and good character of NFL players. Player therefore acknowledges his awareness that if he accepts a bribe or agrees to throw or fix an NFL game; fails to promptly report a bribe offer or an attempt to throw or fix an NFL game; bets on an NFL game; knowingly associates with gamblers or gambling activity; uses or provides other players with stimulants or other drugs for the purpose of attempting to enhance on-field performance; or is guilty of any other form of conduct reasonably judged by the League Commissioner to be detrimental to League or professional football, the Commissioner will have the right, but only after giving Player the opportunity for a hearing at which he may be represented by counsel of his choice, to fine in a reasonable amount; to suspend Player for a period certain or indefinitely; and/or to terminate this contract.

16. EXTENSION. If Player becomes a member of the Armed Forces of the United States or any other country, or retires from professional football as an active player, or otherwise fails or refuses to perform his services under this contract, then this contract will be tolled between the date of Player's induction into the Armed Forces, or his retirement, or his failure or refusal to perform, and the later date of his return to professional football. During the period this contract is tolled, Player will not be entitled to any compensation or benefits. On Player's return to professional football, the term of this contract will be extended for a period of time equal to the number of seasons (to the nearest multiple of one) remaining at the time the contract was tolled. The right of renewal, if any, contained in this contract will remain in effect until the end of any such extended term.

17. RENEWAL. Unless this contract specifically provides otherwise, Club may, by sending written notice to Player on or before the April 1 expiration date referred to in Paragraph 1, renew this contract for a period of one year. The terms and conditions for the renewal year will be the same as those provided in this contract for the last preceding year, except that there will be no further right of renewal in Club and, unless this contract specifically provides otherwise, the rate of compensation for the renewal year will be 90% of the rate of compensation provided in this contract for the last preceding year. The phrase "rate of compensation" as used above means yearly salary, including deferred compensation, and any performance bonus, but excluding any signing or reporting bonus. In order for Player to receive 90% of any performance bonus under this contract he must meet the previously established conditions of that bonus during the renewal year.

18. ASSIGNMENT. Unless this contract specifically provides otherwise, Club may assign this contract and Player's services under this contract to any successor to Club's franchise or to any other Club in the League. Player will report to the assignee club promptly upon being informed of the assignment of his contract and will faithfully perform his services under this contract. The assignee club will pay Player's necessary traveling expenses in reporting to it and will faithfully perform this contract with Player.

19. FILING. This contract will be valid and binding upon Player and Club immediately upon execution. A copy of this contract, including any attachment to it, will be filed by Club with the League Commissioner within 10 days after execution. The Commissioner will have the right to disapprove this contract on reasonable grounds, including but not limited to an attempt by the parties to abridge or impair the rights of any other club, uncertainty or incompleteness in expression of the parties' respective rights and obligations, or conflict between the terms of this contract and any collective bargaining agreement then in existence. Approval will be automatic unless, within 10 days after the receipt of this contract in his office, the Commissioner notifies the parties either of disapproval or of extension of this 10-day period for purposes of investigation or clarification pending his decision. On the receipt of notice of disapproval and termination, both parties will be relieved of their respective rights and obligations under this contract.

20. DISPUTES. Any dispute between Player and Club involving the interpretation or application of any provision of this contract will be submitted to final and binding arbitration in accordance with the procedure called for in any collective bargaining agreement in existence at the time the event giving rise to any such dispute occurs. If no collective bargaining agreement is in existence at such time, the dispute will be submitted within a reasonable time to the League Commissioner for final and binding arbitration by him, except as provided otherwise in Paragraph 13 of this contract.

21. NOTICE. Any notice, request, approval, or consent under this contract will be sufficiently given if in writing and delivered in person or mailed (certified or first class) by one party to the other at the address set forth in this contract or to such other address as the recipient may subsequently have furnished in writing to the sender.

22. OTHER AGREEMENTS. This contract, including any attachment to it, sets forth the entire agreement between Player and Club and cannot be modified or supplemented orally. Player and Club represent that no other agreement, oral or written, except as attached to or specifically incorporated in this contract, exists between them. The provisions of this contract will govern the relationship between Player and Club unless there are conflicting provisions in any collective bargaining agreement in existence during the term of this contract, in which case the provisions of the collective bargaining agreement will take precedence over conflicting provisions of this contract relating to the rights or obligations of either party.

23. LAW. This contract is made under and shall be governed by the laws of the state of _____.

NFLPA Regulations Governing Contract Advisors (Player Agents)

SECTION 1: SCOPE OF REGULATIONS

A. Persons Subject to Regulations

No person (other than a player representing himself) shall be permitted to conduct individual contract negotiations of behalf of a player* and/or assist in or advise with respect to such negotiations with NFL Clubs after the effective date of these Regulations unless he/she is (1) currently certified as a Contract Advisor pursuant to these Regulations; (2) signs the "Standard Representation Agreement Between NFLPA Contract Advisor and Player" with the player (See Section 4); and (3) files a fully executed copy of the Standard Representation Agreement with the NFLPA, along with any contract(s) between the player and the Contract Advisor for other services to be provided.

B. Activities Covered

The activities of Contract Advisors which are governed by these Regulations include: the providing of advice, counsel, information or assistance to players with respect to negotiating their individual contracts with Clubs and/or thereafter in enforcing those contracts; the conduct of individual compensation negotiations with the Clubs on behalf of players; and any other activity or conduct which directly bears upon the Contract Advisor's integrity, competence or ability to properly represent individual NFL players and the NFLPA in individual contract negotiations, including the handling of player funds, providing tax counseling and preparation services, and providing financial advice and investment services to individual players.

---

*For purposes of these regulations, the term "player" shall mean anyone eligible to play in the National Football League, including a player about to enter his rookie season in the NFL.

166

C. Amendments

These Regulations may be amended from time to time by the Officers and Board of Player Representatives of the NFLPA in its sole discretion.

SECTION 2: CERTIFICATION

After the effective date of these Regulations, any person who wishes to perform the functions of a Contract Advisor as described in Section 1 above must be certified by the NFLPA pursuant to the following procedure:

A. Application For Certification

A person must file a verified Application for Certification as a Contract Advisor (in the form attached as Appendix A) with the NFLPA, and pay the required application fee as established by the NFLPA Board of Player Representatives. Certification will be granted hereunder only to individuals and not any firm, corporation, partnership or other business entity. There is no limit on the number of individuals in any one firm, corporation, partnership or other business entity who are eligible for certification.

To be eligible for certification, the applicant must have received a degree from an accredited four year college/university. However, the NFLPA shall have the authority to grant exceptions to this requirement in cases where the applicant has sufficient negotiating experience.

Within forty five (45) days of the filing of an Application for Certification, the NFLPA shall determine whether certification shall be granted to the applicant; provided, however, that this period may be extended for an additional ninety (90) days upon written notification to the applicant before the expiration of the initial forty five (45) day period. Upon receipt of an Application for Certification, the NFLPA may, in the context of reviewing the application, request further written materials from the applicant and/or conduct whatever further investigation it deems appropriate, including an informal conference with the applicant.

B. Interim Certification

During the period in which an Application for Certification is pending, the NFLPA may authorize any person who has filed an Application to provide representational services to one or more players engaged in individual contract negotiations with NFL Clubs if the NFLPA deems such authorization to be in the player's best interest. However, such interim action shall be specifically limited to the terms contained in the NFLPA's authorization and, in any event, shall not constitute a waiver of the NFLPA's right thereafter to deny certification under these Regulations.

C. Certification of Member Contract Advisors Under the NFLPA Code of Conduct

All persons who desire to be certified hereunder, including those who were Member Contract Advisors in good standing under the prior, voluntary Code of Conduct for NFLPA Member Contract Advisors as of the effective date of these Regulations, must file an Application for Certification pursuant to these Regulations. Applicants who were Member Contract Advisors pursuant to the prior Code as of the effective date of these Regulations shall not be required to pay an application fee to become certified, but shall be required to make annual fee payments required by these Regulations.

D. Grounds for Denial of Certification

Grounds for denial of Certification shall include, but not be limited to, the following:

- The applicant has made false or misleading statements of a material nature in his/her application;
- The applicant has misappropriated funds, or engaged in other specific acts such as embezzlement, theft or fraud, which would render him/her unfit to serve in a fiduciary capacity on behalf of players;
- The applicant has engaged in any other conduct the significantly impacts adversely on his/her credibility, integrity or competence to serve in a fiduciary capacity on behalf of players;
- The applicant is unwilling to swear or affirm that he/she will comply with these Regulations and any amendments hereto and/or that he/she will abide by the fee structure contained in the Standard Representation Agreement incorporated into these Regulations;
- The applicant has been denied certification by another professional sports players association.

E. Appeal from Denial of Certification

In the event an application for certification is denied pursuant to this Section, the applicant shall be notified in writing (by prepaid certified mail) of the reasons for the denial. The applicant may appeal such action to the Arbitrator appointed pursuant to Section 5 of these Regulations. Such appeal shall be initiated by filing (by prepaid certified mail) a written notice of appeal with the NFLPA within thirty (30) days of receipt of the notice denying his/her application for certification. The appeal shall be processed and resolved in accordance with the arbitration procedures set for in Section 5(E) through 5(H) of these Regulations, which shall be the exclusive procedure for challenging any denial of Certification hereunder.

F. Suspension or Revocation of Certification

At any time subsequent to granting certification to a Contract Advisor, the NFLPA may, based upon information brought to its attention or acting on its own initiative, propose the suspension or revocation of such certification on any ground that would have provided a basis for denying certification in the first place (see Section 2(D)) and/or for conduct prohibited in Section 3(B)(1) through 3(B)(18) of these Regulations. Any such proposed suspension or revocation must be sent by prepaid certified mail to the Contract Advisor's office for residence (see Section 6). The Contract Advisor may challenge any such proposed suspension or revocation by appealing such action pursuant to Section 6(B) through 6(H). The appeal to arbitration shall constitute the exclusive method of challenging any proposed suspension or revocation of certification.

G. Provisional Certification

The NFLPA may grant a Provisional Certification under these Regulations in cases where the applicant has never represented an NFL player in individual contract negotiations. This Provisional Certification shall expire by its own terms one year after its issuance, and the applicant shall be permitted to conduct individual contract negotiations on behalf of NFL players during such year so long as the applicant has attended an NFLPA seminar prior to commencing such negotiations. In the event that it is not possible for the applicant to attend an NFLPA seminar prior to commencing negotiations, such negotiations may be conducted by the applicant only at the discretion of the NFLPA.

H. Form of Certification

Upon approving an Application for Certification as a Contract Advisor, the NFLPA shall provide the applicant with a written certification in the form attached hereto as Appendix B. (If a Provisional Certification is issued by the NFLPA, it shall be clearly identified as such, with the word "Provisional" appearing in prominent type of the Certification form.)

The applicant will thereupon be authorized to serve as a Contract Advisor in conducting individual player negotiations with NFL Clubs and/or assisting in or advising with respect to such negotiations. In granting either a Certification or Provisional Certification, the NFLPA shall not be deemed to have endorsed any Contract Advisor; nor shall the grant of such Certification or Provisional Certification be deemed to impose liability upon the NFLPA for any acts or omissions of the Contract Advisor in providing representation to any player, whether or not such acts or omissions fall within activities governed by these Regulations.

I. Application and Annual Fees

(1) Application Fees

Each applicant for certification as a Contract Advisor under these Regulations shall submit with his/her fully completed application a one-time fee as set by the Board of Player Representatives. (This payment is not required for those persons who were Member Contract Advisors in good standing under the previous Code of Conduct For NFLPA Member Contract Advisors which existed immediately prior to the effective date of these Regulations, and who apply to become certified Contract Advisors hereunder within a reasonable time.)

(2) Annual Fee

Each Contract Advisor who is certified shall pay an annual fee to the NFLPA, as set by the Board of Player Representatives, to defray the cost of maintaining this agent-regulation system.

SECTION 3: STANDARD OF CONDUCT FOR CONTRACT ADVISORS

The objective of the NFLPA in implementing these Regulations is to enable players to make in informed selection of a Contract Advisor and to help assure that the Contract Advisor will provide effective representation at fair, reasonable, and uniformly applicable rates to those individual players he/she represents, and to avoid any conflict of interest which could potentially compromise the best interests of NFL players.

A. General Requirements

Consistent with this objective, a Contract Advisor shall be required to:

(1) Disclose his/her Application and thereafter upon request of the NFLPA all information relevant to his/her qualifications to serve as Contract Advisor, including, but not limited to, background, special training, experience in negotiations, past representation of professional athletes, and relevant business associations or memberships in professional organization;

(2) Pay an application fee pursuant to Section 2 above unless waived;

(3) Pay the annual fee in a timely manner as established by the Board of Player Representatives;

(4) Attend an NFLPA seminar on individual contract negotiations each year;

(5) Comply with the maximum fee schedule and all other provisions of these Regulations and any amendments thereto;

(6) Execute and abide by the printed Standard Representation Agreement with all players represented and file with the NFLPA a copy of that

fully executed Agreement along with any other contract(s) for additional services that the Contract Advisor has executed with the player'

(7) Advice the affected player and report to the NFLPA any known violations by an NFL Club of a player's individual contract or of his rights under any applicable CBA;

(8) Sign and provide the NFLPA and the club with a copy of any player contract negotiated with that club within 48 hours after the contract is executed (Contract shall be sent by facsimile or overnight mail);

(9) Provide on or before May 1 each year, to every player who he/she represents, with a copy to the NFLPA, an itemized statement covering the period March 1 through February 28 or 29 of that year, which separately sets forth both the fee charged to the player for, and any expenses incurred in connection with the performance of the following services:

(a) individual player salary negotiations, (b) management of the player's assets, (c) financial, investment, legal, tax and/or other advice to the player, and (d) and other miscellaneous services;

(10) Permit a person or firm authorized by a former or current player-client to conduct an audit of all relevant books and records relating to any services provided to that player;

(11) Notify the NFLPA promptly of any significant changes in the contract Advisor's status relevant to continued certification as a Contract Advisor. Specifically, on or before May 1 of each year, a Contract Advisor is required to notify the NFLPA in writing of:

(a) Any change involving employment status since the filing of his/her Application for Certification;

(b) Any change in the list of player(s) Contract Advisor represents since the filing of her/her Application for Certification;

(c) Any disciplinary proceeding initiated against Contract Advisor, or any formal charge or complaint filed against Contract Advisor in his/her professional capacity since the filing of his/her Application for Certification;

(12) For those Contract Advisors who are Member Contract Advisors as of the effective date of these Regulations, and who apply for Certification pursuant to Section 2C above, provide to each player that Contract Advisor currently represents on or before February 1, 1995, a copy of his/her revised Application for Certification as submitted to the NFLPA;

(13) Provide the NFLPA with all materials that the NFLPA deems relevant with respect to any investigation conducted pursuant to these Regulations and in all other respects cooperate fully with the NFLPA;

(14) Fully comply with applicable state and federal laws;

(15) Become and remain sufficiently educated with regard to NFL structure and economics, applicable Collective Bargaining Agreements and other governing documents, basic negotiating techniques, and developments in sports law and related subjects;

(16) Disclose in an addendum attached to the Standard Representation Agreement between the Contract Advisor and player, the names and current positions of any NFL management personnel whom Contract Advisor represents or has represented in matters pertaining to their employment by or association with any NFL club.

B. Prohibited Conduct

Contract Advisors are prohibited from:

(1) Representing any player in individual contract negotiations with any Club unless he/she (i) is an NFLPA Certified Contract Advisor; (ii) has signed the Standard Representation Agreement with each such player; and (iii) has filed a copy of the Standard Representation Agreement with the NFLPA along with any other contract(s) or agreement(s) between the player and the Contract Advisor;

(2) Providing or offering a monetary inducement to any player or prospective player to induce or encourage that person to utilize his/her services;

(3) Providing or offering money or any other things of value to a member of the player or prospective player's family or any other person for the purpose of inducing or encouraging that person to recommend the services of the Contract Advisor;

(4) Providing materially false or misleading information to any player or prospective player in the context of recruiting the player as a client or in the course of representing that player as his Contract Advisor;

(5) Representing or suggesting to any player or prospective player that his/her NFLPA certification is an endorsement or recommendation by the NFLPA of the Contract Advisor or the Contract Advisor's qualifications or services;

(6) Holding or seeking to hold, either directly or indirectly, a financial interest in any professional football Club or in any other business entity when such investment could create an actual conflict of interest or the appearance of a conflict of interest in the representation of NFL players;

(7) Engaging in any other activity which creates an actual or potential conflict of interest with the effective representation of NFL players;

(8) Soliciting or accepting money or anything of value from any NFL Club in a way that would create an actual or apparent conflict of interest with the interests of any player Contract Advisor represents;

(9) Negotiating and/or agreeing to any provision in a player contract which deprives or purports to deprive that player of any benefit contained in any collectively bargained agreement between the NFL and the NFLPA or any other provision of any applicable documents which protect the working conditions of NFL Players;

(10) Negotiating and/or agreeing to any provision in any agreement involving a player which directly or indirectly violates any stated policies or rules established by the NFLPA;

(11) Concealing material facts from any player whom the Contract Advisor is representing which relate to the subject of the player's individual contract negotiation;

(12) Failing to advise the player and to report to the NFLPA any known violations by an NFL club of a player's individual contract;

(13) Engaging in unlawful conduct and/or conduct involving dishonesty, fraud, deceit, misrepresentation, or other activity which reflects adversely on his/her fitness as a Contract Advisor or jeopardizes his/her effective representation of NFL players;

(14) Failure to comply with the maximum free provisions contained in Section 4 of these Regulations;

(15) Circumventing the maximum fee provisions set forth in the Regulations by knowingly and intentionally increasing the fees that Contract Advisor charges or otherwise would have charged the player for other services including, but not limited to, financial consultation, money management, and/or negotiating player endorsement agreements;

(16) Failing to provide to each player represented and the NFLPA the annual statements required by Section 3(A)(9) of these Regulations and/or failing to provide NFLPA copies of all agreements between the Contract Advisor and each player as required by Section 3(A)(6) of these Regulations;

(17) Filing any lawsuit or other proceeding against a player for any matter which is subject to the exclusive arbitration provisions contained in Section 5 of these Regulations; and

(18) Violating any other provision of these Regulations.

A Contract Advisor who engages in any prohibited conduct as defined above shall be subject to discipline in accordance with the procedures of Section 6 of these Regulations.

SECTION 4: AGREEMENTS BETWEEN CONTRACT ADVISORS AND PLAYERS; MAXIMUM FEES

A. Standard Form

Any agreement between a Contract Advisor and a player entered into after the effective date of these Regulations, which is not in writing in the preprinted form attached hereto as Appendix C or which does not meet the requirements of the Regulations, shall not be enforceable against any player and no Contract Advisor shall have the right to assert any claim against the player for compensation on the basis of such a purported contract.

B. Contract Advisor's Compensation

(1) The maximum fee which may be charged or collected by a Contract Advisor shall be three percent (3%) of the "compensation" (as defined within this Section) received by the player in each playing season covered by the contract negotiated by the Contract Advisor.

(2) The Contract Advisor and player may agree to any fee which is less than the maximum fee set forth in (1) above.

(3) As used in this Section 4(B), the term "compensation" shall be deemed to include only salaries, signing bonuses, reporting bonuses, roster bonuses, and any performance incentives earned by the player during the term of the contract (including option year) negotiated by the Contract Advisor. For example, and without limitation, the term compensation shall not include any "honor" incentive bonuses (e.g. ALL PRO, PRO BOWL, Rookie of the Year), or any collectively bargained benefits or other payments provided for in the player's individual contract.

(4) A Contract Advisor is prohibited from receiving any fee for his/her services until and unless the player receives the compensation upon which the fee is based. However, these Regulations recognize that in certain circumstances a player may decide that it is in his best interest to pay his Contract Advisor's fee in advance of the receipt of any deferred compensation from his NFL club. Accordingly, a player may enter into an agreement with a Contract Advisor to pay the Contract Advisor a fee advance on deferred compensation due and payable to the player. Such fee advance may only be collected by the Contract Advisor after the player has performed the services necessary under his contract to entitle him to the deferred compensation. Further, such an agreement between a Contract Advisor and a player must be in writing, with a copy sent by the Contract Advisor to the NFLPA.

For purposes of determining the fee advance, the compensation shall be determined to be an amount equal to the present value of the deferred player compensation. The rate used to determine the present value of the deferred compensation shall be the rate used in Article XXIV, Section 7(a)(ii) of the 1993 CBA.

C. Existing Agreements

Any agreement in existence between an NFL player and a Contract Advisor as of the effective date of these Regulations shall be deemed modified in accordance with these Regulations, except as such agreement shall pertain to the Contract Advisor's fees for the negotiation of NFL player contracts signed on or before the effective date of these Regulations. To the extent that such existing agreement is less favorable to the NFL player than the provisions of these Regulations, these Regulations shall control insofar as they apply to the negotiation of the player's contract with an NFL club. Provisions of agreement(s) which apply to matters other than the negotiation of the player's contract (e.g., financial consulting or money management services), may be considered severable and not affected by these Regulations. Any dispute concerning the proper application of these Regulations to existing agreements shall be resolved exclusively through the Arbitration procedures set forth in Section 5 of these Regulations.

SECTION 5: ARBITRATION PROCEDURES

A. Disputes

This arbitration procedure shall be the exclusive method for resolving any and all disputes that may arise from the following:

(1) Denial by the NFLPA of an Applicant's Application for Certification;

(2) Any dispute between an NFL player and a Contract Advisor with respect to the conduct of individual negotiations by Contract Advisor;

(3) The meaning, interpretation or enforcement of a fee agreement; and/or

(4) Any other activities of a Contract Advisor within the scope of these Regulations.

(With respect to any dispute that may arise pursuant to paragraph (1) above, the procedure for filing an appeal and invoking arbitration is set forth in these Regulations at Section 2(E). Once arbitration has been invoked. the procedure set forth in subparagraphs (E)–(H) below shall apply.)

B. Filing

The arbitration of a dispute under Section 5(A)(2)–(4) above shall be initiated by the filing of a written grievance either by the player or Contract Advisor. Any such grievance must be filed within six (6) months from the date of the occurrence of the event upon which the grievance is based or within six (6) months from the date on which the facts of the matter become known or reasonably should have become known to the grievant, whichever is later. A player need not be under contract to an NFL club at the time a grievance relating to him hereunder arises or at the time such grievance is initiated or processed.

A player may initiate a grievance against a Contract Advisor by (i) sending the written grievance by prepaid certified mail to the Contract Advisor's business address or by personal delivery at such address, and (ii) sending a copy to the NFLPA. The written grievance shall set forth the facts and circumstances giving rise to the grievance, the provision(s) of the agreement between the player and Contract Advisor alleged to have been violated, and the relief sought.

C. Answer

The party against whom a grievance has been filed ("the respondent') shall answer the grievance in writing by certified mail or personal delivery to the grievant and the NFLPA within twenty (20) calendar days of receipt of the grievance. The answer shall admit or deny the facts alleged in the grievance and shall also briefly set forth, where applicable, the reasons why the respondent believes the grievance should be denied. No later than thirty days (30) after receipt of the grievance, the NFLPA shall provide the Arbitrator with copies of the grievance and answer and all other relevant documents. If an answer is not filed within this time limit, the Arbitrator, in his/her discretion, may issue an order where appropriate, granting the grievance and the requested relief upon satisfactory proof of the claim.

D. Arbitrator

NFLPA shall select a skilled and experienced person to serve as the outside impartial Arbitrator for all cases arising hereunder.

E. Hearing

After receipt of the grievance documents pursuant to this subsection (C), the Arbitrator shall select a time and place for a hearing on the dispute, giving due consideration to the convenience of the parties involved and the degree of urgency for resolution of the dispute. Upon written request from either party prior to the hearing, the NFLPA shall provide the parties copies of documents in its possession which are relevant to the dispute. these documents shall include but not be limited to NFL Player Contracts, other salary information, and Standard Representation Agreements.

At such hearing, all parties to the dispute and the NFLPA will have the right to present, by testimony or otherwise, any evidence relevant to the grievance. If a witness is unavailable to come to the hearing, the witness' testimony may be taken by telephone conference call if the parties agree. All hearings shall be transcribed. At the close of the hearing or within thirty (30) days thereafter, the Arbitrator shall issue a written decision.

Such decision shall constitute full, final and complete disposition of the grievance, and will be binding upon the player and Contract Advisor involved; provided, however, that the Arbitrator will not have the jurisdiction or authority to add to, subtract from, or alter in any way the provisions of these Regulations or any other applicable document. If the Arbitrator grants a money award, it shall be paid within ten (10) days. The Arbitrator may award interest at his/her discretion.

F. Telephone Conference Call Hearings

Any hearing conducted pursuant to the provisions of this Section in which the amount in dispute is less than $10,000 shall be conducted via telephone conference call if any party so requests.

G. Costs

Each party will bear the costs of its own witnesses and counsel. Costs of arbitration, including the fees and expenses of the Arbitrator, will borne equally between the parties to the grievance; provided, however, that the Arbitrator may assess some or all of a party's costs to an opposing party if the Arbitrator deems a party's position in the case to be frivolous and/or totally without merit.

H. Time Limits

The time limits of this Section may be extended only by written agreement of the parties.

SECTION 6: OVERSIGHT AND COMPLIANCE PROCEDURE

A. Disciplinary Committee

The President of the NFLPA shall appoint a three-person Disciplinary Committee which may prosecute disciplinary procedures against Contract Advisors who violate these Regulations. The Disciplinary Committee shall consist of active or retired NFL players chosen at the discretion of the President. The General Counsel of the NFLPA shall serve as a non-voting advisor to the Committee and will serve as its Counsel in prosecuting disciplinary actions pursuant to this Section.

B. Complaint; Filing

Disciplinary proceedings against any Certified Contract Advisor shall be initiated by the filing of a written Complaint against the Contract Advisor by the Disciplinary Committee. Such complaint shall be based upon verified information received by the Disciplinary Committee from any person having knowledge of the action or conduct of the Contact Advisor in question, including, but not limited to, players, NFLPA staff, other Contract Advisors, NFL Management Personnel, or other persons associated with professional or amateur football. The Complaint shall be sent to the Contract Advisor by prepaid certified mail addressed to the Contract Advisor's business office, or may be hand-delivered to the Contract Advisor personally at his/her business address. The Complaint shall set forth the specific action or conduct giving rise to the Complaints and cite the Regulation(s) alleged to have been violated.

A Complaint must be filed by the Disciplinary Committee within one year from the date of the occurrence which gave rise to the Complaints, or within one year from the date on which the information became known or reasonably should have become known to the Disciplinary Committee, whichever is later. The filing deadline for initiating a Complaint arising out of facts which are the subject of a Section 5 grievance or any other litigation shall be extended to one year from the date of the Arbitrator's final decision in the Section 5 grievance or final decision in such other litigation.

C. Answer

The Contract Advisor against whom the Complaints has been filed shall have thirty (30) days in which to file a written answer to the Complaints. Such answer shall be sent by prepaid certified mail to the Disciplinary Committee at the offices of the NFLPA. The answer must admit or deny the facts alleged in the Complaint, and must assert and facts or arguments which the Contract Advisor wishes to state in his/her defense. Failure to file a timely answer shall be deemed an admission of the allegations in the Complaint and a consent to the revocation of the Contract Advisor's Certification and/or to any other discipline imposed by the Committee.

D. Proposed Disciplinary Action

Within thirty (30) days after receipt of the answer, the Disciplinary Committee shall inform the Contract Advisor in writing (by prepaid certified mail) of the nature of the discipline, if any, which the Committee proposes to impose, which discipline may include one or more of the following:

(1) Issuance by the Committee of an informal order of reprimand to be retained in the Contract Advisor's file at the NFLPA's offices;

(2) Issuance of a formal letter of reprimand which may be made public in NFLPA publications and other media;

(3) Suspension of a Contract Advisor's certified status for a specified period of time during which Contract Advisor shall be prohibited from representing any NFL player in individual contract negotiations with an NFL club or assisting in or advising with respect to such negotiations;

(4) Revocation of the Contract Advisor's Certification hereunder; and/or

(5) Imposition of a fine not to exceed $5,000.

E. Appeal

The Contract Advisor against whom a Complaint has been filed under this Section may appeal the Disciplinary Committee's proposed disciplinary action to the outside arbitrator by filing a written Notice of Appeal with the arbitrator within twenty (20) days following Contract Advisor's receipt of notification of the proposed disciplinary action. The timely filing of a Notice of Appeal shall result in an automatic stay of any disciplinary action.

Within thirty (30) days of receipt of the Notice of Appeal, the arbitrator shall set a time and place for a hearing on the Appeal. The failure of Contract Advisor to file a timely appeal shall be deemed to constitute an acceptance of the discipline which shall then be promptly imposed.

F. Arbitrator

The Arbitrator shall be the same Arbitrator selected to serve pursuant to Section 5, unless such Arbitrator has previously heard and decided a grievance under Section 5 involving the same Contract Advisor and the same factual circumstances which are the subject of the disciplinary action herein. In such cases, the NFLPA shall select another skilled and experienced person to serve as the outside impartial Arbitrator.

G. Conduct of Hearing

At the hearing of any Appeal pursuant to this Section 6, the Disciplinary Committee shall have the burden of proving, by a preponderance of the evidence, the allegations of its Complaint. The Committee and the Contract Advisor shall be afforded a full opportunity to present, through testimony or otherwise, their evidence pertaining to the action or conduct of the Contract Advisor alleged to be in violation of the Regulations. The hearing shall be conducted in accordance with the Voluntary Labor Arbitration Rules of the American Arbitration Association. Each of the parties may appear with counsel or a representative of its choosing. All hearings pursuant to this Section shall be transcribed.

At the close of the hearing or within thirty (30) days thereafter, the Arbitrator shall issue a decision on the Appeal, which decision shall either affirm, vacate or modify the proposed action of the Disciplinary Committee. The arbitrator shall decide two issues: (1) whether the Contract Advisor has engaged in or is engaging in prohibited conduct as alleged by the Committee; and (2) if so, whether the discipline proposed by the Committee should be affirmed or modified. Such decision shall be made in the form of an appropriate written order reflecting the Arbitrator's opinion and shall be final and binding upon all parties.

H. Time Limits, Costs

Each of the time limits set forth in this Section may be extended by mutual written agreement of the parties involved. The fees and expenses of the Arbitrator will be paid by the NFLPA. Each party will bear the costs of its own witnesses and counsel, and other expenses related to its participation in the process.

SECTION 7: EFFECTIVE DATE; AMENDMENT

These Regulations shall become effective on December 1, 1994.

These Regulations may be amended from time to time by the Executive Committee and/or the Board of Player Representatives of the NFLPA.

Standard Representation Agreement: Player and Agent

This AGREEMENT made this_____day of_____, 199_____, by and between _____ (hereinafter "Player") and _____ (hereinafter "Contract Advisor")

WITNESSETH:

In consideration of the mutual promises hereinafter made by each to the other, Player and Contract Advisor agree as follows:

1. General Principles

This agreement is entered into pursuant to and in accordance with the National Football League Players Association (hereinafter "NFLPA") Regulations Governing Contract Advisors (hereinafter "the Regulations") effective December 1, 1994, and as amended thereafter from time to time.

2. Representations

Contract Advisor represents that in advance of executing this Agreement, he/she has been duly certified as a Contract Advisor by the NFLPA. Player acknowledges that the NFLPA certification of the Contract Advisor is neither a recommendation of the Contract Advisor, not a warranty by NFLPA of the Contract Advisor's competence, honesty, skills or qualifications.

Contract Advisor hereby discloses that he/she (check one):[ ] represents or has represented; [ ] does not represent and has not represented NFL management personnel in matters pertaining to their employment by or association with any NFL club. (If Contract Advisor responds in the affirmative, Contract Advisor must attach a written addendum to this Agreement listing names and positions of those NFL Personnel represented.)

3. Contract Services

Player hereby retains Contract Advisor to represent, advise, counsel, and assist Player in the negotiation, execution, and enforcement of his playing contract(s) in the National Football League.

In performing these services, Contract Advisor acknowledges that he/she is acting in a fiduciary capacity on behalf of Player and agrees to act in such a manner as to protect the best interests of Player and assure effective representation of Player in individual contract negotiations with NFL Clubs. Contract Advisor shall be the exclusive representative for the purpose of negotiating player contract for Player. However, Contract Advisor shall not have the authority to bind or commit Player to enter into any contract without actual execution thereof by Player. Once Player agrees to and executes his player contract, Contract Advisor agrees to also sign the player contract and send a copy (by facsimile or overnight mail) to the NFLPA and the NFL Club within 48 hours of execution by Player.

If Player and Contract Advisor have entered into any other agreements or contracts relating to services other than the individual negotiating services described in this Section, describe the nature of the other services covered by the separate agreements:

_____

_____

_____

4. Compensation for Services

If Contract Advisor succeeds in negotiating an NFL Player Contract acceptable to Player and signed by Player during the term hereof, Contract Advisor shall receive a fee of four percent (4 %) of the compensation received by Player for each such playing season, unless a lesser percent (%) or amount has been agreed to by the parties and is noted in the space below.

The parties hereto have agreed to the following lesser fee:

_____

_____

_____

In computing the allowable fee pursuant to this Section 4 the term "compensation" shall include only base salaries, signing bonuses, reporting bonuses, roster bonuses and any performance incentives actually received by Player. The term "compensation" shall not include any "honor" incentive bonuses (i.e. ALL PRO, PRO BOWL, Rookie of the Year), or any collectively bargained benefits.

5. Payment of Contract Advisor's Fee

Contract Advisor shall not be entitled to receive any fee for the performance of his/her services pursuant to this Agreement until Player receives the compensation upon which the fee is based.

However, Player may enter into an agreement with Contract Advisor to pay any fee attributable to deferred compensation due and payable to Player in advance of when the deferred compensation is paid to Player, provided that Player has performed the services necessary under his contract to entitle him to the deferred compensation. Such fee shall be reduced to its present value as specified in the NFLPA Regulations (see Section 4(b)). Such an agreement must also be in writing, with a copy sent to the NFLPA.

In no case shall Contract Advisor accept, directly or indirectly, payment of any fees hereunder from Player's club. Further, Contract Advisor is prohibited from discussing any aspect of his/her fee arrangement hereunder with any club.

6. Expenses

Player shall reimburse Contract Advisor for all reasonable and necessary communication expenses (i.e., telephone and postage) actually incurred by Contract Advisor in connection with the negotiation of Player's NFL contract. Player also shall reimburse Contract Advisor for all reasonable and necessary travel expenses actually incurred by Contract Advisor during the term hereof in the negotiation of Player's NFL contract, but only if such expenses and approximate amounts thereof are approved in advance by Player. Player shall promptly pay all such expenses upon receipt of an itemized, written statement from Contract Advisor.

After each NFL season and prior to the first day of May following each season for which Contract Advisor has received fees and expenses, Contract Advisor must send to Player (with a copy to the NFLPA) an itemized statement covering the period March 1 through February 28th or 29th of that year. Such statement shall set forth both the fees charged to Player for, and any expenses incurred in connection with, the performance of the following services: (a) individual player salary negotiations, (b) management of the player's assets. (c) financial, investment, legal, tax and/or other advice, and (d) any other miscellaneous services.

7. Disclaimer of Liability

Player and Contract Advisor agree that they are not subject to the control or direction of any other person with respect to the timing, place, manner or fashion in which individual negotiations are to be conducted pursuant to this Agreement (except to the extent that Contract Advisor shall comply with NFLPA Regulations) and that they will save and hold harmless the NFLPA, its officers, employees and representatives from any liability whatsoever with respect to their conduct or activities relating to or in connection with this Agreement or such individual negotiations.

8. Disputes

Any and all disputes between Player and Contract Advisor involving the meaning, interpretation, application, or enforcement of this Agreement or the obligations of the parties under this Agreement shall be resolved exclusively through the arbitration procedures set forth in Section 5 of the NFLPA Regulations Governing Contract Advisors.

9. Notices

All notices hereunder shall be effective if sent by certified mail, postage pre-paid to the following addresses:
If to the Contract Advisor:

_____

_____

If to the Player:

_____

_____

10. Entire Agreement

This agreement, along with the NFLPA Regulations, sets forth the entire agreement between the parties hereto and cannot be amended, modified or changed orally. Any written amendments or changes shall be effective only to the extent that they are consistent with the Standard Representation Agreement as approved by the NFLPA.

11. Filing

This contract is signed in triplicate. Contract Advisor agrees to deliver one (1) copy to the NFLPA within five (5) days of its execution; one (1) copy to the Player; and retain one copy for his/her files. Contract Advisor further agrees to submit any other executed agreements between Player and Contract Advisor to NFLPA.

12. Term

The term of this Agreement shall begin on the date hereof and shall continue for the term of any player contract executed pursuant to this Agreement; provided, however, that either party may terminate this Agreement effective five (5) days after written notice of termination is given to the other party. Notice shall be effective for purposes of this paragraph if sent by certified mail, postage prepaid, return receipt requested to the appropriate address contained in this Agreement.

If termination pursuant to the above provision occurs prior to the completion of negotiations for an NFL player contract(s) acceptable to Player and signed by Player, Contract Advisor shall be entitled to compensation for the reasonable value of the services performed in the attempted negotiation of such contract(s) provided such services and time spent thereon are adequately documented by Contract Advisor. If termination pursuant to the above provision occurs after Player has signed an NFL player contract negotiated by Contract Advisor, Contract Advisor shall be entitled to the fee prescribed in Section 4 above for negotiation of such contract(s).

In the event that Player is able to renegotiate any contract(s) previously negotiated by Contract Advisor prior to expiration thereof, Contract Advisor shall still be entitled to the fee he/she would have been paid pursuant to Section 4 above as if such original contract(s) had not been renegotiated. If Contract Advisor represents Player in renegotiation of the original contract(s), the fee for such renegotiation shall be based solely upon the amount which the compensation in the renegotiated contract(s) exceeds the compensation in the original contract(s), whether or not Contract Advisor negotiated the original contract(s).

If the Contract Advisor's certification is suspended or revoked by the NFLPA or the Contract Advisor it otherwise prohibited by the NFLPA from performing the services he/she has agreed to perform herein, this Agreement shall automatically terminate, effective as of the date of such suspension or termination.

13. Governing Law

This Agreement shall be construed, interpreted and enforced according to the laws of the State of _____.

Contract Advisor and Player recognize that certain state statutes regulating sports agents require specified language in the player/agent contract. The parties therefore agree to the following additional language as required by state statute:

Examine this Contract Carefully Before Signing It

IN WITNESS WHEREOF, the parties hereto have hereunder signed their names as hereinafter set forth.

_____

(CONTRACT ADVISOR)

_____

(Street Address)

_____

(City, State, Zip Code)

_____

(Telephone)

_____

(Fax Number)

_____

(PLAYER)

_____

(Street or P.O. Box)

_____

(City, State, Zip Code)

_____

(In-Season Telephone)

_____

(Off-Season Telephone)

Player's Date of Birth:_____

_____

Print Name and Signature of PARENT or GUARDIAN (if Player is under 21 Years of Age)

_____

(Street Address)

_____

(City, State, Zip Code)

_____

(Telephone)

Florida Statutes Professions and Occupations Code Title 32 (Adopted 1988)

468.451. Legislative findings and intent. The Legislature finds that dishonest or unscrupulous practices by agents who solicit representation of student athletes can cause significant harm to student athletes and the academic institutions for which they play. It is the intent of the Legislature to protect the interests of student athletes and academic institutions by regulating the activities of athlete agents which involve student activities at colleges or universities in the state.

468.452. Definitions. For purposes of [this Act], the term:

(1) "Agent contract" means a contract or agreement pursuant to which a student athlete authorizes an athlete agent to represent him in the marketing of his athletic ability or reputation in a sport.

(3) "Student athlete" means any athlete who practices for or otherwise participates in intercollegiate athletics at any college or university that is located in this state.

468.453. Registration

(1) Each athlete agent must register biennially with the Department of Professional Registration on forms to be provided by the department and, at the same time, pay to the department a registration fee not to exceed $500 * * * for which the department shall issue a registration certificate entitling the holder to operate as an athlete agent for a period of 2 years.

(3) It is unlawful for any person to operate as an athlete agent unless he is registered as provided in this section. Violation of this section is a felony of the third degree * * *.

468.454. Contracts

(1) A student athlete who is subject to the rules and regulations of [the NCAA, the NAIA, or the NJCAA], and who enters into an agent contract with an athlete agent, or a contract pursuant to which an athlete is employed as a professional athlete must notify the athletic director or the president of the college

187

in which he is enrolled that he has entered into such a contract. Written notification of entering into a contract must be given prior to practicing for or participating in any athletic event on behalf of any college or university or within 72 hours after entering into the contract, whichever occurs first. Failure of the student athlete to provide this notification is a misdemeanor of the first degree * * *.

(2) [Requires the same notification to be given by the athlete agent.] Failure of the athlete agent to provide this notification is a felony of the third degree * * *.

(4) An agent contract between a student athlete and an athlete agent must have a notice printed near the space for the student athlete's signature which must contain the following statement in ten-point boldface type:

"WARNING: IF YOU AS A STUDENT ATHLETE SIGN THIS CONTRACT, YOU MAY LOSE YOUR ELIGIBILITY TO COMPETE IN INTERCOLLEGIATE ATHLETICS. PURSUANT TO FLORIDA LAW, YOU MUST NOTIFY THE ATHLETIC DIRECTOR OR PRESIDENT OF YOUR COLLEGE OR UNIVERSITY IN WRITING PRIOR TO PRACTICING FOR OR PARTICIPATING IN ANY ATHLETIC EVENT ON BEHALF OF ANY COLLEGE OR UNIVERSITY OR WITHIN 72 HOURS AFTER ENTERING INTO THIS CONTRACT, WHICHEVER OCCURS FIRST. FAILURE TO PROVIDE THIS NOTICE IS A CRIMINAL OFFENSE."

(5) An agent contract entered into between a student athlete and an athlete agent who fails to provide the notification required by this section is void and unenforceable.

(6) Any student athlete or athlete agent who enters into an agent contract and fails to provide the notification required by this section is liable for damages to the college or university in which the student athlete is enrolled that result from the student athlete's subsequent ineligibility. In addition to damages, if any, awarded pursuant to this section, treble damages may be assessed in an amount equal to three times the value of the athletic scholarship furnished by the institution to the student athlete during the student athlete's period of eligibility.

(7) Within 10 days [of signing the contract or notifying the athletic director or president], whichever occurs later, the student athlete shall have the right to rescind the contract or any contractual relationship with the athlete agent by giving notice in writing of his intent to rescind. Such rescission shall be effective upon repayment by the student athlete to the athlete agent of any monetary amounts paid to the student athlete by the athlete agent, exclusive of travel, lodging, meals, and entertainment, or reimbursement therefor, furnished by the athlete agent to the student athlete. The student athlete may not under any circumstances effect a waiver of his right to rescind, and any attempt to do so shall be ineffective.

(8) Postdating of agent contracts is prohibited, and any such postdated contract is void and unenforceable. * * *

4368.456 Prohibited Acts

(1) An agent shall not publish or cause to be published false or misleading information or advertisements, nor give false information or make false promises to an athlete concerning employment.

(2) An agent shall not accept as a client a student athlete referred by an employee or coach for a college or university located in this state in exchange for a rendition of free legal services, the rendition of legal services for a reduced fee, or any other consideration.

(3) An athlete agent shall not enter into any agreement, written or oral, by which the athlete agent offers anything of value to any employee of or a coach for a college or university located in this state in return for the referral of any student athlete clients by that attorney or coach.

(4) An athlete agent shall not offer anything of value to induce a student athlete to enter into an agreement by which the agent will represent the student athlete. However, negotiations regarding the agent's fee shall not be considered an inducement.

(5) An agent shall not conduct business as an athlete agent if his registration is suspended.

Leading College/University Sports Management and Administration Programs

Adelphi University, School of Education, Dept. of Physical Education, Recreation, and Human Performance Science, Garden City, NY 11530.

University of Alabama, Birmingham, Birmingham, AL.

Albertson College of Idaho, 2112 Cleveland Blvd., Caldwell, ID 83605

Alcorn State University, Dept. of HPER, PO Box 510, Loman, MS 39096

Allentown College, 2755 Station Ave., Carter Valley, PA 18034

Appalachian State University, Health, Leisure, and Exercise Science Dept., Varsity Gym, Boone, NC 28608   *Also:* College of Fine and Applied Arts, Dept. of Health, Leisure and Exercise Science, Program in Health and Physical Education, Boone, NC 28608.

University of Arkansas, Dept. of Health Science, Kinesiology, Recreation and Dance, 306 HPER Bldg. Fayetteville, AR 72701

Baldwin-Wallace College, Sport/Dance/Arts Mgmt. Prog. Berea, OH 44017

Ball State University, Health & Phys. Activities Bldg., Muncie, IN 47306

Barry University, School of Human Performance and Leisure Sciences, Program in Sports Management, Miami Shores, FL 33161-6695.

Baylor University, HPER Dept., Box 7313, Waco, TX 76798-7313

Bemidji State University, 1500 Birchmont Dr. NE, Dept. of Phys. Ed., Health & Sport, Bemidji, MN 56601-2699

Boise State University, College of Education, Dept. of Health, Physical Education, and Recreation, Program in Physical Education, Boise, ID 83725-0399.

Bowling Green State University, Sport Management Division, School of HPER, Bowling Green, OH 43403-0248

Brooklyn College of the City University of New York, School of Education, Division of Secondary Education, Program in Physical Education, 2900 Bedford Ave., Brooklyn, NY 11210-2889.

California State University, Fullerton, Dept. of Kinesiology & Health Prom., Fullerton, CA 92634

Campbell University, Dept. of Exercise Science, Box 414, Buies Creek, NC 27506

Canisius College, School of Education and Human Services, Program in Sports Administration, Buffalo, NY 14208-1098.

Capital University, 2199 E. Main St., Dept. of Health & Sport Sciences, Columbus, OH 43209

Central Michigan University, College of Education, Health and Human Services, Dept. of Physical Education & Sport, Mount Pleasant, MI 48859.

Central Missouri State University, College of Education and Human Services, Dept. of Physical Education, Warrensburg, MO 64093.

Central Washington University, Dept. of PEHLS, Ellensburg, WA 98926

Chadron State College, HPER, 10th & Main, Chaldron, NE 69337

Cleveland State University, College of Education, Dept. of Health, Physical Education, Recreation, and Dance, Cleveland, OH 44115.

Columbus College, 4225 University Ave., Columbus, GA 31907-5645

Concordia University, Faculty of Commerce and Administration, Montreal, PQ H3G 1M8, Canada.

University of Connecticut, 2095 Hillside Rd. U-110, Storrs, CT 06269-1110

Davis & Elkins College, Dept. of Health & Phys. Ed., 100 Campus Drive, Elkins, WV 26241-3996

University of Dayton, 300 College Park, Dayton, OH 45469-1210

Delta State University, Box B-2, Cleveland, MS 38733

Eastern Illinois University, 263 Lantz Gym, Charleston, IL 61920

Eastern Kentucky University, College of Health, Physical Education, Recreation and Athletics, Dept. of Physical Education, Richmond, KY 40475-3101.

East Stroudsburg University of Pennsylvania, School of Health Sciences and Human Performance, Dept. of Movement Studies and Exercise Science, East Stroudsburg, PA 18301-2999.

Elon College, Campus Box 2500, Elon College, Elon, NC 27244-2010

University of Evansville, Dept. of Phys. Ed., 1800 Lincoln Ave., Evansville, IN 47722

Florida International University, Dept. of Health, Phys.Ed., & Recreation, Miami, FL 33199

Florida State University, College of Education, Dept. of Physical Education, Program in Administration, Tallahassee, FL 32306.

University of Florida, 305 Florida Gym, Gainesville, FL 32611

George Washington University, School of Business and Public Management, Dept. of Tourism Studies, Washington, DC 20052.

Georgia Southern University, College of Health and Professional Studies, Dept. of Kinesiology, Program in Sports Management, Statesboro, GA 30460.

Georgia State University, College of Education, Dept. of Kinesiology and Health, Program in Sports Administration, Atlanta, GA 30303-3083.

Georgia Tech, International Sports Business and Economics, Atlanta, GA 30332-0525

University of Georgia, Dept. of Phys. Ed/Sport Studies, Athens, GA 30602

Gettysburg College, Dept. of HPE, Bream/Wright/Hauser Athletic Complex , W. Lincoln Ave., Gettysburg, PA 17325-1426

Gonzaga University, Graduate School, School of Education, Program in Administration of Physical Education and Athletics, Spokane, WA 99258.

Grambling State University, College of Education, Program in Sports Administration, Grambling, LA 71245.

Greenville College, 315 E. College Ave., Greenville, IL 62246

Guilford College, Dept. of Sport Studies, 5800 W. Friendly Ave., Greensboro, NC 27410

Hardin-Simmons University, Irvin School of Education, Dept. of Physical Education, Program in Sports and Recreation Management, Abilene, TX 79698-0001.

Harding University, 900 E. Center, Searcy, AR 72143

University of Houston, 123 Melcher Gymnasium, Houston, TX 77204-5331

University of Idaho, Recreation Dept., Memorial Gym #109, Moscow, ID 83844-2429

Illinois State University, Dept. of HPERD, Normal, IL 61761

University of Illinois at Chicago, Dept. of Phys.Ed., 901 W. Roosevelt Rd., Chicago, IL 60608

Indiana State University, Phys. Ed. Dept., HPER Bldg., Terre Haute, IN 47809

Indiana University, Dept. of Kinesiology, HPER 112, Bloomington, IN 47405-4801

Indiana University of Pennsylvania, College of Health and Human Services, Dept. of Health and Physical Education, Indiana, PA 15705.

Iowa State University, Dept. of Health & Human Performance, Ames, IA 50011

Ithaca College, 953 Danby Rd., School of HS&HP, Dept. of Exercise & Sport Science, Ithaca, NY 14850-7193

James Madison University, Dept. of Kinesiology. Godwin Hall. Harrisonburg, VA 22807

Jersey City State College, Athletic/Recreational Fitness Center, 324-338 West Side Ave., Jersey City, NJ 07305

Johnson & Wales University, 8 Abbott Park Place Providence. RI 02903

University of Kansas, 104 Robinson Center, Dept. of HPER, Lawrence. KS 66045

Keene State College, 229 Main St., Dept. of Phys. Ed., Keene, NH 03431

Kennesaw State College, HPER, PO Box 444, Marietta, GA 30061

Kent State University, 264 Memorial Annex, School of Exercise, Leisure & Sport, Kent, OH 44242

Laurentian University, School of Sports Administration, Ramsey Lake Road, Sudbury, ON P3E 2C6 Canada

Le Tourneau University, PO Box 7001, Longview, TX 75607-7001

Liberty University, Box 20000, Lynchburg. VA 24506

Long Beach State University, 1250 Bellflower Blvd., Long Beach, CA 90640

Loras College, 1450 Alta Vista Dr., Dubuque, IA 52004

University of Louisville, Dept. of HPES, HP Bldg., Louisville, KY 40292

Luther College, Regents Center, Decorah, IA 52101

Lynn University, School of Graduate Studies, School of Hospitality Administration, Boca Raton. FL 33431-5598.

Mankato State University, Phys. Ed. Dept., MSU PO Box 28. Mankato, MN 56002-8400

Marshall University, Div. of HPER, College of Education, Huntington, WV 25755

University of Maryland, Kinesiology Dept., Rm. 2351, North Gym, College Park, MD 20742

University of Massachusetts, Amherst, Curry Hicks Bldg., Rm. 1, Amherst, MA 01003

Medaille College, 18 Agassiz Circle, Buffalo, NY 14214

University of Memphis, Bureau of Sport & Leisure Commerce, 253 Fieldhouse, Memphis, TN 38152

Michigan State University, 134 1M Sports Circle, East Lansing, MI 48824

University of Michigan, Dept. of Kinesiology, Central Campus Recreation Bldg., Ann Arbor, MI 48109-2214

University of Minnesota, 218 Cooke Hall, Minneapolis, MN 55455

Mississippi State University, College of Education, Dept. of Health, Physical Education, and Recreation, Mississippi State, MS 39762.

University of Mississippi, Dept. of HPER, Turner Complex, University, MS 38677

University of Missouri, Health & Exercise Sciences, 102 Rottwell Gymnasium, Columbia, MO 65211

Missouri Western State College, HPERD, 4525 Downs Dr., St. Joseph, MO 64507

Montana State University, Rm. 225, Romney Gym, Montana State University, Bozeman, MT 59717

Montclair State University, College of Education and Human Services, Dept. of Health Professions, Physical Education, Recreation, and Leisure Studies, Program in Physical Education, Upper Montclair, NJ 07043-1624.

Mount Union College, Sports Management Program, Alliance, OH 44601

National-Louis University, 2840 Sheridan Rd., Evanston, IL 60201

University of New Hampshire, Dept. of Kinesiology, New Hampshire Hall, Durham, NH 03824

University of New Haven, 300 Orange Ave., West Haven, CT 06516

University of New Mexico, Dept. of HPPELP, Albuquerque, NM 87131

New York University–Grad, 239 Greene St., Ste. 635, Washington Square, New York, NY 10003

New York University–Undergrad, 48 Cooper Square, Rm. 108, New York, NY 10003

Newberry College, Dept. of Phys.Ed., 2100 College St., Newberry, SC 29108

North Carolina State University, College of Forest Resources, Dept. of Parks, Recreation and Tourism Management, Raleigh, NC 27695.

North Dakota State University, College of Human Development and Education, School of Education, Education Programs, Option in Physical Education/Athletic Administration, Fargo, ND 58105.

Northeastern University, 360 Huntington Ave., 208 Dockser Hall, Boston, MA 02115

University of Northern Colorado, Sports Adm. Program, School of Kinesiology/Phys. Ed., Greeley, CO 80639

Northern Illinois University, PHED Dept., Anderson Hall, DeKalb, IL 60115

Northwestern State University of Louisiana, Dept. of Health & Human Performance, Natchitoches, LA 71497

Ohio Northern University, Sport Center, Ada, OH 45810

Ohio State University, Sports Mgt. Prog., 455 Larkins Hall, 337 W. 17th Ave., Columbus, OH 43210-1284

Ohio University, Graduate Studies, College of Health and Human Services, School of Recreation and Sport Sciences, Program in Sports Administration, Athens, OH 45701-2979.

Oklahoma State University, 103 Colvin Center, School of HPEL, Stillwater, OK 74078-0616

Old Dominion University, Darden College of Education, Dept. of Health, Physical Education, Recreation, and Athletics, Norfolk, VA 23529.

University of Oregon, College of Business, Eugene, OR 97403-1208 **(note: address incomplete; illegible)**

Pacific Christian, Phys. Ed. Dept., 1800 E. Nutwood Ave., Fullerton, CA 92631 **(note: number of address illegible; looks like 1800)**

University of the Pacific, Sport Management Program, Sport Sciences Dept. 94211 **(note: room number in Sport Sciences Building illegible.)**

Pfeiffer College, Hwy. 52 N., Mearheimer NC 28109

Quincy University, 1800 College Ave., Quincy, IL 62301-2699

Rice University, Dept. of HP & HS, PO Box 1892, Houston, TX 77251

Robert Morris College, Program in Business Administration, Narrows Run Road, Coraopolis, PA 15108-1189.

State University of New Jersey, Rutgers, Dept. of Exercise Science & Sport Studies, Loree Gym, PO Box 270, New Brunswick, NJ 08903-0270

Saginaw Valley State University, Dept. of PHE, University Center, MI 48710

St. Cloud State University, College of Education, Dept. of Physical Education, Recreation, and Sport Science, St. Cloud, MN 56301-4498.

St. John's University, 8000 Utopia Pkwy., Jamaica, NY 11439

St. Leo College, Div. of Professional Studies, PO Box 2098, St. Leo, FL 33574

St. Thomas University, School of Graduate Studies, Dept. of Professional Management, Dept. of Sports Administration, Miami, FL 33054-6459.

San Jose State University, Dept. of Human Performance, San Jose, CA 95192

Seattle Pacific University, 3414 3rd W., School of Phys. Ed/Athletics, Seattle, WA 98119

Seton Hall University, W. Paul Stillman School of Business, Center for Sports Management, South Orange, NJ 07079-2697.

Slippery Rock University, Morrow Fieldhouse c/o Sport Management Coordinator, Slippery Rock, PA 16057

University of South Carolina, Dept. of Sports Adm., College of Applied Professional Sciences, Carolina Coliseum, Rm. 2012, Columbia, SC 29208

Southeastern Louisiana University, Dept. of Kinesiology Health Studies, Box SLU845, Hammond, LA 70402

Southern Illinois University at Carbondale, Dept. of Phys. Ed., Carbondale, IL 62901

University of Southern Mississippi, School of Human Performance/ Recreation, Sports Administration Bldg., Southern Station Box 5142, Hattiesburg, MS 39406-5142

Spring Arbor College, Dept. of Exercise & Sport Science, Spring Arbor, MI 49283

Springfield College, Programs in Health Science, Programs in Physical Education, Springfield, MA 01109-3797.

State University of New York, Brockport, 304 Tuttle N., Brockport, NY 14420

State University of New York, Cortland, PO Box 2000, Cortland, NY 13045

University of Tampa, 401 Kennedy Blvd., Tampa, FL 33606

Temple University, College of Health, Physical Education, Recreation, and Dance, Dept. of Sports Management and Leisure Studies, Philadelphia, PA 19122.

Tennessee State University, 3500 John Merritt Blvd., Nashville, TN 37209-1561

Texas A&M University, c/o Dept. of Health & Kinesiology, 158 Read Bldg., College Station, TX 77843-4243

University of Texas-Austin, Kinesiology & Health Ed., Belmont 222, Austin, TX 78712

Texas Wesleyan University, 1201 Wesleyan St., Fort Worth, TX 76105

Tiffin University, 155 Miami Street, Tiffin, OH 44883

Towson State University, Dept. of Phys. Ed., Towson Center Rm. 200, Sport Studies, Towson, MD 21204

Tulane University, Reily Recreation Center 105, New Orleans, LA 70118

United States Sports Academy, Graduate Programs, Dept. of Sport Management, Daphne, AL 36526-7055.

Universite du Montreal, Dept. of Physical Education, Montreal, PQ H3C 3J7, Canada.

University of Alberta, Faculty of Graduate Studies and Research, Faculty of Business, Program in Business Administration, Edmonton, AB T6G 2E1, Canada.

University of Miami, School of Education, Dept. of Exercise and Sport Sciences, Program in Sports Administration, Coral Gables, FL 33124.

University of Nevada, Las Vegas, College of Human Performance and Development, Kinesiology and Sport and Leisure Studies Program, Las Vegas, NV 89154-9900.

University of North Carolina at Chapel Hill, College of Arts and Sciences, Dept. of Physical Education, Exercise and Sport Science, Chapel Hill, NC 27599.

University of Oklahoma, College of Arts and Sciences, Dept. of Health and Sports Sciences, Norman, OK 73018.

University of Ottawa, Faculty of Health Sciences, School of Human Kinetics, Ottawa ON K1N 6N5 Canada.

University of Rhode Island, College of Business Administration, Kingston, RI 02881.

University of Richmond, Dept. of Health and Sport Science, Richmond, VA 23173.

University of St. Thomas, Graduate School of Business, St. Paul, MN 55105-1089.

University of San Francisco, College of Arts and Sciences, Program in Sports and Fitness Management, San Francisco, CA 94117-1080.

University of Tennessee, Knoxville, College of Education, Program in Human Performance and Sport Studies, Knoxville, TN 37996.

University of the Incarnate Word, School of Professional Studies, Programs in Administration, San Antonio, TX 78209-6397.

University of Utah, Dept. of Exercise & Sport Science, HPR N-245, Salt Lake City, UT 84112

University of Wisconsin-LaCrosse, College of Health, Physical Education and Recreation, Dept. of Exercise and Sport Science, Program in General Sports Administration, LaCrosse, WI 54601-3742.

Valparaiso University, Dept. of Phys. Ed., 252 Ath-Rec Center, Valparaiso, IN 46383

Washburn University of Topeka, Dept. of HPED, Topeka, KS 66621

Washington State University, Dept. of Education Leadership & Counseling, Pullman, WA 99164-2136

Wayne State University, College of Education, Division of Health and Physical Education, Detroit, MI 48202.

West Chester University of Pennsylvania, Program in Administration., School of Health Sciences, Dept. of Physical Education, West Chester, PA 19383.

West Virginia University, PO Box 6116, Rm. 265 Coliseum, Morgantown, WV 26506-6116

Western Carolina University, Sport Management, Breese Gymnasium, Cullowhee, NC 28723

Western Illinois University, College of Education and Human Services, Dept. of Physical Education, Macomb, IL 61455-1390.

Western Michigan University, College of Education, Dept. of Health, Physical Education and Recreation, Kalamazoo, MI 49008.

Wheaton College, Athletics; 501 E. College, Wheaton, IL 60187

Wichita State University, College of Education, Dept. of Health and Physical Education, Wichita, KS 67260.

Wittenberg University, Dept. of Health/Sport Science; Box 720, Springfield, OH 45501

Xavier University, College of Social Sciences, Dept. of Education, Program in Sport Administration, Cincinnati, OH 45207-5311.

Index